BRIDESHEAD ABBREVIATED

John Crace is a *Guardian* staff feature writer and columnist, and author of the regular 'Digested Read' and 'Digested Classic' columns. His latest book, *Vertigo: One Football Fan's Fear of Success*, has just been published and he is now writing a play for Out of Joint.

Praise for *Brideshead Abbreviated*

'For the last 10 years [Crace's] 'Digested Reads' have been reason enough to buy the *Guardian*. Taking a well-known novel, he gives a brief distillation of the plot while capturing – often perfectly – the tone of its author. At the same time, he jabs a sharpened elbow into their pomposities and limitations' *The Spectator*

'A swift kick up the backside to some of modern literature's most iconic works. Accurate, merciless and very, very funny' Sarah Waters

'Beautifully observed and poisonously cruel . . . laugh-out-loud funny. Crace's arch style pricks the literary bubble and reminds you that a book is, after all, just a book' *The Lady*

'I've read all these books at least twice – and now I've read John Crace's digested versions I wonder why I bothered' Will Self

'With witty, accurate impressions of writers' styles, this is the best way to appear incredibly well read without getting bogged down in hundreds of pages of James Joyce or Ernest Hemingway' *Reader's Digest*

BRIDESHEAD ABBREVIATED

*The Digested Read of
the Twentieth Century*

∾

JOHN CRACE

arrow books

For Jill

Published by Arrow Books 2011

2 4 6 8 10 9 7 5 3 1

First published in Great Britain in 2010 by
Random House Books
Random House, 20 Vauxhall Bridge Road,
London SW1V 2SA

www.randomhouse.co.uk

Addresses for companies within The Random House Group Limited can be found at:
www.randomhouse.co.uk/offices.htm

The Random House Group Limited Reg. No. 954009

A CIP catalogue record for this book
is available from the British Library

ISBN 9780099505457

The Random House Group Limited supports The Forest Stewardship Council
(FSC®), the leading international forest certification organisation. Our books
carrying the FSC label are printed on FSC® certified paper. FSC is the only forest
certification scheme endorsed by the leading environmental organisations,
including Greenpeace. Our paper procurement policy can be found at
www.randomhouse.co.uk/environment

Book design by Chris Wakeling
Typeset by Palimpsest Book Production Limited, Falkirk, Stirlingshire

Printed and bound by CPI Group (UK) Ltd, Croydon, CR0 4YY

CONTENTS

Foreword · 1

– 1950s –

– 1960s –

– 1970s –

FOREWORD

So MANY BOOKS, so many years ... Compiling any list is an arbitrary, thankless task. Why 100 books? Why not 103? Compiling a list of the 100 classic reads of the twentieth century is more arbitrary and more thankless than most. Inevitably it involves compromise and the omissions are as striking to me as they must be to you.

My choices are almost entirely skewed towards European and American writers. This isn't because there are no great Chinese, Indian or African writers; it's because they are not widely known or published in the west, and there's little fun to be had in parodying a book very few people are likely to have heard of, let alone read. So my selection is conservative; it reflects the consensual view of the western literary canon rather than trying to reshape it.

Even within these parameters, though, there are some key books missing. Where is *Ulysses*? Where is *The Leopard*? Where indeed. When I began this project, I formulated some rules. No author could appear more than once: partly to allow me to include as many different authors as possible and partly because repeating the stylistic mannerisms of a particular author could get ... well, repetitive. So *Ulysses* lost out to *A Portrait of the Artist as a Young Man*, a book I reckoned more readers – myself included – were likely to have finished.

I also decided to divide the book into 10 decades featuring 10 books each. Apart from giving the book a very obvious symmetrical structure, it also offered a good way in to both what was considered important at the time and to tracking different literary traditions –

from the late Victorians to the modernists, the existentialists, the social realists and post-modernists. But it also has its drawbacks. Some decades are far richer in literature than others; in any other decade but the 1950s, *The Leopard* would have made the cut. But rules are rules . . .

It also became harder to decide what constituted a classic the later on into the twentieth century I progressed. Will people still be reading *High Fidelity* in 100 years' time as they now continue to read *Howards End*? Perhaps not, but *High Fidelity* is important – if not for its stylistic brilliance then for creating a new genre of lad-lit. Similarly, no one would claim *Harry Potter* to be a masterpiece but it was and is a cultural phenomenon that turned many kids on to the pleasures of reading.

So I've taken the word 'classic' in its broadest sense. Not just so as to include those books the critics tell us are of lasting literary value, but also those with a wider social significance to the twentieth century. My guess is that most people will find little to quibble with in about 80 of my choices. I suspect there will also be little agreement about which 80 these are. But please feel free to make your feelings known. It's a conversation well worth having.

John Crace
June 2010

– 1900 –

THE WONDERFUL WIZARD OF OZ

L. Frank Baum

Dorothy lived in the midst of the great Kansas prairies with Uncle Henry and Aunt Em. Their house had four walls, for if there had been only three it would have toppled over. Uncle Henry and Aunt Em never smiled; it was Toto the dog that made Dorothy laugh. Today they were not playing, though, for a low wail of wind approached from the north.

Uncle Henry and Aunt Em made it to the cellar before the cyclone struck; Dorothy and Toto were not so fortunate. The house started whirling around and lifted many miles into the air. Dorothy got bored waiting for them to land, so she fell asleep.

She awoke to find herself in a luscious country surrounded by the queerest people. 'Are you the Seven Dwarves?' she enquired of the little men with white beards and pointy hats.

'Good guess,' said one, 'but in fact we are Munchkins. And you are very welcome because your house has squashed the Wicked Witch of the East and freed us from our bondage.'

Just then a little lady appeared. 'Who are you?' said Dorothy.

'I am the Good Witch of the North,' the little lady replied, 'and if you put on the Wicked Witch's silver shoes . . .'

'I'll look like Lady Gaga.'

'. . . you'll have magic powers. Now where would you like to go?'

'Anywhere that Andrew Lloyd Webber is not.'

'Then you must avoid meeting the Wicked Witches of the

3

West and the North-West.' And so saying, she kissed Dorothy on the forehead and took off her magic hat. A sign then appeared on the ground which read *Follow the Yellow Brick Road to see the Great Oz in the Emerald City*.

After Dorothy had been walking for an hour, she came across a Scarecrow that winked at her. 'Are you alive?' she asked.

'Of course I am.'

'Then why don't you move?'

'Because I've got a pole rammed up my arse.'

Dorothy and the Scarecrow started walking. 'How I wish I had some brains instead of a head full of straw,' the Scarecrow sobbed.

'A lot of people back home in Kansas feel the same way,' Dorothy replied, and they carried on walking until they came across a Tin Woodman.

'What happened to you?' Dorothy asked.

'It's a sad story. The Wicked Witch of the East killed my love for a Munchkin by making my axe slip. First I chopped off all my limbs and then I cut out my heart so now I don't feel anything.'

'How would you know it's sad if you don't have any feelings?'

They all chose to ignore this inconsistency and carried on walking until they came across a Lion. 'I want to be very brave,' the Lion said. 'But really I'm a bit of a pussy.'

Eventually the four of them, along with Toto, reached the Emerald City, where they each in turn had an audience with the Great Oz. To Dorothy he appeared as a giant Head; to the Scarecrow as a lovely Lady; to the Tin Woodman as a terrible Beast; and to the Lion as a Ball of Fire. Dorothy asked to be returned to Kansas, the Scarecrow for brains, the Tin Woodman for a heart and the Lion for courage. Yet to each the answer was the same: 'First go with Dorothy to slay the Wicked Witch of the West.'

Off they headed along the West Road, where they encountered Cackling Crows, Beastly Bees, and the Winged Monkeys who were under the Wicked Witch's command. Yet Dorothy wasn't that bothered because she could already see how things were shaping up. The Scarecrow wasn't nearly as stupid as many Republicans she knew, the Tin Woodman was actually a bit of a softy and the Lion was really very brave. So when Dorothy threw a bucket of water over the Wicked Witch of the West, it wasn't the slightest bit surprising when she evaporated.

'The thing with children's allegories,' she explained to the others, 'is not to question anything.'

'Oh dear,' said the Great Oz, when they returned to claim their reward. 'You see, I'm actually a charlatan from Omaha.'

'Are you sure you're not a President from Texas?' Dorothy asked.

'Quite sure. But if I pumped a load of manure into the Scarecrow he would have shit for brains. If I drew a heart on the Tin Woodman he'd be more human than Simon Cowell, and if I gave the Lion a bottle of vodka he'd have Dutch Courage . . .'

'Yes, yes,' said Dorothy testily. 'We get the point. But can you get me back to Kansas?'

'No chance, but you can come with me in a balloon to Omaha.'

'I guess that's better than nothing.' But before she could get in, the balloon flew off without her.

Dorothy wept with frustration. So did the readers. 'I guess we'd better start walking somewhere again,' she announced to her companions, and off they set once more.

Again they faced many difficulties. The Scarecrow rescued them from a smack overdose in a poppy field; the Tin Woodman rescued them from Marauding Trees by chopping down loads of branches; the Lion accidentally scared off a few Tigers; and the Winged Monkeys did the rest.

'Hello,' said Glinda, the Good Witch of the South. 'How can I help?'

'I want to go back to rule Oz because they are used to having an idiot in charge,' said the Scarecrow.

'I want to rule over the Winkies because I'm a right Winker,' said the Tin Woodman.

'The Beasts of the Forest have asked me to be their Lion King,' said the Lion.

'I sense a spin-off musical there,' said Dorothy.

'These three things I can do,' Glinda smiled. 'And what of you, Dorothy?'

'I want to go back to Kansas.'

'You could have done that anytime. All you had to do was click your Lady Gaga heels three times.'

'You mean, we needn't have gone through endless repetitions of the same story,' everyone gasped.

'Precisely so.'

With that Dorothy clicked her silver heels three times and woke to find herself back home.

'Where have you been?' asked Aunt Em.

'I've been to Oz.'

'How was it?'

'I could have done without Andrew Lloyd Webber.'

CLAUDINE IN PARIS

Colette

P AGE ONE AND I am already exhausted! But I can just about raise my head to look at myself in the mirror. How my hair has been shorn! I may be 17, but I do declare I could pass for 15. Still your beating hearts, *mes petits* schoolgirl fantasists!

For the honour of my notebooks, I shall have to explain how I come to be in Paris. Oh Papa, I am as furious with you as I am with my naughty eyebrows! How could you have forced us to leave Montigny after a publisher failed to respond to the delivery of your manuscript on the *Malacology of Fresnois* within half an hour? It was all I could do to find my darling cat, Fanchette, before our train departed.

My memory of our arrival at the apartment in the dismal Rue Jacob is confused in a fog of misery. The effort of unpacking a single box of clothes left me with a brain fever so profound the doctors feared I might never try on a pair of cami-knickers again. The violets by my bedside prolonged my illness for they reminded me of Montigny and it was several months before I was well enough to venture outside.

'We should visit my sister, your Aunt Coeur,' Papa said one day.

'But my hair is far too short!' I complained. 'And I have nothing to wear!'

The whipped-cream living-room couldn't have been more 1900 and I was curious to get to know my aunt's grandson, Marcel, who was waiting there. The days before our dinner engagement passed slowly. I spent my mornings having my bottom pinched –

Ooh la la! – and the afternoons worrying that my breasts were too tiny for my décolletage – *Encore ooh la la!*

It was annoying to be seen in public with Marcel as he was far too pretty to be a boy and everyone stared at him not me. Yet I contained my jealousy and fluttered my eyelashes coquettishly at him.

'I am not a goody-goody,' he said, 'but I will not make love to you. Rather, let me tell you about my dear friend Charlie.'

How thrillingly racy for the Paris *demi-monde*! A boy's forbidden love for another boy! We must become each other's confidante!

'Tell me all about Charlie's naughty bits,' I demanded.

'Only if you tell me all about your Fresnois Sapphism,' he pouted.

How I yearned for a glimpse of Aimée's budding breasts! How I used to delight in beating Luce about the head when I caught sight of her staring at me pulling my silken stockings over my milky thighs! How strange it was she had not replied to my letter! But, no! I would make Marcel wait awhile.

After a few days' tiring shopping, Marcel introduced me to his father, my Uncle Cousin Renaud. Mon Oncle bowed low before me, taking my hands in his and kissing them softly, brushing his silver moustache against my quivering skin. My cheeks flushed with excitement. How could I contain my incestuous feelings for an older man!

'Let me take you to the opera,' he whispered in my ear, 'and thrill you with scandalous tales of men who dress as women while we watch Marcel and Charlie slip away into the night together.'

Paris was muggy that month and men were staring at the sweat glistening on my exposed breasts when I unexpectedly met Luce, dressed in the most expensive fashions, on the Rive Gauche.

'*Ma chère* Claudine,' she said. 'I moved to Paris to escape my horrid papa and threw myself on the mercies of my wealthy 127-year-old uncle, who gives me 30 Louis each month for the pleasure of my flesh! But I yearn for you. My breasts are rounder now; take them in your greedy hands and ravish them.'

She pushed her mouth towards mine and I felt a momentary passionate quiver, before beating her cruelly until she gasped her little death. I dismissed her contemptuously, enjoying her squirm every bit as uncomfortably as the Messieurs who are reading this on the Métro.

'So tell me about all the saucy things that you and Charlie do?' I begged Marcel, as he tried on a crêpe de Chine cravat.

'It is a special love we have,' he replied, guilefully. 'Not like Papa. He is a journalist and he sleeps with any older woman whose nipples harden for him.'

How I hated those other women! And how my own nipples also strangely hardened!

'Do not call me Oncle any more,' Oncle implored, as we shared a bottle of Asti Spumante. 'It makes me feel such a dirty old man.'

'That is precisely why I love to use it,' I said, feeling quite gay. 'I would be your daughter, if I could, as that is so much more shocking. Yet, if you insist, I will call you Renaud.'

'Oh, Claudine! My grey hair is turning blond once more. Let us be wed!'

How I enjoyed the twisted thrill of older men imagining themselves in bed with a submissive teenaged girl! And yet how strangely coy and dated it now seemed!

'You're only getting married to Papa to get his money,' Marcel sulked.

'I cannot marry you,' I cried, thrusting myself against Renaud in a last attempt at titillation. 'I will be your mistress instead.'

'*Non*,' Renaud insisted. 'I may be a dirty old perve, but I am a dirty old perve with family values.'

KIM

Rudyard Kipling

H<small>E SAT ASTRIDE</small> the gun Zam-Zammah, opposite the Lahore Wonder House. Burnished black by the sun, though definitely not a native as he was the orphaned son of an Irish soldier, Kim yonder espied a Tibetan lama.

'Whither goest thou, Most Holy Asiatic man?' he asked.

'I searcheth for the River in which the Arrow of Life has landed,' the lama replied. 'And what, pray, is thy name, boy?'

'They callest me Friend of the World,' Kim said, 'and I shall be your *chela* on your quest to escape the Wheel of Things. But first, lettest me say farewell to my erstwhile guardian.'

'God's curse on all Unbelievers,' Mahbub Ali exclaimed, reflecting the colourful diversity of the Indian sub-continent. 'Since thou musteth go, then sendeth a letter to the British commander in Umballa telling him the pedigree of his stallion is pukka.'

With the natural disguise of the native and the intelligence of the sahib, Kim overheard two brigands talking. There was more to Mahbub Ali's note than met the eye. 'Come,' he said to the lama. 'Letteth us leave on the te-rain before there's trouble afoot.'

'Thou art a doughty fellow,' Colonel Creighton said, glancing at the note. With the natural disguise of the native and the intelligence of the sahib, the Friend of the World realised the Game was on. There was to be fighting in the North! But first, he would remain the lama's *chela* and seek out the River of the Arrow.

'Hit ye not that snake,' the lama cried as they walked along the Grand Trunk Road. 'For within that snake is a fallen man seeking redemption.'

'Actually,' the cobra hissed, 'I was a millipede in my last life and I'm on the way up.'

'How happy we are,' the Sikh and the Pathan declared, sharing their victuals with Kim and the lama. 'We artest truly blessed to enjoy the rich diversity of India.'

'Indeed we are,' the Old Soldier agreed. 'The Mutiny is but a long-forgotten aberration. Verily, those that did riseth up against the Sacred Sahibs were grippest by a Fevered Madness. How else can one explaineth so profane an act against the undisputed benevolence of the Raj?'

With the natural disguise of the native and the intelligence of the sahib, Kim procured some tikkuts for the te-rain and, after many pages on the richness of Indian culture, realised the plot was getting seriously waylaid.

'Forsooth,' cried Kim, 'my parents always toldeth me the Red Bull would beareth me Good News. And thither is the flag of the Red Bull.'

'Behold,' whispered the lama. 'It is the ensign of your father's regiment. Seeeth how the prophecies cometh true.'

'Well, young man,' the chaplain declared. 'Seeing as thou art a pure sahib by birth, the regiment will taketh thee in and schooleth thee at Lucknow.'

'God's teeth,' the Colonel exclaimed. 'With his natural disguise of the native and his intelligence of the sahib, the boy will becometh a top spy in the Great Game once we have taughteth him a feweth lessons. Come playeth the White Man, boy!'

'I musteth returneth to my spiritual quest for the River of the Arrow,' the lama whispered. 'Else I shall be grindeth by the Wheel of Things. Yet letteth me payeth for my *chela*'s schooling and letteth him visit me from time to time.'

'Thou art a mischievous imp, O Friend of the World,' Mahbub Ali groaned some three years later. 'Thy constant scampish cunning and thy boundless romantic idealising of Indian imperialism becometh rather wearing after a whileth. Prithee, forgeteth the fake fakirs and get oneth with the story. Such as it iseth.'

Kim flung himself upon the next turn of the Wheel, learning the arts of the Game, first with Sahib Lurgan and his Hindu servant, and then with Babu Hurree Chunder Mookherjee.

'What the dooce!' cried Babu Mookherjee. 'We neeedeth to find the eveeeeedence of an attack in the north.'

'Taketh no notice of Babu's funny voice,' the Colonel laughed. 'He talketh stupid to letteth you know that though he iseth a well-educated Indian, he iseth stilleth a native and canneth never be oneth of us.'

'Do not thou and I also talk quaintly?' Kim enquired.

''Pon my word tis a bitteth late to thinketh of that. Now get thee hence to the North to playeth the Great Game.'

'Come, *chela*, perhaps the River of the Arrow is to be found in the Karakorum,' the lama said. 'Yet what manner of Un-enlightened strangers shall be found in the mountains?'

'*Da. Niet. Dosvedanya.*'

'Good fortune!' Kim said. 'We haveth cometh upon the Russians, and yet it iseth the Russians who are the enemy of Blessed India. Keepeth them talking while I nicketh their code books and diaries and thence we shall sneaketh off.'

'You haveth the eveeeedence, O Friend of the World.' Babu smiled. 'The Great Game hath beeeeen won.'

'Methinks I hath been looking for the River of the Arrow in the wrong place,' the lama said sadly. 'Wilt thou comest with me to find the Meaning of Life further south?'

'Perhaps I will. For I am Kim. Or am I?'

ANNA OF THE FIVE TOWNS

Arnold Bennett

'THERE YOU ARE, Anna,' cried Mr Henry Mynors, the superintendent of the Bible Class, who had been waiting for her outside the school.

Tall and sturdily built with the lenient curves of absolute maturity, Anna Tellwright stood motionless. This was one of the great tumultuous moments of her life – she realised for the first time she was loved.

How calm and stately she is, Mynors thought, as she took his hand in greeting and they walked together through the forbidding street that united the five contiguous towns that marked the ancient home of the potter. 'I mean to call on your father to discuss business,' he said, 'but I trust you will be in.' Anna's heart shuddered with expectant perturbation.

She sat in the bay window of the parlour, her mind drifting as pages of tedium detailed every last ha'porth of her father's wealth, in case anyone failed to realise he was a tight-fisted bastard.

'Tha' art twenty-wun t'day, lass,' said Ephraim Tellwright, the only person so morally defective as to talk with a t'Staffordshire accent. 'So tha' inherits the fifta' thoosand poond tha' late mutha' left tha'. Burt doan't tha' worra' aboot wha ta do wi' t. Tha' canst leaf that ta me.'

'Thank you, father,' Anna replied, mindful of her duty, 'for I am too feeble to manage it myself.'

'Noo, get tha' sen down to Mr Price. He owes ma' twenta' poonds in rent.'

'Oh, Miss Tellwright,' sobbed old Titus Price, as his son Willie hid quietly in the corner. 'Times are very hard. We are but honest folk trying to make an honest living. I could give you ten pounds now. Will that do?'

How Anna longed to tell Mr Price that he could forget about the rent! And yet she had a duty to her father, whom she knew would not relent on even a half-penny of what he was owed.

'For now,' she said. 'But mind you give me the rest soon.'

Such harshness grated on her soul, yet her passivity allowed her no recourse to graciousness so she pondered these things deep within herself at the Methodist Revival meeting. How she longed to find Christ and yet somehow He did not come despite the playing of the Cornet.

'So, Mr Tellwright,' Mynors said, as he paid him a call later that evening. 'Will you invest in my pottery?'

'Nay, lad,' Tellwright replied. 'Me brass is all tied oop. But ma daughter will. Woan't tha', lass?'

'Whatever you say, father, for I am too stupid to make financial decisions for myself.'

'Thass settled thun. Noo giv Mr Mynors anuther morsel of fat and thun go an lean on Mr Price for more brass.'

Anna was much troubled by this, but she knew her duty was to be obedient to her father even though it was to precipitate the catastrophe that nobody would give a toss about what was to befall Mr Price.

'How nice that you can come on holiday with us to the Isle of Man now that you are monied,' cried Mrs Sutton. 'I do also declare Mr Mynors is enamoured of you.' There had been a time when Anna would have dreaded such a disclosure, but now she merely smiled as if to say, 'Yes I, the shy, dreary one, am beloved by the man desired of all.'

Few men in Bursley took conscious pride in the ancient art of the potter, steeped as it was within the weft of human life, yet Mynors's works were acknowledged to be among the finest available for those of modest means. 'Thrift is a great virtue,' he said to Anna. 'That's why it is for Mr Price's good you must ensure he pays you what is owed.'

'Would you be so gracious as to take a promissory note from Mr Sutton as our pledge?' Titus asked.

'I'll tak' it,' Tellwright answered.

The separation from the tight paternal fiscal grip lightened Anna's mood on holiday and she nearly ventured to initiate a conversation before thinking better of it. Fortunately Mrs Sutton's daughter caught influenza and Anna was able to stay silent indoors and nurse her. It is far better that someone as dull as me should risk infection, she thought, than that Mrs Sutton should be put in jeopardy.

'The fever has passed,' she said after a lengthy nine-day vigil.

Mynors was deeply touched by her servitude. 'You clearly know your place,' he said. 'Allow me to do you the honour of becoming your husband.'

What strange transport!

'He onla wunts ta marry tha' for tha' brass, tha' mis'rable old cow,' Tellwright said. 'Burt doan't let it wurry tha'. Tha' wonst git a betta offa.'

'Shocking news!' cried Mynors. 'Titus Price has hung himself.'

Grieved and confused, Anna fell prostrate. Like Christ she had consorted with sinners. Yet had it been her obedience to her father's will that had precipitated Mr Price's downfall?

'You are the meekest of angels,' said Willie Price. 'Thy soul is pure. My father killed himself because he had forged Mr Sutton's promissory note and was to be exposed.'

Anna looked deep into Willie's eyes and in that moment they somehow knew they were in love. Yet Anna did not break off her engagement to Mr Mynors because she was so unbelievably dull. Instead she gave Willie one hundred pounds and bade him leave for Australia. She never heard from him again. Neither did anyone else, for Willie threw himself down a pit-shaft, an anti-climactic tragedy that moved no one, save those who wished they had done much the same themselves long ago.

HEART OF DARKNESS

Joseph Conrad

THE FLOOD HAD made, the wind was nearly calm and the only thing for it was to wait for the turn of tide. The sea-reach of the Thames stretched before us. What greatness had not floated on the ebb of that river into the mystery of an unknown earth! . . . The dreams of men, the germs of empires.

Between us four was the bond of the sea, making us tolerant of each other's yarns. Which was just as well when Marlow, sitting serenely as a Buddha, began his two-hour, neo-Freudian critique of colonialism.

'This also has been one of the dark places of the earth,' he said didactically, leadenly ensuring we should not miss the parallels between the Romans in Britain and what was to follow. 'Many men must have died here. The conquest of the earth is not a pretty thing. All that redeems it is the idea.'

He broke off a while to let his words hang portentously. We waited patiently for him to continue. There wasn't anything else to do. 'I don't want to bother you much with personal details,' he said eventually. 'But I'm going to anyway.

'When I was a little chap I had a passion for the blank spaces on the map. And there was one, the biggest, the most blank of all, that I had a hankering after. True, by the end of my boyhood it was no longer a blank. It was a place of darkness. Yet like a giant snake, ensnaring me with its phallic symbolism, this mighty river drew me in and I got appointed as a steamboat skipper.

'I crossed the Channel to show myself to my employers and in a few hours I was in the whited sepulchre of their city. I saw the

Company doctor, inspected another map which showed the river coiling snake-like through the darkness and said goodbye to my aunt. It's queer how stupid women are. They live in a world of their own.

'As the steamer made its way along the serpentine channel of the river, we passed several settlements where many niggers lay dying in the service of the Company. We eventually disembarked and, in the company of a vastly overweight, unattractive white man, the very obvious physical embodiment of imperial greed and exploitation, began the two-hundred-mile journey on foot to the Central Station.

'I arrived to find that my steamboat had been sunk and I kept myself to myself, content to overhear snippets of conversation about a man called Kurtz. "Who is this Kurtz?" I asked at last. "He runs the Inner Station," the Manager said. From this reply, I inferred that this man was afraid of Kurtz, as if he held up a mirror to the moral bankruptcy of Dutch colonialism while somehow escaping judgement himself.

'Two months passed, time which I spent being charmed by the snake-like properties of the river as it slithered its way into the wilderness of the jungle id, before my boat was seaworthy and I could set off in search of Kurtz in the heart of darkness. I had on board with me several white men, whom I shall meaningfully call pilgrims, a bunch of cannibals – surprisingly jolly fellows when they were not eating rancid hippopotamus – and my sturdy, silent helmsman. This fine black specimen did not speak, but had he done so would undoubtedly have said, "You are a good man, Mistah Marlow. We niggers have no language or culture worth mentioning. It is just a shame that we've been civilised by those fat Dutch bastards instead of by someone with your more refined sensibilities."

'We stopped briefly at an abandoned settlement where a written note warned of dark, portentous events ahead, and as we neared Kurtz's station on a bend of this vast snaking river, we were becalmed by fog. The screech of savages assailed us from the darkness and a hail of pitiful arrows rained down on the deck. My sturdy helmsman rashly opened a shutter and was struck by a spear. He looked up, grateful that his last vision before he passed into his own heart of darkness should be of me. I patted my pet affectionately as he died, before tossing his body into the murky darkness of the snake-like river. Rather the fishes should eat him, I thought caringly, than the cannibals.

'At last we reached a clearing in the jungle darkness and there we found Kurtz, semi-delirious with disease, being tended by a young Russian man. "It was Kurtz who ordered the natives to attack you," he told us. "They are in awe of his savagery. They treat him like a god." We gathered up his vast stockpile of ivory and I began to read his journal that started as a witness to a noble moral ideal and ended in unimaginable barbarism with the exhortation to exterminate all the savages. Yet somehow I could not bring myself to pass judgement.

'Kurtz escaped during the night and I found him heading back towards the heart of darkness. He talked briefly of his Intended before whispering, "The horror, the horror." We carried him back onboard and set off down the muscular, coiling stream, yet he died before we reached the brightness of the ego.

'I too almost succumbed to illness and it was with a sense of moral fatigue that I visited Kurtz's Intended on my return to Europe. "I hadn't seen Kurtz for nine long years," the Intended murmured. "Pray tell me his last words."

'My heart trembled. She was only a woman and was thus too dim to be told of the horror, the horror, and the moral depravities of the heart of darkness. "They were your name," I said.'

Marlow ceased talking and we turned our heads towards London, once more mindful of the darkness.

THE HOUND OF THE BASKERVILLES

Sir Arthur Conan Doyle

SHERLOCK HOLMES HAD in his hands a stick left behind by a doctor the night before. 'Well, Watson, what do you make of it?' he said.

I sighed. 'Do we always have to start a new story with me humiliating myself by jumping to all the wrong conclusions?'

'Humour me, Watson.'

'Very well, Holmes. It belongs to an elderly man with a huge dog.'

'My dear Watson, your stupidity never lets you down,' Holmes cackled, drawing deeply on a pipe of heaviest shag. 'Our man is in his thirties with a small spaniel.'

'Good God, man! How could you possibly deduce that?'

'Because he's sitting in that chair in the corner.'

'There's no time to waste,' said our visitor, introducing himself as Dr Mortimer. 'I have urgent need of your services. You may have heard of the legendary curse of the Hound of the Baskervilles. For centuries it has been held as but a myth, but recently Sir Charles Baskerville was found dead on Dartmoor surrounded by the paw prints of a giant beast. Today, his only heir, Sir Henry, arrives from Canada and I fear for his life.'

'This is a most interesting problem,' Holmes replied grimly, 'and I fear it will be even trickier than the curious case of Lady Ascot's missing Fortnum & Mason's hamper. Bring Sir Henry to these rooms tomorrow and I shall ponder the matter overnight.

Watson, get me some morphine. It's the only way I can bear to listen to my violin-playing.'

An urgent knocking interrupted our breakfast the following morning . 'Sir Henry Baskerville, I presume,' Holmes said drily.

'The very same,' he responded. 'It really is most intolerable, sir. I've been in the country less than 24 hours and I've already been sent an anonymous letter warning me to stay away from Baskerville Hall if I value my life.'

'Show me the note,' Holmes demanded. 'Hmm. I see it has been fashioned from today's *Times* leader.'

'How could you possibly know that?' I ejaculated.

'Elementary, Watson. Which bit of the paper would you cut up other than that which you had no intention of reading? This problem may turn out to be even more curious than the case of Elton of John's tiara.

'It seems you are being followed, Sir Henry, but I fear the answers are to be found in Devon. I must stay in town to complete my investigations into the disappearance of the Prince of Wales's toothbrush, but Watson will accompany you to Dartmoor.'

Sir Henry's mood darkened as the train sped westward; by the time we reached Coombe Tracey and discovered a prisoner had escaped on the moor, it was thunderous. 'Why did Holmes have to send me down with you?' he barked. 'I've read enough of his exploits to know you're a complete moron who will get everything wrong. And besides, the bits where Holmes doesn't feature are usually fairly dull.'

An eerie howling atmospherically emanated from the moor. 'I don't much like the look of Barrymore the butler,' I whispered to Sir Henry. 'I'd steer clear of the swimming pool.'

Later that night, I observed Barrymore signalling to someone out on the moor. 'Caught you, you bounder,' I yelled.

'Oh, sir, I meant no harm,' Barrymore whimpered. 'The escaped prisoner is the wife's younger brother. He's a murderer with a heart of gold really and we're leaving food out for him.'

'Of course, my good man,' I replied. 'So you're just a red herring and I've got everything wrong as usual.'

Taking our afternoon perambulations out on the moor, Sir Henry and I encountered the local naturalist John Stapleton out with his sister.

'I say, you're a bit of a stunner,' Sir Henry muttered as he doffed his hat to Miss Stapleton.

I rather thought he had caught her fancy too, but she whispered a hasty, 'Stay away,' before her brother pulled her away, laughing satanically as a horse was sucked into the mud of Grimpen Mire.

'That's all very queer,' I said as we returned home. Queerer still was the silhouette of a thin, angular man I glimpsed against the moon. Later that night, Sir Henry went out on the moor alone. A deep growl followed by a desperate scream rent the air. I hastened to the body, fearing the worst.

'Thank God,' I gasped. 'It was only the escaped prisoner dressed in Sir Henry's clothes.'

'Good evening, Watson,' Holmes said, stepping from out of the shadows.

'What the deuce are you doing here, Holmes?'

'I've been hiding on the moor all along and I have the case solved. Stapleton is a distant relative of the Baskervilles and the woman posing as his sister is his wife. She has tried to warn Sir Henry he is planning to kill off everyone to inherit the Baskerville fortune, but Stapleton has silenced her. We must act before he succeeds.'

Fog swept over the moor as a shiny, fire-breathing beast bore down on Sir Henry. Holmes emptied his revolver. The mastiff fell lifeless and Stapleton ran into Grimpen Mire, to be swallowed by the mud.

'See how he painted the dog and placed phosphorus in his mouth,' Holmes said breezily. 'This really has been the most fiendish of cases I've ever encountered, more fiendish even than the abduction of Mrs Slocombe's pussy.'

'Just one thing bothers me, Holmes,' I replied. 'Even if Stapleton had killed Sir Henry, how would he have gotten away with suddenly announcing himself the heir?'

'Shut the fuck up, Watson.'

– 1902 –

THE IMMORALIST

André Gide

*M*ICHEL HAS SPOKEN to us. *Oh, what will you think of our friend? Shall we reprove him or shall we admit that we can recognise ourselves in this tale? Or will we even care?*

My dear friends, thank you for coming. The last time we met was at my wedding. I hardly knew my wife and it was a loveless marriage. I merely felt a *comme-ci, comme-ça* tenderness for Marceline born of pity. Where I was a wealthy, successful classicist, she was an impoverished simpleton. Why did I marry her? To keep my father happy on his death bed.

We travelled south, sleeping in separate rooms, naturally, and it was only after several months that I momentarily slipped out of my self-absorption and realised Marceline was actually quite pretty. But back to me. When we reached Sousse, I felt unwell and casually told Marceline I had spat blood in the night.

She collapsed to the floor with fright. I was enraged. Was it not enough that one of us was ill? Thrilled with the daring selfishness of my thoughts, I summoned a doctor before losing consciousness myself. We were taken to Biskra, where Marceline slowly nursed me back to health. I passed my convalescence observing the nakedness of young Arab boys beneath their thin white *gandourah* and ignoring Marceline.

'I've been praying for you,' she said one day.

'Don't bother. I don't need God's help; it creates obligations.'

Marceline passively accepted her role as a patsy in a thinly disguised Nietzschean treatise and as her reward, after wasting several more months ogling boys, I consummated our marriage in Sorrento during our return journey to France. Her gratitude was touching, but the sense she was but an impediment to my inflated ego was growing daily.

Having come so close to death, I felt an unconstrained need to experience joy by doing whatever I liked, when I liked. To show the courage of my convictions – how I had cast off the shackles of my past – I even declined to visit Agrigentum. How *risqué* was that!

After a few days in Paris spent in companionable silence, Marceline and I moved to Normandy to visit my family's estate. It was there I had a new emotion to deal with: Marceline announced she was pregnant. I was filled with a joy that I expressed by ignoring her, choosing instead to spend my days with my farm manager, Bocage, whose unctuous sincerity I found cloying, but whose son Charles was an utter delight. Apart from his clothes, which were not to my taste.

'I could manage the estate so much better,' Charles teased, as we went out riding together – me playfully slapping his thighs with my hunting crop and allowing my hands to touch his in lingering caresses. Yet his attire was *de trop*: even his beauty could not carry off his peasant chic, so Marceline and I were forced to return to Paris once more.

I was not that concerned by Marceline's fatigue – why should I have been? – for I was weighed down by the seriousness of my Nietzschean crusade, which had led me to reject my bourgeois friends, whose lives were ruled by duty, and to live my life in the *moment*.

It was after delivering a derivative lecture on how Culture kills Life that I met Mélanque, himself an obvious Nietzschean avatar. 'I live life in the *ici et maintenant*,' he said. 'I have no rules other than to do what I want, when I want. It is the only honesty. The past means *rien*.'

'I'm sure the readers will agree,' I said enthusiastically, embracing the New Order with as much speed as a terminally languid member of the French bourgeoisie could muster. 'Another glass of Syrah, perhaps?'

I returned home to find Marceline had lost the baby. For a moment I was distraught, but then I forgot the past and went out looking at boys instead until she had got over it.

'God helped me get better,' she said.

'I got better on my own,' I replied. 'Now God can help you pack up the house while I leer at *garçons*, because we're off to Normandy again as I'm exhausted by your illness.'

Marceline was content to stay in the house, but I preferred the company of rustic proletarians whose primitive responses to stimuli lacked the guile and simulacra of the more refined. I became nocturnal, going out poaching with Bocage's youngest son Alcide on my estate at night. How very, very dare you!

'Don't you fancy me any more?' said Charles one day, after I had been ignoring him for some time.

'Not really,' I replied. 'You've become as big a twat as me and you still have no dress sense.'

Marceline's health was failing so obviously that with the great love I felt towards my impediment, I took her on an arduous journey of symbolic circularity back to North Africa. Annoyingly she seemed to recover at first, but then she grew weak once more.

I, the Superman, felt restrained by her cloying neediness and spent my nights searching out boys. Or girls, if I couldn't find any boys. Marceline was touched by my deep expressions of love when I dropped in on her for a few moments and, when I announced we must move to Biskra after she had started coughing blood, whispered, 'I am not worthy of such a strong man.'

'You're right.' I shrugged. 'But since we're back where we started the book, you can croak now.' And she did! So now I'm off to play with some boys. See you later, alligators.

THE GOLDEN BOWL

Henry James

THE PRINCE HAD always liked his London and, as we join him, he is conversing with his affianced bride, Maggie, daughter of the rich American art collector, Mr Verver.

'You are truly a *galantuomo*,' she had said.

'I know.'

With that they had lapsed into pages of intense introspection, an introspection into the most precise nature of their feelings, feelings which would include the Prince's impecunious state, a state that was of necessity the binding force between them, conferring on Maggie the advantage of European aristocracy and on the Prince the endowment of new capital. They smiled at one another, a smile that lasted for at least another dozen pages, pages which induced an extreme sopor, a sopor that would in time degenerate into unconsciousness.

It was on the Friday before his wedding that the Prince paid a visit to the Assinghams, a couple delicately placed beneath the highest ranks of the upper classes with whom he had been acquainted in Italy.

'Your arrival is most gracious yet unexpected, Your Highness,' said Mrs Assingham, curtseying before the Prince, 'for Miss Charlotte Stant is due for tea.'

Miss Stant made no circumstance of thus coming upon the Prince, and for his part the Prince felt 'safe', 'safe' for being so placed in the innocent coincidence of their meeting that he could interject a note of jocularity, a jocularity tempered by the remembrance of the refinement of their heightened sensibilities, such that it would pass unnoticed.

'Perhaps I could accompany you on an expedition to acquire a present for your bride?' Charlotte enquired.

This little crisis was of a great deal shorter duration than our account of it, but then it could hardly have been much longer save that it had taken five hours including nodding-off breaks to read it. Upon their departure Mrs Assingham apprised her husband of the situation.

'The Prince and Miss Stant had been intimate in Italy,' she said, 'and I do believe that if she had even a little money, he would have bravely married beneath himself. This places me queerly with the Ververs, for perhaps I might have mentioned this fact to them previously.'

Up, up, up, never so high, the Prince walked with Charlotte around the *antiquarii* of Bloomsbury. 'See in the Jew's shop window a Golden Bowl, a Golden Bowl worthy of the selflessness of your bride,' Charlotte said in perfect Italian.

'Trust not the thieving Son of Abraham,' the Prince replied. 'For the gilded crystal bowl has a hidden fatal flaw.'

Overwhelmed by the symbolism, the pair continued their promenade in mute intensity, an intensity borne of the superlative degree of their angularity.

Mr Adam Verver, inscrutably monotonous behind an iridescent cloud, patted the Principino, the Principino who need detain us no longer now that the passage of hymeneal time has been indicated by the arrival of issue to the Prince and Maggie, and wondered whether the actuality of his not having remarried after the death of his wife was preventing Maggie from obtaining the maximum immersion in the fact of her being married.

'I am aware it is you who are young and I who am old,' he said to Charlotte.

'*Au contraire*,' Charlotte answered with tortured logic, a logic in which no one but James believed. 'It is you who are young and I who am old.'

Charlotte questioned whether she was square with Mrs

Assingham, but the place of her marriage to Mr Verver made her placement so, a placement whose matchless beauty allowed her to do nothing in life at all, not that she'd done that much previously, a placement that made her proximity to the Prince an occurrence of immense naturalness such that when Lady Castledean invited them to stay it was only natural they should return to London alone.

'You shall have whatever you want,' the Prince whispered to her, kissing her with passion, a passion that was almost passionless in the denseness of the prose.

For 150 long pages, Maggie considered how she was placed both in regard to the Prince and to her father and Charlotte, a placement that required sentences of breathtakingly meaningless construction, a construction given over to a detailed deconstruction of every nuance in each regard, a regard to which anyone else in their right mind would not have devoted more than a second. She longed to know where she really 'was', yet was as yet uncertain whether the idea was in fact a fact.

'Your behaviour towards me is most unsettling,' Charlotte said. 'Pray tell me how we are placed?'

'We are placed where we always were.'

Having determined that appearing the fool in so far as the Prince and Charlotte were concerned was the best way of serving the Princess, Mrs Assingham was mindful of her position when Maggie summoned her to Portland Place.

'I have bought the Golden Bowl from the Jew and the Prince's duplicity is revealed,' the Princess said.

'Not if I break it,' cried Mrs Assingham, hurling it to the ground.

At this point, the Prince returned, prompting Maggie to retell the coincidence of her having bought the Golden Bowl and the Jew having remembered the Prince and Charlotte, a coincidence no more convincing the second time around.

The Prince fell silent, a silence born of his never having looked a gift fortune in the mouth, and a *froideur* was slowly initiated in his dealings with Charlotte.

'Mr Verver and I are returning to America,' Charlotte announced a month later.

'Charlotte always was a stupid woman,' the Prince said, holding the Princess's hand.

'What was all that about?' enquired Mrs Assingham.

'A load of Golden Bowlocks,' her husband grunted.

THE SCARLET PIMPERNEL

Baroness Orczy

A SEETHING CROWD, human only in name, were demanding the Roi and his beautiful gâteau-stuffing Reine be sacrificed to Madame Guillotine. But this was the year of grace 1792 and the awful peasants were the rulers of France.

Sergeant Bibot allowed the deformed hunchback, driving a cart laden with decapitated aristocrats, through the gates of Paris. 'You fool!' cried Citoyen Tinville. 'Zat was ze accursed Eengleeshman, ze Scarlet Pimpernel, escaping with ze Comtesse de Tournay sewn into ze bodies.'

England had never been merrier and Dover rocked with bucolic laughter. 'God Save the King,' sang the local rustics, before tugging their forelocks as an impossibly handsome young nobleman arrived with the Comtesse de Tournay and her children.

'Come quaff some ale,' ejaculated Sir Andrew Ffffoulkes.

'*Ooh la la!*' the Comtesse declared. 'I can see my daughter eez swooning with desire for you. If only my huzzban waz 'ere too my 'appiness would be complete.'

'Odd's teeth, he will be soon. The League of the Scarlet Pimpernel enjoys a little sport with the Frenchies.'

'And 'ooo eez ze Pumpernelle?'

'Zounds, Milady, I cannot tell you. No one knows the elusive Pimpernel.'

Dover once more fell silent as the peasants prostrated themselves before Sir Percy Blakeney, eight feet tall and the richest dandy in Merrie England, and his wife, Lady Marguerite, a beautiful apparition of five and twenty years and once the cleverest woman in France. Not that that was saying much.

'Well, I'll be demmed,' Sir Percy said. 'I em as wet as a herring.' Even though he was eight feet tall and the richest dandy in Merrie England, no one knew why the cleverest woman in France had chosen him as her husband.

'I deespize you, Milady,' the Comtesse de Tournay cried. 'You betrayed ze Marquis de St Cyr.'

Marguerite wept a quiet tear. Sir Percy had left her severely alone since he had discovered her part in St Cyr's arrest, and yet she could not tell him of the circumstances that would exonerate her from any blame. And now her beloved brother, Armand, was returning to France to save *La Patrie* from the merciless *citoyens*.

'France 'eez in peril,' said Armand. 'Eet needz my lofty *vertus*. Bert one day zoon we will be reunited and Sir Percy will *comprend* ze circumstances zat weeel *completement* exonerate you from blame in St Cyr's *mort*.'

A weaselly Francheman appeared at Marguerite's door. It was Citoyen Chauvelin, ze spymaster in cheff for the République. 'I 'av *une lettre* zat preuvvs your bruzzaire eez un serffant of ze Pumpernelle. Bert if you 'elp *moi* unmask ze Pumpernelle, zen I weeel let Armand go.'

'*Mais* how can I 'elp?'

'Ze Pumpernelle eeze an Eeeengleesh Milord et az *vous* are se pivot de society, you can lead *moi* to eeem.'

Marguerite wept more quiet tears. Sir Percy didn't love her because he didn't understand the circumstances that would completely exonerate her from blame for St Cyr's death, and now she was going to have to betray the magnificent Pimpernel to save her *frère*.

'Odds bodkins,' said Sir Percy, as he entered the ball-room. 'I'll be demmed. This is a tremendous party.'

Marguerite sighed with relief. She had baited the trap as

Chauvelin had asked but only her husband had appeared. So the Pimpernel was steeel at large!

'Madam, I must hie me North at once,' Sir Percy said. Was that his hidden passion she sensed? But why did he leave so suddenly? And why did he have a large map of France stencilled with a pimpernel on the wall?

The cleverest woman in France was perturbed for 50 pages. Zen it struck 'er like a clap of *tonnerre*. Sir Percy *wazz* ze Pumpernelle. *Non! Oui!* And he 'ad always luvvered 'er but 'ad disguizered 'eez feelings and made 'eemself look stupeeed in order not to be deescuvvered.

'*Quelle* fool I 'ave been!' the cleverest woman in France announced. 'He has gone to rescue my bruzzaire et le Comte, bert ee eez riding into a trap. I muzzt hie me to France *aussi*.'

Her heart pounded noisily. Sir Percy 'ad escaped Chauvelin near Calais by singing the National Anthem, but now she 'ad been taken prisoner by ze dreaded Citoyen. Her thoughts were interrupted by the arrival of a four-foot-tall Jew.

'Take me to ze 'ut where ze Pumpernelle, Armand and le Comte are waiting for a *bateau*, you hideous *personne*,' Chauvelin demanded, showing the Frenchman's traditional contempt for the Jew.

'Very well,' the dwarfish son of Abraham replied, whistling the National Anthem.

Armand and the Count were safe, and the cleverest woman in France melted into the arms of Sir Percy who had discarded his disguise as a four-foot descendant of Moses and returned to his accustomed height.

'I weeel nezzaire doubt you again, my savieuurr of France,' she sobbed. '*Je suis* so 'eppy.'

'I'll be demmed,' Sir Percy laughed. 'Now that I understand the circumstances that completely exonerate you from any blame over the death of St Cyr, I rather think I might lurve you too.'

ANN VERONICA

H. G. Wells

A NN VERONICA STANLEY, a young woman of one and twenty years, placed her feet on the train seat in an attitude of defiance that would have given her grandmother a touch of the vapours. She had teetered on the verge of such a resolution before, but now her mind was made up. A Crisis had been reached and the Row with her father must be had.

'You cannot go, Vee,' said her father, a neuralgic solicitor of one and fifty-two years. 'It is simply preposterous to imagine that you can go to a party with the Widgett girls dressed as a Corsair.'

'You old-fashioned Victorian father, you!' she cried, her heart heaving with burgeoning feminism as she slammed the front door shut and bustled along the tree-lined avenues of the London suburb of Morningside Park, to expostulate at length on women's rights.

'I'm all for women getting the vote,' said Teddy, the one and seventeen year-old brother of the Widgett girls. 'Please marry me.'

'Don't be silly.'

Ann Veronica's second offer of marriage came two days later, the day before the Crisis was finally resolved, at a lunch held by Lady Palsworthy for her nephew, Mr Manning. 'I hear you believe women should be allowed a day off from housework,' said Mr Manning, a comely moustachioed man of one and twenty-five years.

'Indeed I do.'

'Jolly good. Pray listen to my poetry. *I would die / I would cry / I would sigh / If I could not lie / Next to thy / Beautiful body.* Marry me.'

This invitation was also rebuffed and Ann Veronica returned

home to barricade herself into her room. This was the night of the party! And she would not kiss her papa goodnight! Tomorrow she would leave for London Town.

She arose at dawn and furtively left the house. How her heart ached with righteousness! She was now a Person in her own Right! She was alarmed to encounter Mr Ramage, a City financier of one and fifty-four years who dribbled lecherously, but once the train was Waterloo-bound her spirits soared.

Finding accommodation was not as easy as she had thought, but Ann Veronica eventually found a room in Bloomsbury and sought ways to earn her living. Fie! Only posts for shop assistants or governessess were on offer. How could one become a Person on just a few shillings a week? Perhaps she had been a little hasty! 'Vixen' her father had called her, declaring he never wished to see her again.

Her resolve hardened. Being a Person was not meant to be easy and she was committed to a Higher Morality. She would abandon her domestic science course at Tredgold's Women's College and study with Mr Russell at Imperial College. How her father would have hated a woman's pursuit of Rationality! Yet how could she afford it?

'I will lend you forty pounds,' said Mr Ramage, suggestively.

'How very generous,' Ann Veronica replied, heading for the laboratories of South Kensington where she was greeted by her tutor Mr Capes, a handsome man of two and thirty-one years who in many ways resembled Mr Wells himself. Staring at him, she felt a Higher Love. Yet was he not a man of scandal, a man who was separated from his wife! She must not declare Herself.

'I'm a committed suffragette who has been to a few Fabian meetings with the Webbs,' she declared, hoping Capes would not detect the Higher Love his presence inspired in her.

'Fascinating,' Capes replied, dissecting a dogfish.

A letter from Mr Ramage arrived, inviting her to join him for a performance of *Tristan and Isolde* followed by dinner at a *cabinet particulier*. 'Do not the dark longings of Wagner's music instil a stirring in your nether regions?' Mr Ramage recklessly declared, thrusting his mouth towards her lips.

Ann Veronica punched him firmly on the chin. 'How dare you!' she cried. 'I am not a Woman of Lower Truth.'

'Did you not understand the ways in which I loved you when you borrowed forty pounds?'

Alone in her room, she sobbed heavy tears of feminist heartbreak. She had a Higher Love for a man who did not even know he was Higher Loved! And how could she repay Mr Ramage forty pounds when all she had was one and twenty pounds and five shillings? She withdrew three and one five-pound notes from her account and sent them to Mr Ramage. They were returned that very day. 'How dare he?' she yelled, flinging the money into the fire. There was just one way out. She must go to prison for being a suffragette.

Ann Veronica wept tears of bitter bitterness in her cell for one and thirty long days. Perhaps she had been too hasty! Perhaps she had been a little too feminist! Yes! She would return home when she was released.

'Glad you've got that women's stuff out of your system, Vee,' her father said.

'Will you marry me now?' Mr Manning asked. 'I would get a takeaway from time to time, to save you some cooking.'

She would! Though she did not love him with the Higher Love she felt for Capes, it was best if such desires were repressed. 'I will,' she said. 'As long as you don't tell anyone.'

'*The Dove of Love / Hath descended from Above!*'

'But no,' she wept three days later. 'I cannot marry you. I must remain true to the Higher Love!'

Ann Veronica ran to Imperial and lay prostrate at Capes's feet. 'I can no longer lie to Myself. I have become the right kind of feminist, the kind acceptable to a man. I love you with all the humility and obedience a woman owes a Man who understands her need for emancipation and Higher Truth.'

'How I have longed to tell you of the Harder, I mean Higher, Love I feel for you. Yet the shame I feel at possessing a wife who doesn't understand me stayed my tongue!'

'I have no care. Take me in your arms and elope.'

'We'll go to Germany and I'll give up my work as a boring scientist to be a trendy writer just like H. G. Wells.'

They climbed every mountain, forded every stream, as the Universe smiled on their Higher Love. 'Together we shall get married and have lots of children, my Dionysus,' Ann Veronica whispered.

'Indeed we shall, my Pallas Athene.'

One and three years later, Capes smoked a cigar, standing by the mantelpiece. 'It's wonderful your father has accepted your radical feminism.'

'I rather think the one and nines of thousands of pounds your masterpiece of a play has earned have soothed his bourgeois sensibilities, my Hero,' Ann Veronica said, while tidying away the glasses. 'But don't ever let us forget the Higher Emancipated Love we enjoyed in Germany.'

'Course not, babe. Now be a good girl and make us a cuppa.'

HOWARDS END

E. M. Forster

ONE MAY AS well begin with Helen's letters to her sister.
Dearest Meg, I am having a glorious time at Howards End. I especially like young Mr Wilcox. We are to be wed.

'You Schlegel sisters are quite the dark horses,' said Mrs Munt. 'It is surely because you are German.'

'Don't be silly, Aunt Juley,' Margaret replied. 'We are the very best sort of cultured Germans.'

It's all over. The Wilcoxes are mercantile; Paul is leaving the book to go to Nigeria – H.

'I don't know what came over me,' Helen sighed. 'We'll hear no more about it,' Margaret exclaimed. 'Let's go to the Beethoven concert.'

We are not concerned with the poor. No one is. But let's imagine someone on the edge of gentility and call him Leonard Bast. See Mr Bast pointlessly trying to improve himself by attending the same concert as the Schlegels. See Helen pick up Mr Bast's umbrella in error. See Mr Bast follow her home.

'I believe you took my umbrella,' Mr Bast insisted, for he is of sufficient impoverishment not to be able to afford the loss. 'I'm always stealing umbrellas,' Helen announced with Bohemian breeziness.

'And you, Mr Bast, are a fascinating specimen of the lower orders,' Margaret said. 'Allow me to patronise you for the rest of the book.'

Taking her card, Mr Bast returned to his squalid lodgings.

'Gawd bless you, Leonard,' said Jacky, the least convincing temptress in English fiction. 'Come to bed.'

Margaret twitched with social embarrassment. The Wilcoxes were moving in across the road.

Dear Miss Schlegel, We are in London because my son Charles is to be wed. Paul is in Africa so we can meet – Yours, Mrs Wilcox.

'How I miss Howards End,' Mrs Wilcox said wanly.

'I too have my doubts about Modernity,' Margaret smiled.

The funeral of Mrs Wilcox was over. Edwardian women understood their obligation to die with little fuss. 'She was a good woman,' Mr Wilcox intoned gravely. 'There's just one thing. She wanted Miss Schlegel to have Howards End. It's most improper.'

Two years had passed when there was a knock on the Schlegels' door.

'Where's my 'usband?' Jacky demanded.

'What are you talking about?' Margaret responded.

The next day an ashen-faced Mr Bast stood before Margaret. 'My wife found your card and reached an unfortunate conclusion,' he said. 'I was walking alone for 24 hours to be with Nature.'

'I too love Nature, Fate and other ideals that start with Capital Letters,' Margaret condescended.

'I'm a clerk with Porphyrion Insurance . . .'

'We'll have to do something about that.'

Margaret had worries of her own. Progress was marching onwards and their home was to be demolished. Where would they live? Just then she espied Mr Wilcox.

'Good day,' she said. 'I am very concerned about my friend Mr Bast. And I am shortly to be homeless.'

'I have heard Porphyrion will smash and I have a house you may rent,' Mr Wilcox replied gruffly.

Margaret's heart skipped. Could it be that Mr Wilcox would propose? 'Would you do me the honour of marrying me?' asked Mr Wilcox. She hesitated for a decorous few days before giving an affirmative response. 'May we live at Howards End?'

'It's too shabby and London is growing so fast it's almost suburban,' he said testily. 'I have rented a Shropshire estate.'

The day of the engagement party did not start well. Charles, disturbed by his father marrying a German, symbolically ran over a cat. Then Helen appeared with Mr and Mrs Bast.

'Porphyrion didn't smash,' Helen sobbed, 'but Mr Bast left his employment anyway. Now he's penniless.'

'Dearest Mr Wilcox,' Margaret pleaded, 'please find work for our pet who has fallen on hard times because of us.'

'A man's future is in his own hands,' he answered swiftly, speaking for Capital.

'Hello again, ducky,' Mrs Bast slurred.

Mr Wilcox blanched. 'I release you from your vows, Miss Schlegel,' he murmured gravely. 'My youthful dalliance has been exposed.'

Margaret's heart was reeling but her head was German. 'I forgive you,' she said eventually.

So Margaret settled for Love, Property and Propriety. All that spoiled her happiness was Helen. 'She is avoiding me,' she wept sagely. 'We must interrupt our self-satisfaction to trick Helen into meeting us.'

'I'm with child,' declared Helen. 'Mr Bast is the father. I took pity and awarded him charity intercourse.'

'Charles must beat the bounder to within an inch of his life,' Mr Wilcox shouted.

Leonard Bast lay dead. His heart had given out spontaneously.

'See how everything is connected,' Margaret wittered. 'You, Me, Helen, Her Baby, Nature, Town, Love and Fate. Even Mr Bast. Let's all be unbearably smug until the First World War starts.'

SANDERS OF THE RIVER

Edgar Wallace

MR COMMISSIONER SANDERS had graduated to West Central Africa by way of the Zulu, Matabele, Bechuana and the Pigmy people, and he now kept watch over a quarter of a million cannibal folk who until ten years ago had never had the good fortune to meet a white man.

You may say of Sanders that he was a statesman for he understood the way of the negro. He knew to treat them like children, for that was the language they understood. When they stepped out of line, Sanders would have them hung or shot with the Maxim, and even the miscreants who were killed thanked him for it. The black man does not respond to kindness. There was once a Mr Commissioner Niceman who tried to engage the Akasava people in a long humanitarian palaver about returning the women and goats to the Ochori. His head was stuck on a pole for his efforts.

So it fell to Sanders to settle the dispute. 'You can keep the women for they have no value,' he said. 'But the goats you must return by nightfall.' The Akasava failed so to do and so Sanders sent in 20 Houssas to string up an entire village. Thus was the problem resolved to everyone's satisfaction.

A month later the child King Peter of the Akasavas, whom Sanders had installed as ruler after his father's death, was once more behaving bellicosely towards the Ochori.

'Why are you acting so?' Sanders enquired, cracking his rhinoceros tail whip hard against the boy's back.

Swish. Swish, swish! 'Ow, Lord!' Swish, swish, swish. 'Because my evil Uncle Sato-Kato made me, Sandi,' Peter yelped.

'Then summon him here.'

Sato-Kato arrived intent on killing Sanders and might even have done so had not Peter taken the spear intended for his Lord. 'That was a close-run thing,' Sanders said to Abiboo, his trusty servant, who had concluded the business by chopping off Sato-Kato's head and eating him.

Now you may have wondered why it was that the Akasawa always chose to attack the Ochori. The truth is the Ochori were congenital cowards. If a stranger were to demand a goat or a woman, they would hand one over without question rather than fight. This gave Sanders many a sleepless night, until one of his spies reported that many cattle had gone missing from the Ochori's close neighbours.

Sanders thought this most odd and went upriver with 20 faithful Houssas in the steamboat *Zaire* to see the lie of the land for himself. After casually ordering three men to be hanged on the grounds that they must have committed some crime or other, Sanders demanded an audience with the king.

To his surprise, Sanders discovered that Bosambo, the least trustworthy man in the whole of Africa, had installed himself as ruler of the Ochori.

'I take it, then, that you have taught the Ochori to steal and fight,' said Sanders.

'Indeed I have, Sandi Lord.'

'Well, that's no bad thing. The Ochori needed to learn how to stand up for themselves. And as long as you remember to do whatever the British government wants, I'll overlook your misdemeanours.'

'Thank you, Lord. It will be a pleasure to serve the British. They are so much more straightforward than the filthy Dutch, French and Italians.'

There came to the country an Englishman named Cuthbert

who took it upon himself to venture into the dark interior, despite being warned against it by Sanders. He was not seen for many months so Sanders headed out into the forest in search of him. He found him delirious, claiming to have bought land from the Isisi and to be suffering from sleeping sickness. Straightway, Sanders summoned Bosambo.

'Why did you sell him lands that were not yours to sell?'

'Because I had no lands of my own to sell, Sandi.'

'And why did you give the man Cuthbert some hemp?'

'Because I had nothing else to give him, Sandi.'

'Very good, Bosambo. Carry on.'

There was another time when the Olari had put a most fearful ju-ju on a Mr George Tackle, who would most assuredly have been sacrificed without a palaver had not Sanders arrived in the nick of time to execute the witch doctor and 1,000 of his accomplices. Mr Tackle, not being well versed in the way of the native, was appalled at Sanders's summary justice and wrote to *The Times* of London to complain in the strongest possible terms.

'The man was a fool,' said Sanders, after he was awarded nine thousand pounds in compensation.

'Do you not think that all these little tales might not become somewhat repetitive after a while, Sandi Lord,' said Abiboo, hurrying to tell Sanders about the latest foul chicanery involving the Akasava, wholesale poisoning and some sacred stones.

'Indeed I do,' Sanders replied. 'But what's a man to do in the face of the native cunning? As long as the negro tries to get the better of the white man, it behoves the white man to teach him a lesson by chopping off his head. Besides, the penny dreadful reader can't get enough of this casual colonial racism. Now prepare the *Zaire* for another trip upriver.'

'Sandi, sir,' Abiboo laughed, clapping his hands with glee. 'How did you manage to persuade the British government to send you 20,000 of the King's finest troops to annihilate 100,000 cannibals?'

'It turned out the sacred stones held large traces of gold. That usually gets the attention of the British government.'

It has been said by some that Sanders was a 'woman-hater', but those who described him thus were those who knew him not. It is true that Sanders had no close female attachments, but he was far from a woman-hater. Rather, he had more than enough on his hands with killing cannibals to contemplate the very idea of romance. Besides which, there were no suitable women with whom Sanders might force an attachment.

Of unsuitable women there were many as a man called Ludley found to his cost, having struck up a liaison with a native woman whose father put him in the cooking pot for his troubles. There he might have burned to death but for the arrival of Sanders, along with 20 Houssas and his trusty Maxims.

'Stop that!' Sanders shouted, before rounding up 120 natives who were cowering in the corner. 'Now, stand still while I put a noose around the lot of you.'

'Why, Sandi Lord?' they cried. 'We have done nothing wrong. It is the ju-ju witch doctor who is to blame.'

'I know that. But I expect you would have committed a capital crime tomorrow, so it's as well to get ahead of myself.'

'Thank you, Sandi Lord. You are indeed wise.'

On the way back downriver, Sanders took Ludley to one side. 'The thing is, man, the native has no memory. So there's no point holding a trial as they would never remember of what crime they had been convicted. Punishing them in advance is the only way to win their respect. And while you're about it, steer clear of the native woman. She may have a fine physique, but she is exceedingly ugly.'

No sooner had he returned home than Sanders heard that the Isisi were playing up once more. 'Head back upriver,' he commanded the steamboat captain. As they neared the village, arrows rained down on the deck.

'Looks like we could be in Queer Street this time, Abiboo,' he said.

'Perhaps not,' Abiboo yelled, leaping up and down. There in the distance, heading upriver, were hundreds of canoes full of Ochori tribesman armed to the teeth. Within minutes 20,000 Isisi lay mutilated beyond recognition on the riverbed.

'Keep up the good work, Bosambo,' Sanders said. 'Your country needs you.'

DEATH IN VENICE

Thomas Mann

O N A SPRING afternoon in 19—, Gustav Aschenbach, or von Aschenbach as he had officially been known since his fiftieth birthday, set out from his apartment in Munich. The morning's writing had overstimulated him. As with many German intellectuals of the early-twentieth century, his mind was feasting on the classicism of his surroundings when he came across a displeasing red-haired man. A strange emotion stirred within him, an emotion he later identified as a desire to travel. He had been too preoccupied with the duties imposed on him by the collective European psyche. He needed an impromptu interlude, a *dolce far niente*.

The author of the massive prose epic about the life of Frederick of Prussia, and creator of *A Study in Abjection*, Aschenbach had first made a name for himself at little more than school age and his reputation had grown steadily ever since. His physical frailty, combined with an overarching self-regard, meant he had few friends, and he had scarcely noticed when his wife had died some years earlier. He slept twelve hours each day, exhausted by the hard labour of twenty minutes' writing and the over-refinement of his existence, yet Aschenbach did not complain, accepting his Teutonic duty was to sublimate his Self in an ecstasy of the will to Art, Beauty and Capital Letters.

He took the overnight train to Trieste and thence headed for the island of Pola. The rain and provincialism soon filled this Apollonian artist with vexation; his destination had been mis-chosen and so he booked his passage to Venice. From the seclusion of his first-class quarters, he gazed down at the hoi polloi before recoiling in disaste at the sight of a lamentably dandified old man, his cheeks carmine with rouge and Asti.

Venice was not enshrined in sun when the ferry docked, a disturbing insult to his aesthetics, and Aschenbach's mood was not improved when a contumacious, red-haired gondolier imposed his services on him. Quite naturally, his thoughts turned to death. For what man does not think of death at such a moment? He disembarked at the Hotel des Bains on the Lido and was reassured to hear the sounds of all the major world languages. And Polish. As he was waiting for dinner he spotted three austere expressionless girls with their extremely beautiful fourteen-year-old brother. He went to sleep in a transport of delight and entered a dreamland where he was a great deal more active than he ever was awake.

The smell of the lagoon was vexatious and Aschenbach was again concerned his asceticism might be compromised. He dressed for breakfast and espied the young boy in the dining room. 'Well, my little Phaeacian with the head of Eros,' Aschenbach said to himself, as would any man of letters overwhelmed by the liquid beauty of Achelous. He went to the sea to watch the Bacchanalia of the simple peasants and escape the complexity of phenomena, yet when the boy, whom he now learned was called Tadzio, once more appeared, romping with the others, he was transfixed again. Tut, tut, Critobulus, he thought, in a manner that his superego confused with paternal fondness, yet which his turbulent id identified with pederasty. Albeit a very high-minded, noble pederasty.

He took a walk around the Piazza and the sickening stench that pervaded the air made him resolve to leave. He sent his luggage ahead, desirous to spend his last few hours in Venice with his Narcissus. 'Adieu, Tadzio,' he said to no one but himself. 'May God bless you even though you are probably going to die young.' Real grief rent his heart. How he longed to turn back! What joy! What rapture! What exclamation marks! His trunk had been sent on to Como by mistake. There was nothing for it but to return to his hotel.

Exhausted by the half-hour journey, Aschenbach spent the following week reclining in a chair, enjoying Oceanus's calming breeze and watching Tadzio's translucent god-like physique. 'O Hyacinthus, O Phaedrus,' he said. 'How I desire to produce prose of limpid sensuousness to match your beauty.' As the days slipped by, Aschenbach dared to hope for a reciprocity of feeling, and once he smiled and mouthed a dignified 'I love you' to the boy's retreating figure.

In the fourth week, Aschenbach heard rumours there was a sickness in the city, yet he could not bring himself to leave. He followed Tadzio more openly, leaning against his bedroom door, enjoying both the city's and his own guilty secrets and the ancient nobility of his debasement. As the stench of gastric juices continued to fill the air, he learned there was a cholera epidemic but still he could not bring himself to tell Tadzio's mother. The consciousness of his complicity intoxicated him and his dreams became full of leaden Freudian archetypes of Saturnalia.

He allowed the barber to colour his hair and cheeks and to paint his lips cherry-red, the mirror image of the Satyr who had so offended his delicate asceticism on the ferry. Apollo had made way for Dionysus. He revelled in his sensuousness, becoming ever more reckless in his pursuit of Phaedrus. He overheard Tadzio's mother say they were leaving and he started to feel unwell. He went to the beach and watched Tadzio wrestle with a friend. Was he beckoning him? He made to rise from his chair, but collapsed, crushed by the weight of the symbolism.

LE GRAND MEAULNES

Alain-Fournier

H E CAME TO our place one Sunday in November 189–. I say 'our place' though it is fifteen years since we left the old school of Saint-Agathe where my father taught and we shall never come back, for one's childhood is a world to which one can never return . . .

I can well remember that first night I spent in my garret, a sickly lonely five-year-old who even then had an unhealthy fondness for over-indulgent nostalgia . . . But enough of that! For now I must leap forward ten years to the arrival of Augustin Meaulnes, a tall, imposing seventeen-year-old youth . . . And how I fell under his spell, a spell so Grand that everyone called him Le Grand Meaulnes!

One afternoon, as my father ordered Moucheboeuf to collect my grandparents from the station, I noticed a strange expression, an expression I had only ever previously seen in Robinson Crusoe – don't ask how – cross the face of Le Grand Meaulnes . . . And then, when no one but me was looking, he arose and made his way to the trap. And like a Roman charioteer he disappeared into the misty forest, a forest redolent with the metaphors of childhood . . .

And three long days was he gone, days I spent wondering if my childhood happiness would ever return. And then! A knock on the window pane . . . It was Le Grand Meaulnes! How agitated he was! And how the joyous innocence of childhood seemed to fade as he scribbled silently in his notebook . . .

Eventually he spoke . . . 'I have been on a great adventure, François,' he said. 'As I drove through the mists of the Sologne, I found myself transported into a land I did not recognise . . . At last I fell asleep and awoke in the barn of a lost estate where the workers invited me to join the preparation for the wedding party of Frantz de Galais, the Parsifalic son of the Seigneur.'

'Are you sure you had not been taking *les champignons magiques* . . . ?' I enquired.

'*Mais non*,' he replied. 'All this is very normal for tales of French adolescent whimsy. Now where was I? *Oui*, I was walking by the lake and I met the most beautiful woman in the world. I looked at her, she looked at me, we looked at each other . . . And it was a great and beautiful thing. And then she says to me in stilted French, "I am Yvonne de Galais, sister of Frantz de Galais. Please do not follow me again . . ."

'And then there was a big commotion . . . Frantz appears, declaring that Valentine, his bride-to-be, has abandoned him and he no longer wants to live . . . Mysteriously was I put in a carriage and fell asleep once more only to be awoken two leagues from Saint-Agathe by the sound of a distant gunshot . . .'

Le Grand Meaulnes sobbed. 'And I still do not know where I have been. So I cannot retrace my steps to the resting place of my childhood happiness!'

For weeks I watched Augustin feverishly sketching, trying to create the map that would take him back to his lost childhood, as the other children plotted with the unknown Gypsy, heavily bandaged around his head, who had mysteriously arrived in the village to steal the notebook from him . . . And, alas, steal it he did! Yet soon the Gypsy, Le Grand Meaulnes and I became friends, united in a very French nostalgic whimsy. And he gave it back . . .

'Promise me,' said the Gypsy. 'That if ever I go *whoo, whoo* you will drop everything and come to my aid.'

And later that day, while dancing in the street, the Gypsy pulled away the bandages, revealing himself to be Frantz de Galais . . . Who would have thought it? Or believed that Augustin would not recognise him? 'I was so unhappy when Valentine dumped me I tried to shoot myself in the head,' he explained.

And with that he vanished, leaving Le Grand Meaulnes sobbing. 'My only chance of finding my childhood happiness has gone. I must hie me to Paris to walk the streets of Paris searching for Yvonne in perpetuity, where I shall find she is already married.'

Guess what? A year and a half later I was chatting to my Uncle Florentin and it turns out he lives in the very same village where the lost estate is situated . . . *Oui, sérieusement!* It's called Les Sablonnières and Yvonne isn't even married. In fact, she still remembers my friend, and my Uncle Florentin is having a party to reunite us all!

'Everything is not right,' Le Grand Meaulnes cried on his arrival. 'This is not the estate of my childhood, it is the estate of my adulthood. And I want my childhood. But, yes, I will marry Yvonne, I suppose, even though she is looking a bit rough.'

A distant echo cut through the melancholia of the wedding night. '*Whoo, whoo . . .*'

'It is Frantz,' Le Grand Meaulnes whispered. 'I cannot come back here to my childhood until after I have brought Valentine and him together . . .'

The months passed and Yvonne grew larger, for she was with child . . . And yet still Le Grand Meaulnes did not return.

'How I love Le Grand Meaulnes even though I only spent one day with him,' Yvonne wept. 'It is all my fault he has gone . . .'

'Fear not, for one day can seem a lifetime in adolescence . . . especially if you're reading this,' I said, perhaps unnecessarily as she had collapsed and died shortly after giving birth to a baby girl . . .

My nostalgic reveries continued apace without Yvonne . . . Why did Le Grand Meaulnes not return? I picked up his diary and started reading, something I could well have done a year ago. *I have been a very* mauvais personne, it said. *While searching for my childhood in Paris, I seduced another girl who naturally turned out to be Valentine. So I felt a bit guilty about betraying Frantz, and I dumped her . . . And then I felt very guilty about dumping her so I went looking for her but could not find her. Growing up is very painful, n'est-ce pas? And now I cannot rest until Valentine and Frantz are married . . .*

Well, fuck me! Le Grand Meaulnes finally returned with Valentine and Frantz . . . And they are married . . . Le Grand Meaulnes picked up his child and looked wistfully into the middle distance. 'I guess that if I get killed in the First World War there's a chance this book will be remembered as a classic of lost childhood.' And with that he strode towards the front line . . .

THE WAY BY SWANN'S

Marcel Proust

FOR A LONG time, I went to bed early. For a very short time, I fooled people into believing I wrote in short sentences, yet then as I hovered in that indeterminate space between sleeping and waking, as after metempsychosis thoughts of an earlier existence are unintelligible, the memory of my bedroom in Combray with its pitiless quadrangular cheval-glass came flooding back, which is more than the servants did, whose absence seemed to emanate from a Merovingian past, leaving me to wonder, in my increasingly delicate health, whether Maman would come to kiss me goodnight before M. Swann, whose red hair, cut Bressant-style, so contrasted with the icy pallor of the cocotte Odette, whose prolonged absences with M. de Charlus you might have chosen for yourself before embarking on this book, for there is so much of insignificance written that, with its endless circumlocutions, you can safely ignore vast chunks of this, arrived for dinner, a dinner of Madeleine cakes infused in tea from which still clearer memories of my childhood, though refracted through a very adult voice, came racing back.

Combray, from far away, is no location for a writer steeped in the semiotics of Bergotte, whose desire to recreate through memory, though one cannot say for certain since memory informs our comprehension of ourselves and yet somehow obscures it, hiding our latency, our very identity, through an inability to discriminate between the trivial and the consequential, creating an epic, some say endless, stream of consciousness that reminds me, as the fragment of the Vinteuil Sonata I caught through the very same window that some years later I was to overhear the violinist's daughter and her woman lover, the embodiment of Evil, laughing at his death while walking along the way by Swann to observe both the hawthorns, to whom I sobbed, 'You are not the one who tried to hurt me,' and the church's steeple which framed the village skyline, of the devotion of Françoise to Aunt Léonie, whose frailty more than matched my own, for it was her very hypochondria, not that one of my refinement would ordinarily stoop to use such a term, for the illnesses in our memory were of the gravest nature, such as those experienced by the greatest of Proustian illuminati, Alain de Botton, hastened her passing and at whose funeral I was shocked to notice that the Duchesse de Guermantes, on whose beauty I had often had cause to dwell when inclined to partake of the periwinkles and forget-me-nots along Guermantes path, was not quite so radiant as I had first imagined, and yet less time had passed between the imagination and the memory than I had thought, though that may not be how it feels to you.

Through the fissures of memory seeped knowledge of Swann's love affair, a passion that occurred some thirty years previously and which you might have imagined out of place within the confines of the narrative, yet such is the distortion of memory, a subject to which I will return in still greater distortions until the present memory is unrecognisable to the original, a derangement that will even allow you to imagine you are following this and, stranger still, enjoying it, as one would perhaps derive enjoyment from the knowledge that someone is no longer hitting you, that I find myself remembering the petit-bourgeois social gatherings of the Verdurins, observations of which, to the uninformed reader, will seem like the minutiae of social climbing described with the name-dropping of the inveterate snob, yet which to the literati is a wonder of intricate remembrance and knowing self-deceit, where Odette, a regular guest herself, secured an invitation for Swann, despite his Jewishness, for the Verdurins liked nothing more than to widen their acquaintance with people they could patronise, and at that point they had no cognisance of his friendship with the Prince of Wales, for as yet also Swann had not fallen for Odette as the Verdurins had made her appear less available than she truly was, but when he noted her resemblance to Bellini's 'Zipporah', a painting on which I will digress for many pages, he believed himself in love and that love was at first reciprocated, yet within months his visits went unanswered and so strange were the jealousies and memories that circled Swann's mind that he could not quite accept she had betrayed him with the Duc de Forcheville and countless other lovers, of both male and female gender, despite the evidence and entreaties of his friend M. de Charlus, and it was only when the doctor's wife explained how Odette thought so highly of him that he came to his senses and returned to his circle of Dukes and Princes, while wondering how he could have been attracted to a woman so clearly not his type.

The aural emotional accretion of the Vinteuil Sonata offered another opportunity to repeat the subjectivity of memory, and as I thought of Florence and Balbec, how at odds my impressions of them had been in contrast to my expectations. my mind recalled that summer when I travelled each day to the Champs-Elysées, rapt in the desire to see Gilberte, whom I knew to be Swann and Odette's daughter, and lost in the intense solipsism that would mark my writing, unable to see that because I believed myself in love with her it did not mean she loved me, and, on those days she chose not to come, I felt bereft, a feeling that draws me back to the quotidian sense of futility I experience in the Bois de Boulogne, a pointlessness with which you are surely now familiar, *n'est-ce pas*?

TARZAN OF THE APES

Edgar Rice Burroughs

'DASH IT,' SAID John Clayton, Lord Greystoke. 'These beastly Europeans mistreat the blacks even more than we do. There will be a mutiny, I'll be bound.'

'Oh, John, my love,' said Lady Alice, bursting into uncontrollable sobs as the mutineers cast them ashore. 'What's to become of us now we've been stranded in this savage jungle?'

Clayton stiffened his upper lip, quickly fashioning a castle out of fallen lumber before shooting a pride of lions for dinner. The months passed slowly, and Alice had abandoned hope of rescue when a large 300-pound ape battered at the door. 'Faith, we are doomed,' she cried, swooning in terror.

''Tis a shame she never recovered to see our baby,' Clayton murmured to himself, stretching a panther skin into a lampshade and looking at his time-piece. 'Gosh, is that the time? I'd better conveniently expire myself.'

Kala had dropped her baby, and her shoulders heaved with anthropoid despair. 'Never mind,' said Kerchak, the great ape, handing over the hairless creature they had found in the abandoned castle. 'Have this one instead.'

Tublat did not like the simple boy thing his wife had brought home. Yet Kala loved her Tarzan dearly, and as the years slid by he blossomed into a superior intelligence, effortlessly slaughtering every animal he encountered with his bare hands and swinging from tree to tree with muscular, film-star panache.

Prowling through the jungle one day, Tarzan came upon an

abandoned castle. He did not realise the desiccated skeletons inside were his parents and so paid them scant attention. Instead he picked up a book. What were these strange markings? What did 'N is for Negro' mean? Within 20 minutes Tarzan had taught himself to read and write.

Bolgani the Gorilla interrupted his learning; within minutes the pair were locked in mortal combat. The battle was fierce. Bolgani breathed his last and Tarzan's head was barely attached, hanging by the thread of his jugular vein.

'Oh, poor Tarzikins,' Kala wept, drawing him to her hairy breasts. Tublat hollered with rage. How he loathed his adopted son! He smote him hard, but Tarzan avoided his smiting and twisted his jugular vein around Tublat's throat. 'Never underestimate the Oedipus complex,' he laughed.

Tarzan subjugated every beast in the jungle and lorded over the stupid black natives with his good looks and cunning; but in his heart he longed to meet his own kind.

'What are we doing here?' Professor Porter enquired.

'How would you know?' his beautiful 19-year-old daughter Jane replied. 'You are an absent-minded professor.'

'We are lost,' wailed Clayton, now Lord Greystoke since the disappearance of his uncle. 'The sailors have stolen our treasure and left us in the scary jungle. But we have each other!'

Jane sighed. How she yearned for a tall, fit stranger with flowing locks.

Tarzan watched them, enjoying a movement in his breech-cloth he did not understand, yet not displeased that his manhood which had hitherto seemed trifling compared to other apes' was growing larger. Yet how could he convey his feelings, if he could not talk? He would worry about that later: first he must dig up that large chest those sailors had buried.

The Professor and Clayton were in peril. Tarzan wrote a hurried note for Jane – *Me Tarzan, You Jane, Me Have You* – and raced through the trees to rescue them. Jane's heart leapt when she read the note, but joy turned to despair as a lioness grabbed her arm and dragged her into the undergrowth.

Tarzan grunted with happiness as he slit the lioness's throat and held Jane in his arms. 'Oh, Tarzie,' she purred, toying with his flowing locks and admiring his diamante necklace. 'You could be an Olympic swimmer. Or the lead guitarist with Spinal Tap.'

Their bliss was short-lived. A French captain, D'Arnot, had appeared from nowhere and been abducted by cannibals. 'Blast,' Tarzan said to himself. 'Now I'll have to rescue him as well.'

'Oh, father, I am so sad,' Jane cried. 'Tarzie has not returned and our boat has come to take us back to America.'

'*Je suis inconsolable qu'elle soit partie,*' said Tarzan, having learnt French while he was nursing D'Arnot. '*Je* will go . . . er . . . *en Amérique* to find her.'

'*Je peux* teller *que vous êtes vraiment un* gent, *parce que vous ne mangez pas des personnes comme les* darkies,' D'Arnot replied. '*Je* bet *que vous êtes vraiment le* long *perdu fils de* Lord Greystoke.'

'Ha!' sneered the wicked Canler, to whom Jane's father was greatly indebted. 'Now you'll have to marry me as your father has lost the treasure.'

'Not so *vite,*' Tarzan hollered, leaping through the branches to rescue Jane from a forest fire. 'I have the treasure.' Jane's heart raced as Tarzan kissed her passionately. Yet bestiality was one thing, marriage to a simian quite another.

'I am promised to Clayton,' she sobbed, 'though I do not love him. I cannot have sex with another species, however much I want to.'

Tarzan saw Clayton's happiness and could not bear to reveal his true aristocratic identity. 'I'm an apeman, I'm an ape ape man, I'm an apeman, the apeman,' he sang, swinging his way out of the book and into the sequel.

THE GOOD SOLDIER

Ford Madox Ford

THIS IS THE saddest story I ever heard. Yet I do not know how best to set it down, for in the dawn of modernism this is an experimental narrative of recovered memories and broken time-frames that loops and skips, to leave you as confused and frustrated as myself.

We had known the Ashburnhams for nine years in Nauheim and had assumed an intimacy that only comes from not talking to each other. You will gather from this that my wife, Florence, had a 'heart' and, by the way I cleverly manipulate the pluperfect, that she is now dead.

Captain Ashburnham, Edward, who had had a successful military career in India, and his wife, Leonora, whom I loved though without the sex instinct – far too much effort for one so languidly detached as myself – would dine with us each night. Florence and I were Americans abroad, Teddy and Leonora the perfect British gentry; together we were good people who never did anything very much.

It was 1913 when Florence grasped Teddy's arm as we were visiting a Protestant relic and I noticed Leonora whiten. I suppose that a more engaged and reliable narrator might have been disturbed by his wife's display of intimacy, but I was satisfied when Leonora explained her reaction as that of an injured Irish Catholic.

Besides, Florence had given me no reason to suspect she had been Teddy's lover for nine years. If I had heard strange cries emanating from her locked bedroom, to which she retired alone each night at nine o' clock, then I understandably assumed they were the consequences of acute arrhythmia. So I assured Leonora I would only insult her co-religionists once per chapter, and thought no more about it.

It was only after Teddy had died that Leonora told me of the Kilsyte case where he had improperly kissed a servant girl, of his attachment to Major Basil's wife, of his affair with Maisie Maidan, and of his unfortunate *amour* with the mistress of a Russian grand-duke that had cost him £40,000 and forced Leonora to take control of his assets to save them from bankruptcy.

And yet, in my familiar annoyingly perverse manner, I judge Teddy to have been a good man, who was kind to his tenants and small animals, and it is hard not to acknowledge he was trying to keep his philandering in order because each mistress was better bred than the last. If he had a fault, it was that he was a sentimentalist; and if I had a fault, it was that I was so absorbed in being the perfect stylist, repeating the perfect adjectives to ever more perfect effect, that I failed to notice my IQ was hovering near zero.

Did I mention that Maisie Maidan had died on the 4th of August? Perhaps not. How artfully artless of me! But then everything important in Florence's life had happened on that date. She had been born on the 4th of August and we also got married on that day – one I remember well as it was the last time I showed any passion. Not sexual, of course, but by hitting my darky servant for no good reason, other than that is how a gentleman from Philadelphia behaves.

And of course poor Florence committed suicide on that date, not that I realised she had killed herself at first, but then as I had turned stupidity into an art form, it was at least in keeping for me not to notice. Leonora tells me the first thing I said was, 'Now I can marry the girl.' I don't recall that, but even though Leonora is a Romanist, I see no reason to disbelieve her.

Ah, the girl! Leonora's ward, Nancy Rufford. Silly me again for not mentioning her earlier! Teddy was a good man and I honestly believe he was struggling to maintain propriety in his feelings for the young woman, and that Florence might have misunderstood his intentions. Not that that is why she took her own life. Rather it was that she had returned to the hotel to find me talking to one of her relatives and assumed he must have told me about her inappropriate sexual liaison before we met.

He hadn't, as I only discovered later, though I see now her family had once tried to warn me about the affair, that had also begun on the 4th of August, but it's hard to heed such advice when one's head is located so securely inside one's rectum. But Florence wasn't to know that when she swallowed the Prussic acid.

I suppose the deceived husband ought to have been angry with Teddy, but I was a sentimentalist too and I truly loved him so much that some critics suspected me of being a closet homosexual. The person I really hated was Leonora. It was she who had pimped for Teddy, she who had led me to believe I might marry Nancy.

It was Leonora, too, who had conducted her own Papist affair with Rodney Bayham and had married him after Teddy's suicide. Yes, it quite slipped my mind that Teddy took his own life when Leonora forced Nancy to return to India. Nancy went quite mad on the boat and Teddy never forgave himself.

So now I sit, the American millionaire, waiting for the next 40 boring years to pass, listening to Nancy repeating the word 'shuttlecock'. Sometimes I even think of Teddy lying in the barn with his throat slit and how I saw him take out the penknife but was too exhausted to stop him. Yes, it is a very sad story.

THE THIRTY-NINE STEPS

John Buchan

'Richard Hannay,' I kept telling myself. 'Here you are with plenty of money to amuse yourself and you're yawning your head off.' That afternoon I had made up my mind that if nothing had happened by the end of the next paragraph, I would return to the Cape.

As I was turning the key to my Langham Place flat, I noticed my next-door neighbour at my elbow. 'I've been observing you a while,' he said, 'and you seem like a cool customer who's not afraid of playing a bold hand.' I listened while he told me about a plot engineered by the Jew to bring Russia and Germany to war.

'To thwart this fiendish scheme I have to stay alive until June 15th when the Greek Premier, Karolides, comes to London,' he continued, 'but the enemy are close on my tail. So I've bought a corpse from Harrods that the Boche will think is me and left it in my flat to cover my tracks. Now I just need somewhere to hide.'

'Wouldn't it have been easier to go straight to the British government?' I asked.

'That would have rather ruined the book.'

I liked the cut of his jib.

'Thank you for playing the white man,' he said. 'Scudder, at your service.'

Several days later I found him dead on my living room floor. I had seen bodies before in Matabeleland, but this was different. Scudder was white. I was in the soup. I would be suspected of his murder and the Boche would know I knew their plans. I had no choice but to lie low in Scotland for 20 days. I found his notebook, persuaded the cockney milkman to lend me his cap by saying 'Gaw blimey, guv'nor', and escaped to St Pancras.

I jumped off the train near Galloway, easily escaping the attentions of the police with my *veldkraft*. Alone that evening in the heather, I opened Scudder's notebook and saw it was written in cipher. With my hallmark cool logic, I had it cracked in 10 minutes.

What I read shocked me to the core. The Jew plot was eyewash. This was bigger than just killing a dago, it was the Boche Black Stone planning to infiltrate the British establishment, kill a Frenchie, steal our plans and sneak out at high tide by the 39 steps at 10.27pm. I stole a car and drove like the wind, escaping the police a second time by driving over a cliff and hanging on to a thorn bush for dear life.

I set off on foot, encountering Sir Harry, the Liberal candidate, on the road. Something about his aristocratic demeanour made me trust him.

'You are in a pickle, Mr Hannay,' he said. 'You should talk to my godfather, Sir Walter Bullivant, the PS at the FO who lives in Wiltshire.'

I bade him farewell and continued until I came to a remote farmhouse. '*Ich* have been expecting you,' the Black Stone sneered, locking me into a store room. I had unwittingly stumbled on the enemy's lair. I quickly found some explosives, blew a hole in the wall and hid in a dovecote, before running 20 miles to the derelict cottage of a roadman I had befriended earlier.

'Ach, I have no time for the polis,' he said, 'and I can see you're a gentleman. You can hide out here.' I could sense my exploits would already have stretched the credulity of a 9-year-old and that I needed a break, so I conveniently succumbed to a recurrence of my malaria for a week.

Eventually my strength returned and I ran through the night from Scotland until I came across a fisherman by a Wiltshire riverbank. It had to be my contact.

'I'm an innocent man, Sir Walter,' I gasped.

'Don't worry, old boy,' he replied. 'Scudder told me all about you before he was killed.'

Unaware of what a bizarre coincidence it was that I had been directed to Sir Walter or what a complete waste of time my Scotch adventures now were, I fell into a dreamless sleep. I awoke to a sense of anticlimax and a strangely familiar face leaving a private meeting with Sir Walter and four British and French generals.

'That wasn't Lord Alloa,' I said, bursting into their room. 'That was the Black Stone!'

'Good God!' Sir Walter cried. 'The Boche are privy to our secrets.'

'Not quite yet,' I replied. 'The Black Stone will want to tell the Boche in person. If we can find him before he gets home to Germany, Britain will be saved.'

I pushed Allied High Command to one side and studied the maps until I found a pier in Kent with 39 steps where high tide would be at 10.27pm. 'There, unless I'm very much mistaken,' I said, 'we shall find the Black Stone.'

'Arrest him quickly,' Sir Walter insisted.

'Not so fast. We Brits play by the rules and we can't arrest him until we know he really *is* the Boche.'

I settled down to a long game of bridge with the Black Stone. Damn him, he was good. Just as I was beginning to wonder if he might be British after all, he made a fatal error.

'Only a German would have bid no trumps.'

'*Gott im Himmel*, Hannay. Ze game is *hoch*!'

A PORTRAIT OF THE ARTIST AS A YOUNG MAN

James Joyce

Once upon a time and a very good time it was there was a moocow that met a nicens baby tuckoo . . . His father told him that story. When you wet the bed it is warm then it gets cold then it smells. His mother had a nicer smell than his father who was younger than his Uncle Charles and Dante.

The wide playgrounds of Clongowes were swarming with boys and he was caught in the scrimmage.

– Tell us Dedalus, do you kiss your mother? Wells asked.

– I do, Stephen replied not knowing if it was the right answer. Or indeed why he had recalled this particular snatch of conversation at all. But he thought it must be important for the very reason that he had recalled it and his mind soon slipped to God. He knelt down to pray.

Oh God, please help me find a voice
That's recognisably James Joyce.

It was the holidays, his father and Dante were rowing over something called politics. What was this politics thing?

– You're a sinner Simon, Dante said to his father, and so is Parnell.

Parnell was dead. He might die too. Was it cancer or canker? Brother Michael had given him no medicine so maybe he was not ill. He went down to classes and Father Dolan was in a wax because he had not been writing but Father Arnall had told him to scut as he had broken his glasses.

– You are an idler, Dedalus, Father Dolan had said, striking him with the pandybat. His eyes smarted with the injustice and he went to see the rector.

Huroo, the other boys shouted and this was important as it ended the chapter.

He was older now so his prose became less childish and he sat day-dreaming of *The Count of Monte Cristo* for he was growing weary of his parents' company. The sounds and smells of Dublin were fresh and complex to him and he struggled to keep up with all the footnotes. A friend invited him to a party at Blackrock.

– Hello, said a girl named Emma.

– I cannot talk, he replied, for serious young men need no distractions from their solipsism. Far better I should stalk you on the bus and write Byronic epics.

Oh sweetest, fairest E . . .
I have a terrible dile . . .
This verse, this gentle poet knows,
Is just as dire as his prose.

– Things are set fair, Stephen, his father said but he knew better. He had heard his mother say his father had lost all his money and Stephen would not be returning to Clongowes.

– You have heresy in your essay, said Mr Tate. Heresy! What did he care for heresy at Belvedere College? The teachers and his classmates were fools. They did not understand his meta-morphosis. Cardinal Newman would have felt his pain. He yearned to lose the shackles of his religion, of his very Irishness, yet there was no voice inside him save an annoying protean adolescent know-all.

He spent the money he had won for his brilliance on his family and cringed with shame at his father's antics. Where is my greatness? He cried to himself as he wandered alone through the streets of Dublin.

– Fancy a kiss, dearie, the woman said and he tried to resist but she pulled him close and he surrendered to her swoon of sin. Day after day he allowed himself to lust with ladies of darkness. Disgust and remorse were etched in his soul and he felt God's wrath upon him. Mad! Mad! What had he done? But how could he bear the shame? And what would E. think?

– *Peccavi*, he said in Latin to feel the purity of Saint Francis Xavier.

– *Peccavisti*, the priest answered. You have allowed yourself to be tempted by the pleasures of a straightforward narrative. For too many pages now you have written sentences that follow meaningfully on from one another. Your only hope is to join a seminary.

Yes! He would be a priest. He would give his Soul to the Ciborium! And yet there was E. whom he had not seen and as he walked along the beach and saw a woman who wasn't E. dancing in the sand he knew he could not become Christ's disciple. He had transcended his Catholic bonds! He was an aesthete.

Stephen grew weary of the shallowness of university life. How his friends loved to prattle on about Irish nationalism!

They stand and argue all long day
About Parnell's lover, Kitty O'Shea

Had he not resolved these temporal feelings when he was but twelve? An artist could not be tied to statehood!

– There is the matter of the tundish, the dean said. Stephen railed at the insensitivity of the Englishman. The language he is speaking is mine, he thought. I am Irish yet I am forced to speak English. What kind of voice, what kind of life is that!

– I have seen the birds swirling symbolically in the sky and I cannot go to church with my mother, Stephen declared. Nor can I be myself. I must get me thither to France.

– Don't go, his friends begged. Save us from *Ulysses* and *Finnegans Wake*.

1. March, I have a voice, a voice I have, a voice that is mine a scutting, smugging, oozing voice.

2. April, Icarus can crash and burn. I don't give a Simian's whether any of you understand a sourfavoured word.

3. May, My clarity lies in my opacity, my penetratability in my impenetrability. And you, poor suckers, have fallen for my myth of genius.

TARR

Wyndham Lewis

PARIS. A CITY wasted on the Parisians. A city where Artists with a capital A go to make Art with a capital A. Though only English Artists, of course; the Germans merely make art with a small a, for the juxtaposition of art and German is but an oxymoron, yet still the sluggish Germans come to the Vitelotte Quartier and it behoves the English to patronise them civilly.

Frederick Tarr met Hobson in the Boulevard du Paradis. It was not a meeting that either party had intended for both were too self-absorbed to be aware of the other's existence.

'Your hair is too long,' said Tarr .

'*Au contraire*, it is yours that is too short,' Hobson wittily retorted. 'And are you not too friendly with the Germans?'

'If you are referring to my fiancée, Fräulein Bertha Lunken, then of course I am ashamed! For that is the point! Mwa-ha-ha! Art is the very opposite of one's Appetite, and as my Art is the epitome of refinement then it behoves me to partake of my Appetite among the lumpen Germans!'

Tarr strode briskly onwards, reflecting on Hobson's complete absence of personality – a trait one might have thought would have made him an ideal main character instead of a bit part who was never to be seen again – until he reached Bertha's bourgeois-bohemian studio.

'I am, of course, naked,' she said daringly.

'I'm afraid I have to end our engagement for it is compromising my Art. But by ending it I am somehow allowing us to remain together, my little Milch Cow.'

Bertha caught her breath from the orgasm she had mysteriously just had. 'Of course,' she said nonchalantly. 'Do as you will.' She was not as nonchalant as she outwardly appeared, yet understood that nonchalance was the means by which Artists were caught. For his part, Tarr was perplexed by her nonchalance and wondered . . . For our part, we were bored senseless with the banality of the self-consciously Modern.

'But don't you see?' cried Wyndham. 'This is a brilliantly savage satire on Art and Sexuality.'

'The point of satire, Wyndham,' we replied, 'is that it should be both funny and choose targets worthy of attack. This fails on both counts. Perhaps you find yourself identifying too closely with those you wish to make fun of – though we use the term "fun" loosely. In which case, you might have thought twice before giving up the day job.'

Otto Kreisler cracked his whip Teutonically, for he was indeed a German. 'Ach! I find myself without money again,' he said. 'My father, who has married my fiancée, has once more failed to send me my allowance and I have nothing left to pawn.'

'Perhaps you should sell a painting then,' suggested Louis Soltyk, a narcissistic Polish dandy.

'Do not be ridiculous! I am an Artist; this means I never actually do any Art as I spend too long talking about it. I am also a German Artist, which means even if I did create Art it wouldn't be any good. So therefore I demand you retract your outrageous slur!'

'Very well. Then allow me to introduce you to the amazingly rich Anastasya who has escaped from her bourgeois family to live in Parisian Bohemia.'

Kreisler was nothing if not open to importuning money from his acquaintances and wondered how best to raise the subject of his impecunious state. Unfortunately, before such an occasion arose, Soltyk took Anastasya's arm and led her out into the street.

Gott im himmel! Donner und blitzen, Kreisler thought with all the clichéd power of the stereotypical German. How then would he find the 20 francs he needed to retrieve his dinner jacket from the pawn shop in time for Fräulein Liepmann's party? *Teufel*! Of course. He would Bohemianly go as he was.

Bertha espied Kreisler walking to the party. Ha! The very man, she thought. What better way to prove her nonchalance to Tarr, her darling Sorbert, than by being seen talking intimately with Kreisler.

'As you can see, I have no dinner jacket!' Kreisler declared loudly, before kissing Bertha roughly in the Café Berne. Bertha was surprised by his forcefulness yet did not complain for she was both a Bohemian and a woman. Besides, Tarr could not now doubt the seriousness of her nonchalance!

'See how Kreisler kissed Bertha,' exclaimed Fräulein Liepmann. 'And see how he has got drunk and insulted everyone. Worst of all, he isn't even wearing a dinner jacket. He really is a disgrace to we Germans!'

Tarr had been contemplating Time and Space and other matters of Proto-Nietzschean urgency when he had heard of Bertha's involvement with Herr Kreisler and found to his surprise a stirring in his Appetite. Perhaps this *Homme Sensuel*, this *Homme Egoiste*, this *Homme Tosseur* might find some time in his otherwise punishing daily schedule to partake of tea with her.

Bertha found herself lying semi-naked on the chaise-longue, posing for Kreisler as he attempted his matchstick representation of her in the finest tradition of German Vorticism. Not that he had requested her to expose her pendulous breasts, but her Bohemian spirit obliged her to make the gesture.

Throwing down his pencil in anger, Kreisler grabbed her roughly, forcing his sweaty body on hers. Once the shocking deed was done, Bertha noticed her arms were covered in bruises. It had been a terrible act, yet in some way she felt herself more drawn to Kreisler, for his brutality yet again strengthened her appearance of nonchalance towards Tarr.

'Good day again, Herr Kreisler,' said Tarr, as he took tea with him and Bertha for the tenth day in a row.

'We do not need you here,' Kreisler replied.

'I only come to prove to you that I am an Artist and that I have relinquished my Appetite for Bertha's adipose body and that I am indifferent to the attachment you both share.'

Bertha kept silent for she was both a woman and nonchalant in her desire for Tarr, yet Kreisler rose up, smiting Tarr with his whip, shouting he had no need of his approval.

'I'd best be going back to not painting,' said Tarr.

Kreisler's Germanic anger knew no bounds and he strode purposefully into the Café Berne where he hit Saltyk twice upon the cheeks. 'That is for insulting me,' he declared. Saltyk was not sure quite what injuries he had inflicted on the German, but his honour was at stake. A duel it reluctantly must be. Saltyk fell dead, accidentally shot before the duel could take place, and Kreisler made haste for the border where he hung himself in prison.

'Thank God that is over,' said Tarr to Anastasya. 'At least it was only a Pole and a German, so no harm done. Please tell me you are not a German . . .'

'Indeed I am not. I am Russian,' she replied as he rubbed his hands along her plump, equine thighs. 'Good, then I shall marry you. For perhaps I am now ready for my Art and Appetite to co-exist.'

'I'm pregnant with Kreisler's baby,' cried Bertha.

'Then I shall marry you,' said Tarr, 'and carry on seeing Anastasya at tea times. Maybe that's better for my Art after all.'

So Bertha and Tarr got married. They divorced within two years. Tarr continued to see Anastasya but remarried a woman called Ruth Fawcett. He still never produced any Art. So he could have written this.

THE AGE OF INNOCENCE

Edith Wharton

'SORRY I'M A bit late,' Newland said, though both he and Ellen knew that what he was really saying was that he loved her deeply, yet did not want to compromise her by making her his mistress. When Newland Archer opened the door at the back of the box, the curtain had just gone up on the garden scene. 'Darn it,' he thought. 'I have arrived ten seconds unfashionably early. All New York knows you are not supposed to make your entrance until Marguerite is two bars into her aria.' Newland's annoyance dissipated when he realised that no one who was anyone in New York society had witnessed his horrendous faux-pas.

During the interval he turned his gaze towards his beloved, the divine May Welland, seated in the Mingott box opposite, and frowned when he saw that her cousin, the Countess Ellen Olenska, was in her party. How very awkward! What would New York think of the reintroduction of the scarlet woman into society? Yet how typical of the Mingotts to be so brazenly protective of their own! No matter! He would rise above New York's pettiness and his reputation would be unstained!

Archer made his way to the Mingott box and sat down next to May. They looked into one another's eyes and felt no need to speak. Their thoughts were as one. Newland knew that May had understood he wished their betrothal to be announced that very night at the Beauforts' party.

The engagement would normally have been quite the talk of

New York, yet it was the return of Mrs Mingott's other grand-daughter, the Countess Ellen, that dominated the conversation of the finest salons.

'I hear she left her husband and hid with his secretary for a year before returning to New York,' said Mr Sillerton Jackson. '*Quelle scandale!* How racy these Europeans are!'

'How dare you, sir!' Newland exclaimed. 'You will find she left her husband to escape his beatings.'

'No matter,' replied Mr Sillerton Jackson. 'A New York wife would take a beating in private. I find myself most compromised by our acquaintance as you are to be married into the Mingott family.'

Mr Sillerton Jackson's sentiments were echoed throughout New York society and for several weeks it appeared as if no one would attend the Mingott ball, until Mrs Archer, sensing the shame that might accrue to her own family by her son's impending engagement to a Mingott, persuaded her cousins, the van der Luydens, New York's most powerful family, to invite the Countess to tea.

'Thank goodness for that,' New York society sighed. 'We can go to the Mingotts' party after all.'

Sitting in his office some months later, Newland was irritated to be summoned to see his employer, Mr Letterblair. Although nominally engaged as a lawyer, Newland had far better things to occupy his mind than the grubbiness of commerce; there was, for instance, the compelling question of whether New York was wearing its waistcoats with one or two buttons undone this season.

'Mrs Mingott has requested your assistance,' said Mr Letterblair. 'It appears that the Countess Olenska is seeking a divorce. The family find that most embarrassing.'

Archer understood the gravity and delicacy of the situation and took a carriage to the Countess's residence. 'You must realise that New York will expel the Mingotts from society if you pursue this action,' he said, 'and that my engagement to May will also make me an outcast.'

The Countess looked down, a maelstrom of emotion racing through her bosom. 'Very well,' she said. Newland sensed the passion beating in his own breast. 'I must see you again soon,' he implored.

'Come and see me for ten minutes in a few months' time when I am staying in Skuytercliff,' she whispered, overwhelmed by feelings that could not be expressed in New York society. 'And now I have a party to attend.'

Newland urged his horses on as the carriage raced along the coast road. 'Sorry I'm a bit late,' he said, though both he and Ellen knew that what he was really saying was that he loved her deeply, yet did not want to compromise her by making her his mistress.

'I've got to go now,' Ellen replied, 'I have to fend off Beaufort's unwanted attentions,' though both she and Newland knew that what she was really saying was that she loved him deeply, yet did not want to compromise him by becoming his mistress.

Rocked by the intolerability of the situation, Newland took a few more weeks off work to go to Florida to see May. 'We must get married this year,' he begged her. 'You only want to do that because you are frightened you may go off me,' May replied. 'Don't think I am unaware that you once had feelings for a Mrs Rushworth. If you have any outstanding obligations to her, then I am happy to release you from your promise to me.'

Newland felt a surge of love for May. Particularly as she didn't seem to have guessed the true nature of his feelings for the Countess. 'No, my darling,' he declared. 'It is you whom I adore.'

'Why do we have to honeymoon in Europe?' May enquired, as they docked in London. 'Because it is our Henry James moment,' Newland replied.

'Well, I shall be quite glad when we are back in America.' Locked in the loveless marriage decreed by New York, Newland was tormented by his passion for Ellen, a passion made still more tormented by New York having turned its back on her once more for refusing her husband's offer of a reconciliation.

'We should not see quite so much of Ellen now,' said May. Had she sensed his true feelings for Ellen, Newland wondered. How strange that the emancipation he admired so much in Ellen he should seek to deny to May!

Newland hurried to Boston. 'It's been two years since I last saw you and I wanted us to spend another five minutes together,' he cried, touching Ellen's hand. They kissed, a kiss that announced both of them accepted they might have intercourse some time in the next few years.

'I will throw off the shackles of New York and elope with Ellen,' Newland boldly wondered.

'I'm pregnant,' said May, having secretly been aware of her husband's feelings for Ellen all along.

'Maybe I won't be going anywhere after all,' Newland muttered.

'I am returning to Europe,' Ellen announced, and all New York breathed a sigh of relief at such a satisfactory conclusion to the affair.

Twenty-six years later, Newland stood outside Ellen's Paris apartment with his son, Dallas. May had died some years earlier and Dallas had suggested they make the visit now that New York society was so much more casual in its mores.

'Come on up,' said Dallas.

'I don't think I will, after all,' said Newland. 'The imagined love is so much more real. And besides, she's probably a right minger now.'

SIDDHARTHA

Hermann Hesse

IN THE SHADE of the sallow wood, Siddhartha, the handsome Brahmin's son, grew up with his friend Govinda. He had learned to pronounce Om – the word of words – when he was two weeks old and love stirred in all who knew him for they recognised in him a Holy Man. Yet Siddhartha himself was troubled; neither his heart nor soul was full.

He meditated for decades under the banana plants, breathing in the Consciousness of the Cosmos, before whispering to Govinda: 'I cannot find the Atman's dwelling place here. I must join the Samanas.'

'You cannot leave,' his father wept, though in his heart of hearts he knew his son had already left, for he was a wise and noble man. Siddhartha levitated gently, hovering above Govinda's outstretched hands. 'Come, my friend,' he said. 'It is time to transcend our Destinies. Whatever that means.'

For two thousand years Siddhartha fasted among the Samanas, the sun's fierce rays bleaching his bones. His asceticism was legendary, yet still Atman eluded him. 'No matter how far I get away from the Self, I always come back to the Self,' he wept.

'Truly, you are too deep for these Samanas losers,' Govinda replied. 'Perhaps Paulo Coelho the Illustrious Buddha can help with your divine quest.' The two New Seekers left the forest, full of hope they could teach the world to sing, and made their way to Coelho's yurt.

Coelho sat, smiling and inscrutable, as he preached the teachings of the here and now and the now and then. 'You are a man of Peace,' Govinda whispered. 'I will follow your illustrious path.'

'But I must be on my way,' Siddhartha said. 'For if I am he as you are he as you are me and we are all together, then who is the Walrus?'

'You have found the gap between the single and Eternal worlds,' Coelho nodded gravely. 'Be on your guard, O Clever One, against taking too many drugs.'

Siddhartha pondered these things in his heart. In searching for Atman, he had lost himself. 'And me,' the last remaining reader echoed, but Siddhartha did not heed this warning. 'River is River, Earth is Earth, and another joint wouldn't hurt,' he sang as he asked the Bryan Ferryman to take him across the water to the village. There he met the ethereal Kamala, whom he wooed with his poetry.

Kamala the serene courtesan pulled him towards her and together they ascended the tree of love in a frenzied, hurried century of Tantric bliss, while a chorus of lutes and sitars played outside their window. Once they had uncoupled, Kamala intuitively understood Siddhartha was too spiritual to be bothered with the chores of parenthood and let him depart with a profound 'See you now and Zen, babe' to pursue his Destiny.

Siddhartha went to live among the ordinary people and there he learned the art of acquisitiveness. People trusted him with their money and for five hundred years he found that the more he lost, the more he seemed to gain. 'Congratulations, Grasshopper,' said Sir Fred Goodwin, 'you have found Nirvana.' Yet deep within him, Siddhartha knew he had lost the Path. He yearned for the simplicity of Om sweet Om.

He returned to the river where Govinda was sitting in the lotus position. Yet his old friend did not recognise him. 'I am not the same person I was yesterday, nor the same person I will be tomorrow,' Siddhartha explained. 'Er . . . quite,' Govinda replied, anxious to be on his way.

Siddhartha sat down for a millennium and thought deep thoughts of Omness. 'The river is never still yet it is always the same river,' he eventually announced to the Bryan Ferryman. 'There is no such thing as time.' 'I think you'll find there is,' the Bryan Ferryman replied, 'if you listen to Brian Eno for twenty minutes.'

Crowds gathered as news spread that Coelho the Illustrious Buddha was about to enter Nirvana. Among the throng was Kamala, accompanied by her son. 'I have been bitten by a snake and am dying.' She smiled beatifically. 'But now I have found you, I am at One with your Oneness.'

Siddhartha held the boy to his bosom, as the final chords of 'Ommagomma' signalled Kamala's reincarnation as a Deity. 'What will you teach him?' the Bryan Ferryman asked. 'He don't need no Education, he don't need no thought control,' Siddhartha replied. 'Let him find his own frigging Atman.'

One night the boy disappeared and Siddhartha wept. 'Don't cry,' the Bryan Ferryman said. 'He is too young to comprehend the depth of your love. Only on the Dark Side of the Moon will he see the Divinity of your paternal neglect.' Siddhartha knew this was true and opened the cage to give the brightly plumed Omming Bird its freedom.

As the Dawning of the Age of Aquarius slowly turned to Dusk, Siddhartha experienced a strange feeling of contentment. He could laugh when the river laughed. He was Atman. He was Earth, Wind and Fire.

'But I won't be going on tour with them,' he said to Govinda. 'Because the meaning of life is there's no place like Om.'

THE PROPHET

Kahlil Gibran

Almustafa, the chosen and the beloved, who was a dawn unto his own day, whatever that might mean, had waited twelve years in the city of Orphalese for his ship that was to return him back to the isle of his birth.

Then, in the twelfth year, he climbed the green hill far away without the city wall and looked seaward: and lo! He beheld his ship. His joy flew far over the sea but then a sadness descended upon him.

Long had been his days of pain at being forced to write in the absurd style of the not very profound mystic, yet many had been the naked children who had walked with him and his soul cried out for them. Yet he could not tarry.

So he said unto himself many more meaningless and contradictory statements until he reached the city. There the priests and priestesses said unto him, Fain, do not go away from us. Much have we loved you, though speechless has been our love. Sadly, we've chosen this moment to put that love in words for otherwise you would have been out of here and we'd all have breathed a sigh of relief.

Then a woman named Almitra stepped out of the sanctuary. Prophet of God, in search of the uttermost, please tell me what you know of Love before you go.

He looked profoundly into the middle distance before uttering. I feel it in my fingers, I feel it in my toes, Love is all around me, And so the feeling grows.

And what of Marriage? Almitra asked.

Sometimes you shall be together, Sometimes you shall be apart.

And then a woman who held a babe unto her bosom said, Speak to us of Children.

People of Orphalese, your children are not your children. Especially if they are adopted or have been kidnapped. You may give them your love but not your thoughts, for the children invariably know best. So if they want to eat loads of sweets and beat the crap out of one another, you shouldst stand back and let them.

Then a rich man said, What of giving?

You give but little when you give of your possessions. So by all means hang on to your dosh. Thou really only givest in the truest sense when thou dost also receive. And the rich man went away and scratched his head.

Then another said, Speak to us of Work.

Work is a real bummer unless you are a bit blissed out and stoned. So fain would you do anything that does not fill you with love. Like watching daytime TV. And there was joy in the hearts of many 1970s hippies who believed they were reading the meaning of life.

Then a woman said, Speak to us of Joy and Sorrow.

Fain would you feel Joy without Sorrow. Joy and Sorrow are as one. Joy is Sorrow and Sorrow is Joy. So have a good laugh if your entire family is wiped out in a car crash.

Then weaver said, Speak to us of Clothes.

Fain would you wear Clothes. Clothes are merely the trappings of a bourgeois culture that would seek to try and make you get a job. Better by far to go naked and let it all hang out, man.

Then a judge said, Speak to us of Crime and Punishment.

If a person does wrong then society is to blame. It is you who should be locked up and not some poor hippy who was laying a quarter-ounce of grass on a fellow dopehead.

Then a lawyer said, What of our Laws?

There are no Laws except the ones you choose to obey. So if

you fancy axeing someone to death or abusing several children, then be my guest.

Then a woman with a blister said, Speak to us of Pain.

What can I tell you of Pain, you who have worked your way through pages of this meaningless, turgid drivel?

Then a dropout said, Speak to us of Self-Knowledge.

And he answered, saying: Self-Knowledge is to be found within your soul. Go forth and take a few tabs of LSD and watch the snakes crawl up the walls for a few hours, and then bleat on about how you've had a consciousness-raising experience.

Then a teacher said, Speak to us of Teaching.

No man can reveal to you aught but that which already lies half asleep in the dawning of your knowledge. Which means you are born knowing how to do algebra, speak seven different languages and fly to the Moon.

Then a chatterbox said, What of Talking?

Fain would I talk. People only talk when they have nothing to say. Just watch my lips.

Then an astonomer said, Master, Speak to us of Time.

There is no Time. Even though it may not feel like it while I am still droning on. Today is yesterday is tomorrow is my birthday so where is my card?

Then a loner said, What of Friendship?

And the Master said, I am he as you are he as you are me and we are all together. I am the Eggman, They are the Eggmen, I am the Walrus. Goo Goo G'Joob.

Then another moron said, What of Pleasure?

Pleasure is Freedom but Freedom is not Pleasure. Let not Regret becloud your mind for that is not Pleasure unless your Regrets are a source of Pleasure in which case it is.

Then the Priest said, Speak to us of Prayer.

You'd better start Praying this doesn't go on too much longer.

And lo! Their wish was granted as the ship did dock and The Prophet and his Sad Profundity were taken away from them.

Thank you Master, they all cried. Your leaving has taught us the meaning of Relief.

Then Almitra cried, Why is he called The Prophet?

And Gibran spake, It is a misprint for The Profit. For that's what I have made out of the Gullible's insatiable desire for Platitudes.

GENTLEMEN PREFER BLONDES

Anita Loos

MARCH: A GENTLEMAN frend and I were dining at the Ritz last evening and he said that if I were to write down my forts then I would soon have written a book. I tell him my name is not Joyce James so though I am happy with the streem of conchusness shitick he can forget all the durrty bitz. I do do a lot of finking though especially now my frend Mr Eisman, the button king, has taken time away from Washington CD to edukate me at the Colony Club.

All this late night edukashun is very tiring so I am glad Mr Eisman has bought me an emrald and told me he doesnt want me appearing in any more movies though that nice Mr Chaplin is keen to see a lot more of me. Mr Eisman is now on button bizniss somewear so my friend Dorothy came over and we met a reel life English Lord but he was a bit dull cos he droned on about Tibet and didn't give us nuffink. We also met a riter called Conrad Joseph who was boasting about how he had rittun a book called *The Nigger of the Narcissus* and I told him that wuznt very nice and he could have used the word Negro and he'd be better off selling posh clothes that Mr Eisman could by me.

Fings have been getting quite complikated what with Mr Eisman being away and I have to confess I have developed a bit of a crush on Willie Gwynn who has been sending me orkids every day and with a gentleman Mr Lanson who wants me to call him Gerry and is very rich which is nice. But then Mr Eisman came back and said iit would be good for me and Dorothy to continue our edukashun away from New Yoik men in Europe.

April: So here we are on the ship on the way to France and I seem to have met a man who wants to give me lots of prezents on account of the fact I am so cleva and am happy to hold his hand and somefink else. Dorothy says this book is in danga of being a one trick wunda but I tell her she is a woman of no refinement and its not my fault if I started riting this as a joke on a train as a way of taking the piss out of Mr Mencken, a man to whom I was unakountably attracted but who spent his life chasing blonde bimbos, and then blow me down the book gets published an becomes an instant bestsella.

Bless me if on the boat I didn't meet the District Attorney from Little Rock, Arkansaw, who tried to persuede the judge I was gilty of shooting Mr Jennings in the lungs when I had fit of histerix but luckily the judge and jury didn't believe his nasty insiniuashuns and told me I could go home if I changed my name to Lorelei. Which I dun. And now Ive met some more lords an that, Oh I've already done that, maybe they were a bunch of counts instead, and what with them all having given me prezents and expecting me to hold their hands when Mr Eisman is around, which he isnt now but will be soon, Dorothy and I are going to go to Lundun rather than Paree.

May: Me and Dorothy have been bought a lot of dinners and fings which is nice and last night we went to a salon where I met Mrs Wolf. 'What's the time?' I asks. She looks down her nose at me and says I spose you fink vats funny and vat people will fink me and Dorothy are femnist ikons cos we go round doing xaktyly wot we want and getting loadsa prezents and stuff for holding fings. I tells her not to get to hoity-toity az I only wanted to know ver time cos I have a date with a luvverly gentleman Sir Francis Beekman whom I call Piggie when he kisses I an vat I spose that one day wimmin might try to reclaim me and Dorothy as a forerunner of Thelma and Louise but I ain't that bovvered eiver way as Piggie has just spent £10,000 on a dimond tiara for me and he is famus for being well mean.

June: Me and Dorothy have scarpered to Paree well quick as Mr Piggie is not that happy about the tiara. It didn't take nearly so long to get to Paree as it did to Lundun which is well odd as vey are both the same distunts from New Yoik but nevva mind. I expect you can guess wot happened here so I needunt go into to many detailz aboiut how Mrs Piggie sent to lawyers to try and get the tiara back and Dorothy maid a very funny anti-Semitic joke an I got to keep the tiara while sending Mrs Piggie home wiv a paste. Mr Eisman shows up an sayz we should move on to be edukated in the Central of Europe and we take the train to Munchen where I am amazed at the amount of kunst there are hanging around. Anyway, I keep mentioning the kunst cos I was worried you wouldnt get the gag an just to make sure I couldn't help noticing how many Germans were waving their sossidges around and I did have a hard time – arf! arf! – sleeping when Mr Eisner was around. I then went on to Vienna where I met Mr Froyd who told me I could do with a few more inhibitions to dream about and I also met a nice gentleman callt Mr Henry Spoffard who is very rich and wants to marry me.

July: I know this book is not ver long but between you an me it ran out of steam a long time ago, after all itz basikly ver same gag ova an ova but here I am bak in New Yoik so ill ty to rap this up as kwik as possibul. So you can forget Mr Eisman an I nearly forgot Mr Spoffard as Dorothy says hes a minger an shed much rather marry his farver as he will croke sooner. I kan see her point even if she is well unrefined and has neffa shot anywun espeshully as I haff met a nice Mr Montrose who says he does specialust art movies an that I can be a star. Mr Montrose was not ver happy when I said I wanted to dump Mr Spoffard cos he was hoping Mr spoffard could finance my career in filmz though it doesn't look like I will be needing many costumz. So I am getting married to Mr Spoffard and I think I will be ver happy as I wont haf to see much of him. Ve end.

THE GREAT GATSBY

F. Scott Fitzgerald

I'M INCLINED TO reserve all judgement, yet when I came back from the east last autumn I wanted no more privileged excursions. My family are prominent Middle Westerners, yet after the Great War I decided to go east and learn the bond business. It was a warm season so my father rented me a small bungalow at $80 a month on Long Island Sound, and one evening in that summer of 1922 I drove over to dinner with my second cousin Daisy and her enormously wealthy husband, Tom, whom I had known at college.

'Black people are taking over the world,' said Tom, making himself unsubtly unsympathetic.

'You haven't met our baby yet, have you Nick?' Daisy asked.

'Neither have you, apparently,' her companion, Miss Baker, said evenly. 'She's now three years old.'

'Well let's not worry about her,' Daisy laughed, drinking another cocktail. 'She's only a symbol of neglect.'

The telephone rang in the hall and Tom left the table without a word. Daisy chattered a while and then excused herself.

'Everyone knows Tom has another woman in New York,' Miss Baker whispered to me. 'I'm Jordan, by the way. I sense we're going to have an inconsequential affair.'

Tom mannishly invited me to meet his girl the following week. I tried to demur but he was insistent, and that Sunday we stopped by Wilson's car repair workshop near the ash heaps on Main Street. A roundish woman appeared. 'I've got to see you,' Tom said intently. 'Take the next train into the city.'

'My husband doesn't suspect a thing,' Myrtle Wilson laughed as we all got drunk.

'Just don't mention Daisy,' said Tom.

'Daisy, Daisy, Daisy.'

Tom punched her hard and broke her nose. I've wondered since whether I should have intervened, but that might have compromised my role as a semi-detached observer. So I left quietly with my moral authority still unblemished.

Every Friday a corps of caterers came down to provide for my neighbour's legendary parties at his exquisite shore-side mansion. Some said that Gatsby had once killed a man, but no one seemed to know or care who he was, as they came uninvited from miles around to enjoy his seemingly limitless hospitality. I was the exception, as his manservant had delivered an invitation to me earlier in the week, and soon after I arrived I went looking for my host.

'You look very familiar, old sport,' said a man with piercing, friendly eyes.

'And you are?' I enquired.

'Jay Gatsby, old sport.'

I apologised for not recognising him, having believed him to be much older. It emerged that we had served in France at the same time and I confess that I instantly warmed to him. 'I'm inclined to believe that you really are who you say and that you did go to Oxford,' I said patronisingly.

I see that from what I've written so far, you might think that I was not quite as detached from the fast set as I would like you to believe. So allow me to mention that I also worked extremely hard. And now that's over, I can return to the story. To my surprise, Gatsby courted me assiduously, once even introducing me to his shady Jewish associate.

'He wants you to invite Daisy and him to tea,' Jordan told me later. 'They were lovers before the war and he bought the house just to be close to her. He's been heartbroken since he learned Daisy had married Tom.'

Gatsby told me much later he had been born James Gatz, the son of an impecunious westerner, and had decided to reinvent himself when he was 17. He had never told Daisy he was penniless when they first met, and by the time he had money she was already wed. Yet even before he had trusted me with the truth, I had been happy to effect the introduction, and he and Daisy rekindled their passion with a sincerity that was in marked contrast to the superficiality of my relationship with Jordan.

The weeks slid by in easeful contentment, but eventually Tom grew suspicious. 'She doesn't love you,' he said cruelly one day.

'She does,' Gatsby cried. 'It's you she never loved, old sport.'

'I've loved you both.'

'Gatsby is a bootlegger,' Tom shouted. 'He's not one of us.'

Gatsby and Daisy sped off in Tom's car, while Tom and I followed in the coupé. We came across the body of Myrtle Wilson lying dead in the road. 'She ran out towards the car and it didn't stop,' said a bystander.

I advised Gatsby to make a dash for Montreal, but he refused. I had guessed that it had been Daisy driving, but his nobility went unrewarded. Tom and Daisy refused to see him and society closed ranks. Greater tragedy soon followed. Tom did nothing to correct Mr Wilson's belief that it was Gatsby who had killed his wife, and one morning Wilson shot him by the pool before turning the gun on himself.

Gatsby's death passed almost unmourned except by me and his father. I couldn't hate Tom and Daisy. They were just a bit careless. And with that profound observation, I casually dumped Jordan. It was time to retreat from the green orgastic light of the east back into the safety of my provincial squeamishness.

MRS DALLOWAY

Virginia Woolf

Mrs Dalloway stiffened on the kerb, waiting for Big Ben to strike. There! Out it boomed. She loved life; all was well once more now the War was over.

Clarissa recalled that summer with Peter Walsh. What was it he had said? She couldn't quite remember, yet somehow the lack of clarity felt profound. Was not this impressionistic stream of consciousness confirmation of her place in the avant-garde? Such a pity, then, that so often she seemed so shallow. And yet. Was not Peter due back from India soon? A noise like a pistol shot rang out.

The violent explosion that so shocked Clarissa – or was it Mrs Richard? – Dalloway came from a motor car. Was it the Prime Minister's? Septimus Warren Smith did not care, as his wife, Lucrezia, helped him cross the road. 'I will kill myself,' he said, as an airplane curved overhead, its smoky trail a modernist symbol.

'Dr Holmes says you must rest,' cried Rezia.

Interrupting. Always interrupting. Could she not understand the significance of his shell-shock as a counterpoint to post-war superficiality?

Big Ben struck out again, the bell throbbing with masculinity from within its Freudian tower. Mrs Dalloway's mind turned to matters of love and that first kiss she had once shared with Sally Seton. How thrilling it felt to hint at lesbianism!

The doorbell rang. Who could it be? It was Peter. 'How lovely to see you,' she said. There was so much he wanted to tell her. How he had been heart-broken when she had chosen Richard.

'I'm in love,' he blurted out. 'With a married woman.'

'How interesting,' said Clarissa, lost in solipsism, yet somehow acknowledging their shared sense of unfulfilment. 'Why don't you come to the party tonight?'

Peter marched furiously. Clarissa might be aging into comfortable respectability, but he still felt young and vibrant at 50. He sat down in Regent's Park, his mind tired of repetitious memories of how he had once loved Clarissa to distraction. How could she have married a man with no tremulous love for Shakespeare? Why must his images contain so many portentous adjectives? And why must everything be a question?

Septimus and Lucrezia had also stopped in Regent's Park. The war. Milan. Now he only saw demons. And occasionally visions of Miss Isabel Pole whom he had once loved. There. He couldn't make it any clearer he wasn't homosexual, he told himself.

Big Ben struck twelve as Septimus and Rezia stepped into Sir William Bradshaw's consulting rooms.

'Your husband has served with distinction in the war,' Bradshaw said to Lucrezia. 'He is a very troubled man who needs time away in one of my homes.'

Richard Dalloway was happy to take luncheon with Lady Bruton and help her compose a letter to *The Times*. He supposed he had some influence as a Member of the House, though he was aware of his limitations.

'Peter Walsh is in town,' said Lady Bruton.

'Splendid,' Richard replied. Had not Peter once loved Clarissa? Perhaps he should tell Clarissa that he loved her, too. But first he would buy her some flowers.

Big Ben struck three as he entered the house. His mouth opened, but the words would not come. 'Here,' he said instead, thrusting the flowers into Clarissa's arms, before rushing back to the House.

He wanted to say he loved me, Clarissa thought, yet he couldn't. We are trapped like icicles in the coldness between youth and old age. She sighed as Big Ben struck something or other and went to visit her daughter, Elizabeth, at Miss Kilman's house. How she hated Miss Kilman whose religious, lesbian tendencies were taking Elizabeth away from her.

Rezia tried to release Septimus from his horror. 'Be still,' she said. 'The doctors will soon be here to take you away.'

Septimus trembled with the intensity of his condition 'I'll give it you,' he cried, hurling himself out the window on to the railings below.

The ambulance took the body away as Big Ben struck again. How annoying, thought Peter, to be so constantly reminded that all the action was taking place on one day. How heavenly to see you, Clarissa had written. What could she mean?

The Prime Minister had arrived. The party was a success. And yet, somehow, Clarissa felt disengaged. Maybe if she did a little more and thought a little less her life might be more rewarding, but it was too late in the book for that.

The doorbell rang. It was Sally Seton – or Lady Rosseter as she was now called. 'I heard you were having a party and I thought I'd come along uninvited to tie up a few loose ends.'

Peter spied Sally in the corner. 'How sad that Clarissa's life is so empty,' he remarked. 'And Richard is not bound for greatness.'

Indeed, she thought, and you have not exactly fulfilled your youthful dreams either. But she kept that to herself, content in the compromises of her own life.

'One of my patients committed suicide today,' Bradshaw announced. 'Delayed shell-shock is a terrible condition.'

Clarissa's eyes glazed over. Just like yours.

THE PAINTED VEIL

Somerset Maugham

'I THOUGHT I heard someone try the door,' cried Kitty. 'What's to be done if it was Walter?'

'Dash it all, I've left my solar topee downstairs,' said Charlie.

'Well, I don't care if Walter does find out. I hate him.'

'Is that the time? Must bolt.'

Of course it was stupid for them to have retired to her bedroom after tiffin, but how hateful it was that neither she nor Charlie was free! What a ghastly woman Dorothy was! A good mother and an able Assistant Commisioner's wife, yes! But so old!

Coming to Hong Kong, Kitty had found it hard to reconcile herself to her husband's lowly position as a bacteriologist and within three months of marriage had known she had made a mistake. It had been her mother's fault.

Mrs Garstin was a stupid woman who, disappointed by her own husband's lack of preferment, had focused her ambitions on her prettiest daughter, Kitty. Yet despite the attentions of many admirers, Kitty had reached the age of twenty-five as yet unmarried, and when her younger sister had secured herself a baronet Kitty had panicked and accepted Walter Fane's offer of marriage.

For a while Kitty had hoped Walter might improve, but once she had succumbed to Charlie Townsend's assured athleticism she could no longer fool herself that Walter was anything other than a short, ugly, charmless nonentity.

'I'm afraid you've thought me a bigger fool than I am,' said Walter.

So he did know! Maybe it was for the best!

'Charlie and I are in love,' Kitty sobbed, her chest heaving. 'We shall be wed.'

Walter laughed a cruel laugh. 'Townsend will never leave his wife,' he sneered. 'You are just his plaything. If he promises to leave Dorothy, I will give you a divorce. Otherwise, you must come up country with me to Mei-fan-tu where I've offered to take charge of the cholera epidemic.'

How awful! No parties and a fatal disease! It was social suicide!

'Oh, Charlie,' Kitty wept. 'Walter is a beast. We must be wed as you promised.'

'Steady on, old girl,' Charlie said. 'A chap says a lot of things he doesn't mean with his trousers down. You go off with Walter; cholera isn't so bad as long as you don't get it. Must bolt!'

Walter and Kitty barely spoke as they travelled by chair through the inscrutable Chinese hinterland. How frighteningly yellow were the faces that surrounded them! But such a relief to be met by a white man on their arrival! Even if he was bald and ugly.

'The name's Waddington,' the man said. 'I've cleaned out your hovel since the last missionary died here, so you should be all right. Mind if I pour myself a bottle of whiskey? Helps ward off the cholera! Ho ho!'

Walter would depart their bungalow early each morning and come home late, leaving Kitty to indulge her overwrought fantasies. How she longed to die and yet to live! But as the days passed she began to spend more time with Waddington exploring the village, and found herself reaching a new level of understanding. How shallow she had been up till now!

'Mind the corpses, there's a good girl,' Waddington said in a jocular state of semi-inebriation. 'Come and meet the French missionaries.'

'The Holy Spirit moves in mysterious ways,' said the Mother Superior. 'Your husband is a saint for trying to save the coolies, and you are a saint for being by his side.'

How wrong they were to think she was here by choice! But how she had misjudged her husband! See how the nuns felt his nobility! Perhaps if she were to pray she could find a state of grace and love him! Maybe she could even learn Taoism from Waddington's inscrutable Chinese wife! How fat and sleazy Charlie began to seem!

'Come quickly,' Waddington said. 'Walter is dying.'

'Forgive me, please,' Kitty begged.

'The dog it was that died,' Walter gasped before breathing his last.

Delirium. Or perhaps it was the last line of Goldsmith's elegy that she hadn't read yet somehow knew! If only she could cry for Walter like the stupid, round-faced coolies!

'You must stay with us,' said Dorothy, on Kitty's return to Hong Kong.

'I hear you are pregnant,' Charlie laughed when they were finally alone. 'I hope it's mine. With any luck it's a girl; Dorothy and I only have boys.'

'You are a fat, coarse, shallow brute,' Kitty shouted. 'And I've never loved you.' But even as she tried to resist him she thrust herself against him in a ridiculous plot twist and begged him to take her. How could she have done it again! She would have to return forthwith to Blighty and pay for her sins by living with her mother!

'I'm afraid your mother is dead,' her father said on her return. 'And I've never much cared for you, just as you've never much cared for me. I'm off to the West Indies, so you're rather on your own.'

How right that she should be abandoned! She had never loved him properly! And yet there was time for them both to make amends.

'My daughter and I will come with you,' she said.

'OK then,' her father shrugged. 'May God's bounty be with us all!'

THE TRIAL

Franz Kafka

SOMEONE MUST HAVE been telling lies about Joseph K., for without having done anything wrong he was arrested on the morning of his thirtieth birthday. 'You don't seem to be taking this very seriously,' said the Inspector as the warders looked on. 'I won't say I regard it as a joke,' K. replied dismissively, 'but it must be a matter of unimportance because I cannot recall the slightest offence that might be charged against me.' 'We are mere servants of the Law,' the Inspector said, 'so I can't confirm if you are charged with an offence; only that you are under arrest. Proclaiming your innocence does not redound well upon you. Now I suggest you go about your business at the Bank.' K. stared helplessly as the warders left his neighbour's room in disarray. 'I can explain everything,' K. said, smothering a receptive Fräulein Bürstner in passionate kisses, pleased to have explained nothing.

K. was informed that a short enquiry into his case would take place next Sunday. The caller had not specified a time and K. had not seen fit to ask for fear of lessening the sense of alienation. He entered the building and turned towards the stairs to take him to the Interrogation Chamber and was annoyed to find there were three further staircases leading to the attic. 'You are one hour and five minutes late,' the Examining Magistrate said. 'I recognise there is a great organisation behind you,' K. cried, 'but the warders are corrupt and this trial is unjust.' 'Bravo!' a voice shouted from the gallery and K. was pleased to see he had some support. 'Don't count on it,' the Examining Magistrate cried, 'for in this dystopian world nothing is at it seems and even the observers in the gallery are Court Officials.'

During the next week K. waited for a new summons that never came. Pausing only for solipsistic paragraphs of ever greater length, to mark both his gradual mental disintegration and a lingering sense that everyone might be guilty of something even if it was only to be alive, he presented himself at the Court once more. 'Why have you come on a day when there's no one sitting?' the wife of the Law-Court Attendant enquired, throwing herself at K. rapaciously. K. accepted her advances, not questioning why every woman seemed to find his air of self-congratulation so irresistible. 'I have come to prove my innocence,' he said for the umpteenth time. 'But no one is ever innocent,' the woman replied, just in case anyone had missed the point.

In the next few days, K. found it impossible to exchange even a word with Fräulein Bürstner, though he did contrive an elliptical exchange with her friend Fräulein Montag. 'How would it be if Fräulein Bürstner were to vanish as mysteriously as she appeared?' she enquired. 'The great advantage of an unfinished novel that gets stitched together after your death,' said K., 'is that everything can seem far more symbolic than you ever intended and generations of critics can read almost anything they like into it.'

K. looked on distastefully as the Whipper beat the warders. 'It's your fault!' the Whipper cried. 'If you hadn't spoken out against them in Court, I wouldn't have to punish them.' 'I acknowledge my culpability,' K. said, 'and I understand the futility of fighting the System. If I weren't in such a hurry to feel alienated by the Deputy Manager of the Bank, I would offer to be birched in their place.'

'You need an Advocate,' said K.'s uncle, taking him away from further digressions on futility at the Bank and leading him across the City. 'You must be Joseph K.,' said Leni, the Advocate's nurse. 'And as I'm a woman I must find you so bewitching that I have to have sex with you immediately.' 'You have not created a good impression,' the Advocate observed, when K. eventually appeared several hours later. 'I was discussing your case with the Examining Magistrate and your failure to join us did not go unnoticed.'

With episodic inevitability, K. went to visit Titorelli, the Court Painter. 'I have been told you can help me,' he said. 'It is true that I too can go on for pages about the opacity of the Law,' Titorelli replied, 'and I may be able to put in a good word with a Lower Judge. But my real function is to discourse wryly on the three possible acquittal verdicts, none of which will offer you satisfaction.' Struggling for breath and crushed by symbolism, K. ran from the building. 'You too are a Court Official and every building is a Court Building.'

As the winter months dragged on, K. decided he no longer wanted the Advocate to represent him. 'That's not a good idea,' the Advocate said. 'As I have described for the best part of thirty pages, the Law is infinitely serpentine and you cannot hope to win without me. And don't be disturbed by Leni making eyes at that man pretending to be a dog. He's merely a client of mine called Block whose case has been going on for five years and Leni adores the accused.'

'If you go to the Cathedral to meet a client who is not going to turn up,' said the Deputy Manager, 'you can meet a Priest instead who will deliver yet another tangential parable on the implacability of the Law.' 'Enough!' cried K. 'I know that I really ought to be drawing the whole thing out for another four years or so and that the legal Process has barely got under way, but I can't stand it a moment longer. Just allow me one last fleeting reference to Fräulein Bürstner and let the warders stab me through the heart. Let me feel the point of pointlessness.'

LADY CHATTERLEY'S LOVER

D. H. Lawrence

THE CATACLYSM HAS happened, but we've got to live. This was more or less Constance Chatterley's position. Her husband Clifford had returned home from the war a cripple, unable to have children. He was not downcast for he could propel himself in a motorised bath chair, yet his being was a blank of insentience.

Constance was a ruddy-faced woman who had known the sex thing as an eighteen-year-old girl in 1913 when she had roamed the woods near Dresden with German guitar-playing youths. Twang-Twang! Her father could tell that *l'amour avait passé par là* on her return for he was a man of experience, and was now concerned she was condemned to life as a *demi-vierge*.

Clifford and Connie had returned to Wragby Hall in 1920, yet despite the proximity of his family seat to the earthy Nottingham-shire mining village of Tevershall, there was no connection between the two. The Chatterleys lived in the world of ideas and books, where Clifford's insubstantial writing had brought him a certain celebrity in the empty milieu of the well-to-do London literati.

'The penis is a much overvalued organ,' he declared to Connie. 'But if you are desperate for a child, I would be happy to overlook an act of sexual congress on your part and to raise whatever it may bring as my own.'

Connie was fading by the hour, her body deprived of warm life seed, and she found a connection in the physical contours of the Irish writer Michaelis. He was an outsider with the nobility of a

Negro! A man despised for being arriviste! And yet he had the tiny, disconnected penis of the London Modernist. She felt nothing when he entered her and he had his crisis all too quickly, leaving her to achieve her own by rubbing herself abstractedly against him.

'This is my England,' Clifford said, vibrating with the Bitch-Goddess of Success, as he pointed to his gamekeeper working on the estate. Connie's eyes strayed to the man's red moustache and his strong, Nottinghamshire loins. How she longed for the integrated life! How dare she be defrauded of her womanhood!

Later that day she walked alone to the gamekeeper's hut. 'What's your name?' she asked. 'And what are you doing?'

'Mellors, mi' lady,' he replied. 'Ah've bin killin' a bad pussy.'

Oh Persephone! Oh anemones and crocuses! Connie hated him for defying her by using the earthy Nottinghamshire dialect instead of the received pronunciation he had acquired in the Army that made him acceptably common; yet her womanhood was set afire with sexual symbolism. He was like the lonely, erect pistil of an invisible flower. He was a wounded lion, bound by his class to the pain of his rejection by his wife.

The mental excitement for Clifford had gone. It was Money and Society he sought! The Power of being Upper Class! By day he was taken down the mines to view his mastery of the Bolshevik workforce; by night, he rested his head like a child on the ample bosom of his housekeeper, Mrs Bolton.

Clifford, the Great-I-Am, never so much as touched Connie. A tear fell to her wrist as she watched the chicks breathe New Life. She felt detached as Mellors' buttocks rose and he thrust inside her, but her womb opened up to him and she felt a wave of culmination as he emptied his seed. He had made her reconnect.

'We came arf together tha' time,' he said.

Connie, Clifford, Mrs Bolton and Mellors all thought their separate deep thoughts of Hopelessness and Eternity, yet Connie knew she must not lose her Bacchante passion. Maybe she would have a baby. Go to Venice with her sister even.

'I love you, Mellors,' she whispered.

'Th'art a good cunt,' Mellors said. 'Best bit o' cunt.'

'And what I need is the swarthy ever-ready cock of a horny-handed son of the soil who is actually a little bit middle-class and can quote Latin. Fuck me till I fart.'

Clifford became evermore tainted with commerce, his disconnection from Nature laid bare as his bath chair got stuck in the mud. How furious! How impotent!

'My life is like Persepolis,' said Mellors, for once eschewing his Nottinghamshire vernacular. 'I had a lot of good fucking with my wife, Bertha. Before, I thought only black women came naturally. But then she left me.'

'Let's both get divorced and live in Phallos world,' Connie gasped.

He took her like an animal. 'I like it that tha' shits and pisses and my John Thomas longs to fuck tha' secret places.' The purity of her sexuality could not be denied as she surrendered her arse and they fucked and shitted and pissed all that last night.

London, Paris and Italy felt barren in comparison to her belly that was swelling with Mellors' fertile seed. She dared not tell Clifford she was pregnant, for she was in a Funk. If Mellors' Phallos had entered Bertha, was it not tainted with Commonness?

'You will have to pretend Duncan Forbes is the father,' said her father. 'He is a posh aesthete and he'll be happy to go along with it if he can see you naked.'

'It's not true,' cried Connie, as Clifford buried his infantile, crippled frame deeper into Mrs Bolton's swinging breasts. 'I love Mellors. I must live with the man whose cock I love and in whose arms I strive for the bliss of a continuous Nottinghamshire orgasm.'

'There will be no divorce,' Clifford shouted, toying with his nappy. 'It's just a *nostalgie de boue*.'

I am chaste but long to fuck tha', Mellors wrote. *My John Thomas may be drooping but it lives in hope.*

MEMOIRS OF A FOX–HUNTING MAN

Siegfried Sassoon

M Y CHILDHOOD WAS a queer and not altogether happy one. My father and mother died before I was capable of remembering them. I was entrusted to the care of my unmarried Aunt Evelyn who lived in a large old-fashioned house. My aunt rarely went out, and as I was an only child my solitary existence was enlivened only by Dixon, a perfect gentleman's servant, who taught me to ride.

While attempting to dissuade me from the unmanly habit of riding side-saddle, Dixon filled my head with impossible tales of daring-do at Lord Dumborough's hunt, an unimaginable five miles distant, and I spent many years wondering if I, too, might carve my way through the countryside on a mighty steed.

I will not waste any words recounting how I spent my time in those years before Dixon first persuaded my aunt to let me make the epic journey to Lord Dumborough's hunt because, in truth, I did almost nothing. I was a sickly child and Mr Pennett, the solicitor who managed my yearly income of £600, insisted I should be educated at home, so I never actually got to make any friends.

Not that that was any great concern to me as I rode Mr Star along the lanes to my first meet. How big everything seemed to a youth as callow as myself, and I kept myself out of harm's way towards the rear of the pack, admiring the precocious sporting talents of Denis Milden, a boy no more than a year older than my fourteen. 'To be sure, Master Milden is a handsome rider,' said Dixon, as we returned home. 'But you are no booby yourself.' My heart swelled with pride and I resolved to become the best huntsman of my generation.

Throughout the summer months there was no hunting to be found in the county, so I had even less to do than usual. It was only the occasional cricket match that reminded me I was alive, with the Butley Flower Show Match an annual highlight. How well I remember my first; standing around in the field doing nothing for hours on end, then coming in to bat at number 11 with just one run required. Their fastest bowler, a wide-hipped oik named Sidebottom or something similarly working-class, delivered the ball which I blocked. The batsman at the non-striker's end shouted 'Run' and so we did. What joy unconfined as I walked back to the pavilion for a jam scone and a glass of fresh milk!

Mr Pennett was most put out when I wrote to let him know I was discontinuing my studies at Cambridge. 'A gentleman ought to work for his living, Mr Sherston,' he said. '*Au contraire,*' I replied. 'I am far too busy hunting to bother with anything so plebeian as work. Besides I have a private income.' Dixon was thrilled at the outcome and took me to Tattersalls to purchase a new horse. 'You will never make a top-class sportsman without a finer mount.'

I bought Haraway, a goodly horse, for 45 guineas and, with Dixon's help, set about preparing him for the new hunting season. My riding had come on in leaps and bounds, aided in no small measure by the purchase of a new pair of Ashbridge boots, and I was exceedingly gratified to be on the receiving end of several compliments when the Dumborough Hounds reconvened. It was at this meet I encountered Mr Stephen Colwood, the well-connected son of a local parson, whose large private income also enabled him to do next to nothing throughout the year.

'Come, Georgie,' Stephen said. 'There is better sport to be had at the Ringwell where Lieut-Col CMF Hesmon and other aristocrats are to be found.' As my groom and personal valet, Dixon was also thrilled he was to be allowed to breathe the same air as Lieut-Col CMF Hesmon, and he advised me to make a trip to my London tailor to buy some newer hunting attire.

Mr Pennett was not amused when I told him I had considerably overspent my allowance. 'Master George,' he said. 'A man must work to live within his means.' 'Fie, Pennett,' I replied. 'I have no intention of becoming a *petit-bourgeois* like yourself. Give me £100 and be done.' I remained extremely diffident around those whom I considered my social and sporting superiors, but my confidence was improved no end when I won the Heavyweights race at the Point-to-Point and I was most gratified the following day when the Master approached me on horseback to enquire if I had seen which way the fox had gone.

The next five or six years were among the busiest one could imagine, with scarcely a day passing in the winter months when I was not galloping through frosty field in search of Mr Reynard. Such a punishing schedule had necessarily required me to buy several more horses, among them the thoroughbred Cockbird whose natural balance saved me many a fall, and Dixon had his work cut out to maintain them to my standards. Yet he never faltered in his duty for he was a man who instinctively knew his place.

Do not imagine I was idle during the days when there was no hunting to be had. On such mornings I was be found with my head buried in *Horse & Hound* or perusing the cricket fixtures for matches where I might maintain my batting average of 7 in the upcoming season.

Aunt Evelyn was thrilled I had developed into a competent huntsman, never more so than when Denis Milden invited me to hunt alongside several Marquesses at the Northamptonshire where he had been asked to serve as Master of Foxhounds. It would have been churlish to refuse and that season ranks among my fondest memories of this period of my life, as Denis and I moaned about the work-shy lower orders who had brought the country to near standstill with a coal strike.

My memories blur slightly as the seasons collide with one another, for it never occurred to me – or you, I suspect – that I might one day have cause to write my experiences down in a book, but I do recall waking up one day to find that we were at war with Germany. Though for what reason, I still struggle to recall as the breakout of hostilities came as a complete surprise after a hard-fought cricket season for the village team in which I managed to average 3.7 with the bat.

As a gentleman, I naturally volunteered to join the Yeomanry and the first year of the war passed with me in mourning for my separation from the noble Cockbird. So used to scrubbing my back and ironing my clothes, Dixon was also shattered to be torn from service to me and died of loneliness a few months later.

I did, however, manage a few days' hunting with the Packlestone, while home on leave, but those long days at the Front were nothing but dismal dinginess, punctuated by news of the loss of various friends with whom I had once hunted. How I came to hate the war for transforming the Elysian lifestyle of the very rich into a communitarian pot-pourri of mud and shrapnel! How glad my aunt's maid Miriam would have been to have succumbed to pneumonia before she had to witness my reduced circumstances! And as I lay shivering in Hidden Wood one Easter Sunday, I couldn't help thinking Christ Himself wouldn't have bothered to rise from the dead if He couldn't go hunting.

AS I LAY DYING

William Faulkner

DARL: JEWEL LOOKS ahead, his pale eyes like wood set into his wooden face as he stares at the log-built house. That's so as you know this is a rough-hewn poetry. There I go again. Cash is sawing at the box; Addie Bundren couldn't want a better carpenter. Chuck. Chuck. Ma watches him build her box. She wants it like that. Flesh and blood.

Cora: The Lord sees everything. That's the last you'll hear of me.

Jewel: 'I durnt see why she holts on,' I says. 'Ahm a' leaven with ma hoss.'

Dewey Dell: Lafe took me in the cotton field and he said his sack was full and he was going to empty it into my sack and so it was because I could not help it I knew Darl knew and he said not to tell pa as it would kill him what with ma dyen.

Anse: Durn that road. Durn that rain. Durn them boys. They should be here for her dyen. That fool son a mahn Vardaman has caught a fish in a puddle.

Darl: 'She wants ta be buryened in Jefferson. She tolt me that,' pa says. Cash carries on sawing. She looks like she's a goan. Death's just a function of the mind. *It must be the cue for me to write a sentence in random italics.*

Vardaman: My fish is not fish now it's dead. They kilt my ma. My ma is a fish.

Dewey Dell: I am guts and he is guts and I am Lafe's guts and it took her 10 days to die and I go to the barn and feel my body begin to part and open up the alone.

Vardaman: I don't suppose you made much of that but you ain't seen nothen yet. Cash gives me a banana. Is that her? Is she a rabbit? It be hacked to pieces. My fish is in that box. It needs to breathe. I pick up Cash's augur and drill through the lid.

Faulkner: This multi-voiced experimental fiction isn't going quite as well as planned. The characters still seem much the same and I keep lapsing into third-person observation. Still, at least it's not entirely clear who's who or what's going on, so I must be doing something right. *Maybe I should throw in a few more italics.*

Darl: He bored straight through the box into her face. A hard rain falls. 'I have done my duty to the Lord,' pa says and I reckon he dun hit. Cash is sawing the wagon. 'It ain't balance,' he grunts. I don't know if I am or am not. And nor do you.

Cash: My 15-point plan. 1. Carry on sawing. 2. Except. 15. That's it.

Tull: They placed a veil over her face so the augur holes didn't show. Anse shaved badly as a mark of respect. He had no teeth. The Lord giveth and the Lord taketh away. 'How far did you fall?' I ask Cash. '300 feet and one quarter of an inch,' he answers. 'My leg hurts a bit. It's falling off.'

Jewel: 'I been on ma hoss and the bridge is down,' I say. 'We never git to Jefferson.'

Darl: Jewel's mother is a horse. Vardaman's mother is a fish. Mine's a flying pig.

Dewey Dell: I wish I had lived I wish I had let her die I wish I knew what I wished and by the way I killed Darl. 'No you didn't,' says Darl.

Tull: The river is riz. I suspicioned the mules would not make it across.

Darl: Jewel always did a lot of sleeping. We thought he was seeing a woman or a hoss but it turned out he was working at night to buy a hoss. Ma always did treat him different; I heard her crying and I knew that I knew sure as I knew about Dewey Dell. *The dark torrent runs. Sorry, I was getting poetic again. Maybe I should use italics for that bit.* The wagon has tipped and the mules are drowned.

Faulkner: Son of a bitch. I thought I was writing a modernist tragedy of Mississippi country folk. Seems like it's turning into a farce.

Addie: I guess you were expecting a stream of unconsciousness sooner or later. I took Anse and then he took me and I had Cash and he violated my aloneness and then I had Darl but then Anse died for me and I did not lay for him instead – Lord forgive me – I lay with Brother Whitfield and had Jewel and then I had Vardaman and Dewey Dell with Anse to say sorry and now I'm going back in my box.

Darl: Cash was lyin by the bank with another broken leg and a broken back. 'It ain't hurten,' he says. Pa goes off to get more mules and ma starts smellen like old cheese. A bit like this story.

Dewey Dell: I goes to chemist and tries to buy something to make my guts go down like Lafe said but the chemist gives me notten so I gets some cement and Darl sets Cash's leg and glues him to the top of ma's box.

Jewel: Son of a bitch, pa sold ma hoss to buy some mules.

Darl: Jewel looked like a figure in a Greek frieze – Durn it where did I get that metfor from as I ain't never seen a Greek frieze – as he pulled the coffin out the blaze.

Cash: My leg ain't hurten even though it's turned black. Darl smashed the cement with a sledgehammer. I not blinken.

Darl: Ma is smellen so I tried to burn her but now we dug her into a hole.

Dewey Dell: I went to another chemist and I still couldn't get rid of the baby *do you think I could have some italics too* oh look pa's comen down the street with a woman.

Anse: Check out the new Mrs Bundren.

THE HIGHWAY CODE

GENERAL
ALWAYS BE careful and considerate towards others. As a responsible citizen you have a duty not to endanger or impede others in the lawful use of the King's Highway. Good manners are as desirable on the road as elsewhere: commoners should always give way to their betters. If in doubt about order of precedence, consult *Debrett's Peerage*.

Children
Especial care should be taken of children and urchins. Always make sure children are unrestrained in the back seat so that in the event of an accident they can be thrown clear.

Led animals
Sheep drovers should walk in front of their flock, ringing a bell at 30-second intervals to warn approaching vehicles of the hazard.

Speed
Carefully regulate your speed at all times. Travelling in excess of 30 mph may endanger you and others. If you are going to overtake, allow at least half a mile of clear road as it will take you that long to get past a vehicle almost as slow as your own. Do not cut in once you have completed an overtaking manoeuvre: it is very, very rude.

Corners and bends
If the road suddenly forks to the left or the right, it does not mean

that the road has disappeared. You have just come to a corner. Try to follow the road and you will continue on your way. If you should miss the corner and drive into a ditch, wait for a police constable to pull you out and make you a nice cup of tea.

White lines

These marks in the road are not Morse code, warning of an imminent German invasion. These lines designate the middle of the road and you should endeavour to keep left of them at all times, except when overtaking. Beware of Johnny Foreigner who likes to drive on the wrong side of the road.

Alcohol

It's not really the business of us Government bods to tell a fellow how much he should drink, especially as, in our experience, one's driving is often improved no end by a couple of quick snifters. But it is probably best not to get several sheets to the wind, so the law reluctantly demands that a chap should restrict himself to half a bottle of the finest malt and a chappess should stick to five G&Ts.

Roundabout thingies

Be very careful if you come to one of these new-fangled thingies as we don't really know how they are supposed to work. Best avoided as they are the work of the devil.

Obstruction

Never leave your vehicle parked in the middle of the road, even if you have arranged for a member of staff to come along and remove it within an hour. It can be jolly inconvenient for the three people who might get held up behind you. Likewise, do not stop to chat to a friendly constable on point duty. He is a very busy man and needs to concentrate at all times.

Lights

Do not use your headlights unnecessarily. They may be, with advantage, switched off when following another vehicle which you do not intend to pass. Should you change your mind about overtaking, try not to follow the car in front into the ditch when he drives off the road in shock when you suddenly appear as if from nowhere.

Motorcyclists

It's been brought to our attention that various leather-clad oiks have taken to riding motor-propelled bicycles exceedingly quickly along the King's Highway. This is to warn you that we've got our eyes peeled for you lot, chummies. Any trouble and you'll end up in Chokey.

Drivers of horse-drawn vehicles

Remember that you are marginally more slow-moving than other vehicles and that some road users may parp their horns and frighten your steeds. If a queue does build up behind you, it is often as well to turn round and doff your top hat as a sign of courtesy, in recognition of their forbearance and patience. Should someone then be disobliging enough to complain at being made to drive at a walking pace, you may give them three lashes with your whip.

Dogs

Animals can be a danger to themselves and others. Any dog not on a lead should be taught to look both ways and bark loudly before crossing the road.

BRAVE NEW WORLD

Aldous Huxley

'WELCOME TO THE Central London Hatchery and Conditioning Centre,' said the Director to the ring of fresh-faced students gathered round him. 'We'll begin at the beginning.

'This is where the ova are fertilised by male gametes. The Alphas and Betas will remain bottled in their incubators while the Gammas, Deltas and Epsilons are brought out after 36 hours to undergo Bokanovsky's Process. Each embryo will be budded to create 96 identical twins. It's one of the great instruments of social stability as it makes everything more uniform.

'Ah, Mr Foster,' he continued, spotting a manager of indeterminate age, but then it was impossible to tell how old someone was in the year After Ford of 632. 'Would you care to explain the rest of the process?'

'Oh, thank you sir,' Foster replied. 'The embryos are monitored along the conveyor belt and are conditioned according to what caste they are going to be. The expectations of the Gammas and Epsilons are lowered by giving them less food and training them to hate flowers and music. It's important they should be fulfilled in their stupidity, so that they can do the really boring jobs without moaning to us Alphas.'

'Marvellous,' said the Director, stifling a yawn.

'And then, of course, we have to teach them erotic play. In the days when Our Ford was still alive, children used to stay with their mothers and fathers until they were 20 and formed abusive monogamous relationships. And now I'm going off to play a complicated game of Obstacle Golf. Long live Mustapha Mond,

Resident Controller for Western Europe. To consume is to live. Old is bad, new is good . . .'

'Quite so,' the Director interrupted. 'If I'd wanted a thesis on the dystopia of eugenics and 1930s American consumerism I'd have asked for an essay. But it's supposed to be a novel, you fool. So lay off the high-concept stuff for a bit and introduce a few characters.'

'Er . . . This is Lenina Crowne.'

'You've been going on rather too many dates with Henry Foster,' Fanny said to the pneumatic Lenina. 'It's a long time to be going out with the same man. And it's not as if Henry hasn't been sleeping with other women. He's very conventional. Why don't you go out with the meaningfully named Bakunin or Trotsky?'

'Good Ford, no,' Lenina replied, 'but I might take up Bernard Marx's offer of a holiday in the Savage Reservation in New Mexico. He's a bit ugly but nothing that a few grammes of soma can't put right.'

Even after some soma, Bernard couldn't let himself enjoy the Orgy-Porgy and the Sexophones of the Solidarity Circle. He felt different from everyone else. Even Epsilons liked the social body; he just wanted to be alone with the pneumatic Lenina.

'If you maintain this kind of attitude, you will be sent to Iceland,' the Director said. 'Try to be more infantile when you get to the Savage Reservation. I went there once with a Beta Minus girl about 25 years ago. She got lost and I never saw her again.'

Bernard remembered just what a clunky piece of plotting the Director's last speech had been when he and Lenina came across two Savages on the Malpais Reservation.

'I may be a toothless old crone now but I was once a Beta Minus Beauty,' said Linda. 'I was left for dead here by my Alpha Plus and gave birth to John.'

'To be or not to be, that is the question,' John cried. 'I am her son who was brought up in the traditional ways of yore. I am of

Nature and have drunk deep of the forbidden mystical texts of Shakespeare and the Bible. How I long to be crucified.'

'And how your condition speaks to me,' Bernard replied. 'Allow me to take you back to London.'

Bernard looked around the room contentedly. Women wanted to sleep with him now he'd come back with the Savages, got the Director the sack and was a Celebrity. And tonight he would introduce John to the Arch-Community Songster.

'Tomorrow and tomorrow and tomorrow I'm not coming out,' said John, springing into life after bizarrely taking a back seat for 50 pages.

'We all hate you really, loser,' the Arch-Community Songster whispered to Bernard.

'Oh John, your mean and moody silences have sent me into raptures of lust,' the pneumatic Lenina declared, unzipping her zippicamiknicks. 'Take some soma and sleep with me.'

'Neither a borrower nor a lender be, I love you too but I want some foreplay, you strumpet,' he shouted, before rushing to the hospital to watch his mother die of old age.

'So,' said Mond eventually. 'You'd better go off to the Falkland Islands, Bernard, where you can be on your own-ish. But what shall we do with you, John?'

'Is there no pity sitting in the clouds? I would quite like to have a dreary, portentous chat with you about Shakespeare, science and religion before going off to live on my own in a lighthouse in Surrey.'

He was tormented by visions of Lenina and flagellated himself ceaselessly. Yet still the tourists came to visit him. 'I don't know about you,' he cried, 'but I've had just about enough of this book.' And with that, he hanged himself.

MORE PRICKS THAN KICKS

Samuel Beckett

IT WAS MORNING and Belacqua was stuck in the first *canti* of the moon. He was in stasis between Infernal allusion to Dante and a youthful homage to Joyce. The Master. 'What would Stephen Dedalus do?' he asked himself. Perhaps a lengthy contemplation on the nature of the perfect loaf of bread, a perambulation round Dublin pitted with testy interlocutions with the grocer and then back to his aunt's for dinner. Yes! That would be admirable. Though perhaps with a little more Divine Comedy than the self-regarding Stephen.

'Christ!' he said, as his aunt placed the lobster in the boiling water. 'It's alive! Well, it's a quick death. God help us all.'

It is not. We're only at the end of the first story.

'Where are we?' Winnie asked.

'Where are we ever with Beckett?' Belacqua murmured. 'Character, plot, meaning; just nihilistic abstract ideas to fill in time before we die.'

They were walking in the mountains near Dublin and Belacqua sensed his impetigo playing up. 'What ails you?' she enquired. He scoffed at the notion of a sequitur. Linearity was for fools who wondered how such an unattractive, indolent sot could prove quite so irresistible to women.

'Here is where I take my *sursum corda*,' he said, entering the Martello tower.

'Then I shall see my acquaintance Dr Sholto at the lunatic asylum.'

He stole a bicycle and rode like the wind to the public house. The Master was slipping through his grasp. He needed to smell the streets of Dublin, to reconnect with that lyrical blankness where words filled the page, simple words, obscure learned words, invented words, words , words and yet more words criss-crossing the blankness until the story was done even though nothing had been said. Nothingness was the meaning. He cast his mind back to the trituration of the child in Pearse Street and the woman who had sold him seats in heaven. Jesus! He must be even more pissed than he imagined.

Whither next? It was the night before Christmas and Belacqua was sitting in the inn, discoursing on the perfect amplitude of women over a glass of porter. 'It is vital the Alba's red dress be closed at the back or I shall be forced to withdraw my favours,' he told the Polar Bear.

'I wish that it weren't,' the maid replied, 'because then we would be spared your witless, solipsistic, Empedoclean observations of the Hexenmeister and the Lebensbahn.'

'Come sir,' said the police sergeant while Belacqua cleaned up the vomit he had catted all over his boots. 'If only it was as easy to rid you of your verbal excesses.'

'Give it time,' said Vladimir and Estragon.

The Alba's party ululated with the Joycean banter of a sockdolager, as Belacqua rang the doorbell. 'You are soaked through,' the Alba shrilled. 'We must take off your clothes.'

'Jesmatgenachtheilhitler,' he replied, for it had been a while since he had experimented with language. It was a cold night as he walked home and the pain in his abdomen grew worse. He squatted by the pavement and evacuated himself loudly. The pain remained. There was plenty more shit to come.

The Toughs lived out in Irishtown and their daughter Ruby had invited Belacqua to lunch. Belacqua will be familiar to you but Ruby will not, so if you will forgive the authorial intrusion the Master bade me make, I shall tell you a little about her. There again, I might not.

'Those skirts are an encumbrance to our walk,' he said. 'Let us walk naked to the summit and try to kill ourselves.'

The revolver's bullet fell harmlessly *in terram*. *L'Amour et la Mort n'est qu'une mesme chose*. I bet the Master could never pun in French!

Belacqua bestrode the fields, lamenting that his fiancée Lucy did not allow him to be a cicisbeo. A vagabond urinated powerfully in a sulphurous yellow stream. JJ would be proud. His bitch, the mighty Tanzherr, disturbed Lucy's mount and she fell crippled to the ground. But Tempus Edax and he is now married to her.

Her death two years later came as a timely release to the narrative and Belacqua unfeasibly became Dublin's most sought-after squire. It was Thelma bbbbogsss who had the pleasure of becoming his second bride. 'Be my attendant, Mister Hairy Capper,' Belacqua commanded, handing him Lucy's ring to pay for the wedding. 'But don't spend more than £10.'

'Why are you so beastly?' Thelma ejaculated to the clarion ring of the Unbuttoned Symphony.

'Because it is in the tradition of drunken Irish modernism. Now, I do declare, my carnation has gone west.'

The same could be said for the story, for if the narrative was in need of hospitalisation then so was Belacqua, who was having a tumour the size of a brick removed that dreary morning. He knew how Stephen would await his destiny, but not a bourgeois poltroon. With references to Grock and Democritus? With a passing sexual reverie? Why no! There must be another loud and copious evacuation.

By Christ! He did die! They had forgotten to ausculate him!

Smeraldina, the third Mrs Shuah – did I neglect to mention that Thelma had passed on – she of flabby thighs and pendulous breasts, surveyed her husband's corpse in its Ulysses carrier. Was all that remained a Kleinmeister's Leidenschaftsucherei (thank you, Mr Beckett) or a parodic corpsulence (thank you, Mr Crace)?

'Come, lady,' Hairy cried. 'Let me be your antiphlogistic.'

She took his hand. 'I still can't see the moon.' So it goes, the world, a temporal void where everything goes back to where it started.

RIGHT HO, JEEVES

P. G. Wodehouse

'Jeeves,' I said, 'may I speak frankly?'

Hold on a minute, I seem to have gone off the rails here.

I don't know about you but I often find it dashed hard to know where to begin. Perhaps I should have started with Cousin Angela's encounter with a shark and our holiday with La Bassett.

'I don't think it really matters,' said Jeeves, 'because all your stories are pretty much the same.'

I thought I detected a slight edge to Jeeves's last remark, but Bertram Wooster isn't the sort of chap to bear a grudge, especially when he's just had a few snifters. So I might as well start with the arrival of Gussie Fink-Nottle.

'I'm in a terrible pickle,' Gussie said. 'I've developed a pash for Miss Madeline Bassett but I am unable to talk to her about anything other than newts. Jeeves suggested I dress up as Mephistopheles, but after a side-splittingly unfunny adventure with a London cabby I never got to the fancy dress party where I planned to declare myself.'

Having spent some time with the hound-like Bassett in France, I couldn't quite understand Gussie's attraction. But a pash is a pash and Gussie was no oil painting himself, so I thought I should help him out.

'You can't rely on Jeeves for *les affaires de coeur*,' I said. 'Miss Bassett is staying with my Aunt Dahlia and it just so happens she has asked me to give the prizes to the oiks at her local grammar school. I told her we got the PM at Eton, but she insisted the riff-raff would be thrilled to get an idiot in spats. So you'll do nicely instead.'

I convinced Gussie that prolonged proximity to La Bassett would do the trick and he departed happily, leaving me to admire my new white mess jacket in the mirror.

'It is rather exuberant, sir,' said Jeeves.

I was used to this kind of rebuff from him, but Bertram Wooster isn't the kind of man to mistake a servant's repressed sexual passion for sartorial authority.

'I think you'll find that the chaps at Drones reckon it's quite the thing.'

'Precisely, sir. A telegram, sir.'

'Good God, Jeeves!' I cried. 'My cousin Angela and Tuppy Glossop have called off their engagement. Aunt Dahlia has summoned us both to Brinkley Court to resolve this emergency.'

'It was Jeeves I wanted, actually,' Aunt Dahlia said, 'but sadly you come as a pair. He's a whizz at everything.'

'What ho, Aunt Dahlia, that's a bit of a chizz. And how's Uncle Tom?'

'Don't call him that, it reminds me of a black fellow with a banjo.'

'But you love all that casual racism.'

'I know, but I'd still rather talk about that nice Mr Hitler.'

'It's been ghastly,' said Tuppy. 'I told Angela it was a log and not a shark that chased her, and she called me a fat bore and one thing led to another.'

I was debating whether to mention that my dear friend Tuppy *was* a fat bore, but Jeeves saved me from that embarrassment. 'Perhaps if you were to engage Miss Angela in conversation, sir,' he said, 'she would realise that Mr Glossop was not quite as fat and boring as she thought.'

'Don't be ridiculous, Jeeves,' I replied. 'You have no feeling for the highly strung female temperament. All Tuppy needs to do is refuse his dinner and show he is pining for her.'

'You complete fool, Bertram,' Aunt Dahlia shouted. 'Our marvellous chef, Anatole, has given in his notice because Tuppy wouldn't eat his dinner.'

Even by my own trivial standards it felt as if the plot was scraping the barrel but in for a penny in for a pound, so I started gassing to Gussie.

'I still can't talk about anything other than newts,' he said.

'Perhaps it might be a good idea to give Gussie a nip of gin before the prize-giving,' I suggested to Jeeves.

'If you say so, sir.'

'Gosh, Jeeves, we are in a pickle now,' I said, scratching my noddle. 'It was all going so swimmingly. Gussie had proposed to La Bassett, but then she called it off, Angela is now Gussie's paramour and La Bassett proposes to marry me instead.'

'You're right, sir. A confirmed bachelor never marries.'

'But what shall I do?' I wept, admiring my white mess jacket.

'We've nothing to lose any more, sir,' Jeeves sighed. 'As this book's holed beneath the waterline. But you could try something ridiculous such as ringing the fire alarm and watching everyone try to save the one they love. Gussie will run to Madeline and Tuppy to Angela . . .'

'And will you run to me?'

'No, sir.'

We were all gathered outside Brinkley Court and Jeeves's plan appeared to have backfired as the unhappy couples were still not talking to one another.

'Perhaps if you were to cycle nine miles to the village that might help, sir?' Jeeves said.

'Jolly good,' said Aunt Dahlia. 'The couples are reunited and Anatole is staying.'

'It seemed that what was required was for you to absent yourself for a while so that everyone could focus their hatred on you while you were away,' Jeeves explained later.

'Would you kiss me if I never wear the white jacket again?'

'It's a possibility, sir.'

TROPIC OF CANCER

Henry Miller

I AM LIVING AT the Villa Borghese. We are all alone and we are dead. The cancer of time is eating away at us. There are no more books to be written. Not that this will stop me. Then this is not a book; it is a libel, a kick in the gob of Art, a transgression that will radicalise gap-year students with its daring use of the word 'cunt'. Some may even vote Lib Dem.

Chaos is the score upon which reality is written. You, Tania, are my chaos, the cunt that transforms my Life into Art, the cunt that transforms my sentences into those of a failed creative writing student. I daringly think of my penis and lesbians. *My anecdoctal life*. There's Carl, Boris, Fillmore, Van Norden; all Jews. And Tania, the loveliest Jew of all. For her I would become a Jew. Why not? I am as ugly as a Jew. Where is your bulging warm cunt now, Tania? Your husband cannot inflame your cunt as I can. I will even bite off your clitoris!

Did I not warn you of my Art? For yes, that is what I call this chronicle that lesser mortals do not dare explore, rather than the desperate misogynistic ramblings of an emotionally stunted adolescent who will say anything to get noticed.

Indigo sky swept clear of fleecy clouds . . . Oh, yes, I can drop in the odd *writorly* description that will give some critics a hard-on almost as big as mine, so that our semen may gush in torrents along the gutters of Paris, washing over the feet of every whore.

Mr Wren has come to rent the Villa Borghese. I fuck his cunt of a wife while he is not looking and then wander the streets penniless as ever, for it of course never occurs to me to do a proper job. I am too important for that. I am an Artist. I do not even have a *sou* for a cunt of a whore so I go to the Jardin des Tuileries and impale my cock on a nude statue. I then siphon some gasoline from a Citroën to get drunk, before spunking into the petrol tank.

Boris and I contemplate our book. We decide it will be colossal in its pretentiousness. No shit. Then Elsa brings her German cunt to the café where we have cadged a Pernod from Moldorf and I am forced to reluctantly lubricate her shrivelled fanny. No sooner had Elsa departed than Germaine and her rose-bush cunt appeared. I quite liked both Germaine and her lusty cunt, though separately of course. So I fucked her, too.

Ideas are pouring from me like sweat – though none of them original. Yet living in the Present is enough. I do not even have to write well. All I need is to bang out words and readers will mistake their repetitions, dullness and lack of structure for the energised radicalism of the liberated Artist!

In Paris I am a free man; in New York I was subjugated by malign maggots. What luck! Today I have befriended a rich Hindu, Nanantatee, who is dim enough to believe in my Talent. I take him to a whore house where I am in the process of desultorily pleasuring Mona's cunt, when I hear a commotion from next door. The Indian has shat in the bidet! *Quel faux pas!*

'Come quickly, Joe,' says Carl. We all call each other Joe. It is our amusing affectation. 'I have just been for a ride in a carriage with a rich cunt in the Bois de Boulogne. But I can't be bothered to fuck her as my hair is falling out and I have syphilis. Can you fuck her for me? If it helps, I will watch while you cunt her and masturbate over your back.'

It's an attractive proposition. I check my diary but find I have just spent five francs on a hairless cunt. How ugly an object is a hairless cunt! 'Perhaps you could try Van Norden,' I reply.

There came a time in any experimental narrative where the writer felt the need to change tense and thus it was I drifted into the past for a few chapters to indicate just how Bohemian my life had become. Days passed when I would idly remove my fingers from the clap-infested cunt of a rotting whore and Van Norden and I would walk to the American Express bureau to see if any of our rich relatives had sent us any money to subsidise our pointless lifestyles. Invariably they had rarely chosen to do so and we would return home, relating to one another our dreams of rutting lesbians and broken penises scattered on the pavement.

Inadvertently I once found myself with a job as a proof-reader. The money was useful for cunting, but the bourgeois sellout of being salaried left my Art severely compromised and I was pleased to quickly lose my job and revert to hanging around with rich Russian women who would first let me cunt them for free and then give me a few francs to cunt a toothless, warty whore.

I am now back in the present. The whore is weeping because she has just lost a child. 'Perhaps you would like another,' I say, unbuttoning my trousers and wiping the yellow gonorrhoeac pus that oozed from my thickening penis. She falls on it avidly with false ecstasy while I count the piss stains on the floor. She leaves the room. I steal her money and join Fillmore for dinner.

Oh, what it is to be inhuman! I feel an exaltation. Show me a man who over-elaborates, I think, and I will show you a Great Man. Show me a man with no sense of self-parody, everyone else thinks, and I will show you a self-obsessed American.

A trip to Le Havre introduces me to a more provincial fucked-out cunt of a bitch whore, but my life is rendered truly meaningless when I am offered a trivial job as exchange professor of English in Dijon. God, what a soulless place! If Paris is a whore of a city, then Dijon is her asshole. Throughout my days there, I barely think of cunt.

A letter from Fillmore offering money ended my misery. I left Dijon without even saying goodbye. How good it was to be back in the cafés where statuesque negresses offered you cunt for a few francs and my deluded pisshead friends allowed me to imagine I was an Artist in the spirit of Proust and Matisse!

'I have a problem with Ginette, a toothless whore,' says Fillmore. 'She is pregnant and I am mad with syphilis. My cock is a chancre of sores and my stools soaked in blood.'

'Take some morphine and go to a madhouse,' I suggest, while dipping my rotting penis in the cunt of some cunt friend of that cunt Ginette.

Yet even that was not enough to shake off the cunt Ginette. 'You must leave Paris and return to America.' He gives me 2,500 francs and leaves. I wonder briefly what I should do with the money. Before realising I have enough to stop writing.

OF MICE AND MEN

John Steinbeck

T HE FIRST MAN stopped short in the clearing just south of
Soledad. 'Sure is a lonely place,' he said. 'That bastard bus
driver coulda dropped us at the ranch.'

'What ranch?' said his huge companion.

'So you forgot awready, Lennie,' the small man replied. 'You
son-of-a-bitch. God you're a lot of trouble. I could live so easy
without you.'

'But we gonna get us some land and have some rabbits,
George.'

'I was only kiddin', Lennie. Lonely guys like us gotta look after
one another. Say, what's that you've got in your pocket?'

'It's only a mouse. I was pettin' it. I like to pet things.'

'Well you squashed it, you crazy bastard. You don' know your
own strength. You don' say nuthin' when we get to the ranch. If
you get into trouble like you did at the last place, you hide out here
in the brush.'

'You was supposed to be here yesterday,' the boss said as they
made their way to the ranch the following day.

'Bus driver gave us a bum steer,' George replied.

'Can't the big guy speak?'

'I ain't sayin he is bright. But he's a good worker and lonely
guys like us gotta stay together an' follow our dream of gettin'
some land.'

'An' some rabbits,' said Lennie.

'Ever' one of us out here is lonely, son,' said the boss. 'You ain't
no different.'

'Ain't that the truth,' said Candy, the one-armed swamper. 'All I got is my broken-down ole dawg.'

'At least you ain't a nigger with a crooked back,' said Crooks, the crippled negro stable-hand.

'Have any of you lazy bastards seen my wife,' a voice shouted.

'Who's that?' asked George.

'That's Curley. He's the boss's son,' said Slim. 'He's mean and handy in the ring, so you take care notta cross him. His new wife likes to give men the eye.'

'Is she purty?' Lennie asked. 'I like pettin' purty thangs.'

'You stay away from her,' George said. 'You pet her an' you sure to squash her. Besides there ain't no place for women among us lonely guys in the Dust Bowl. Women just troublesome whores. 'Tween you an' me, Lennie an' I got run outta Weed after he touchta girl's dress and she hollered rape.'

'Don' you worry,' Slim replied. 'Carlson's dawg just had puppies so we can give 'un to Lennie to pet. An' while we're about it, we can shoot Candy's useless mutt an' give him a pup as well.'

'That souns like a met'for for me bein' washed up too,' Candy cried as the shot rang through the yard.

'Have youse bin' messin' with ma wife,' Curley yelled at Lennie.

'Don' you pick on Lennie. He ain't done nuthin' wrong. He jus' simple,' cried George.

'Ain' you reelised yet that 'mongst us lonely men, the weak pick onna weaker,' said Curley, landing several blows on Lennie.

'I jus' like to pet thangs,' smiled Lennie, grabbing hold of Curley's hand and crushing it into splinters. 'Tell me agin 'bout the lan' an' the rabbits we gonna git, George.'

'You ain't getting nuthin' Lennie,' said Slim. 'It's ever' lonely guy's dream to get some lan', but nobody ever does it.'

'Ah've got some money saved up,' Candy whispered. 'Mebbe we could get some lan' together.'

'An' some rabbits,' Lennie said.

'You one mad bastard,' said Crooks. 'What you doin' messin'

'bout here while the others are out at the cat-house? I mebbe a nigger but youse a moron so that makes me better'n you.'

'I wanted to pet my pup,' Lennie answered.

'Well you steer clear of my horses, d'ya hear? I don' wan' them squashed an' all. But say, I gotta dream too. So how 'bout I come an' work with you, George an' Candy?'

'Hello boys,' Curley's wife pouted. 'D'ya thank I'm purty? I coulda bin a movie star if I hadna' married that dis'poin'men'.'

'You git off to bed naw,' George said, returning from the cat-house. 'Us lonely men doan need no fancy women turnin' our heads. We jus' gonna bunk down together like lonely men should.'

'Say, whad'ya doin' in the stable?' Curley's wife said the following day.

'I bin' pettin' the pup,' said Lennie. 'But it seems ta not be movin'.'

'That's cos you gonna squashed it, you clumsy big bwoy. Why don' you play with my purty hair instead?'

'Oh naw,' Lennie said. 'Ah've gonna' squashed her too. George gonna be real mad with me. Ah'd best hide out in that lonely clearing near Soledad.'

George heard the men coming for Lennie. 'What you gonna dun' this time?' he said, placing his arm round Lennie's shoulder.

'We still gonna get us some lan', George?'

'We sure are, Lennie.'

'An' rabbits?'

'Lotsa rabbits,' George said, putting his gun to the back of Lennie's neck and pulling the trigger.

'What's bin happenin' here?' Slim asked.

'Ah've just killed the American Dream.'

'But it ain't such bad news for the rabbits.'

TO HAVE AND HAVE NOT

Ernest Hemingway

Spring: you know how it is early in the morning in Havana when the bums are asleep and only the real men are still drinking.

'We'll give you a thousand apiece,' said the one who spoke good English.

'I don't take anything to the States that can talk,' I replied.

'You saying we are *lenguas largas*?'

'No. I just want you to remember I once had some principles.'

The three Panchos left the bar as a car pulled into the square. A nigger fired a Tommy gun from the back, spraying a scree of bullets across the street, and the three Panchos fell lifeless. A final stray round busted off the top of a bottle of whiskey and I drank the lot. Some nigger.

I went down to the quay where the man, Johnson, who had chartered the boat was waiting. We baited up and were soon hooked into a marlin. Must have been 1,000 pounds. Johnson struck too soon and lost it. Lost the rod with it. I could have pulled it in one-handed while I nailed some rum, but you get used to schmucks in this business.

He never gave me the 880 dollars he owed me. I was down to my last 40 cents with my wife, Marie, and the girls to feed. Frankie came in with a Chink. So it's yellow stuff, I thought.

'You take twelve Chinese to the mainland. I give you 1,200 dollars,' Mr Sing said.

'It's a deal,' I replied. I could smell the double-cross. Some Chink.

Mr Sing sculled the last of them out to the boat and I pulled him on board. I took the money, cracked his arms, cracked his neck. It was either kill him or let him kill the other twelve. I took the boat back into shore and offloaded the Chinks. There were no easy choices for the Have Nots.

FALL: 'I'm shot,' said Wesley.

'You ain't shot nearly as bad as me,' said Harry.

'Why have we slipped into a third-person narrative?'

'Don't go asking no difficult questions, you rummy nigger.'

He hadn't expected the Cubans to open fire when he was running liquor. The boat was holed, the booze was holed and he was holed. His arm was hanging by a tendon, but he could still raise a bottle to his lips.

'Captain Willie's boat is gaining on us and we ain't never gonna make the Keys,' Wesley gasped.

'I'm the third most important person in the America administration and that makes me a Have,' a man shouted from the oncoming vessel. 'And you're not fishing.'

'Don't you worry, Harry,' said Captain Willie. 'I'm a Have Not and I won't let him take you.'

'You shot niggers ain't no use to an tough Have Nots,' Harry whispered to Wesley. 'I'll dump the booze. Maybe we get it back later. I could use some whiskey.'

WINTER: *Albert speaking*: 'What happened to your arm, Harry?' the Bee Lips lawyer asked.

'Ain't got no use for arms when I got your hands in my pocket.'

'You wanna make some money takin' some radicals back home to Cuba?'

'I'm not at all sure about that,' I said.

'You're just another scared Conch wasting away on seven

dollars a week,' Harry growled. 'You're only here to be the loser.'

Harry: I don't want to fool with it, but then what choice have I got? I certainly ain't got no choice about being in a book with endless pointless voice changes. Just feels like I'm being used, being spat out into three novellas that are passed off as a book. But then a Have Not's gotta do what a Have Not's gotta do.

Bee Lips came back. 'So you're on then?'

Harry drank a case of whiskey. It was good to be back in the third person.

'You're a good man and a good husband, Harry Morgan,' Marie said.

'I'd have liked a son.'

'You too much of a man to have a boy.'

'And you may be fat now, old woman, but you still make me hard.'

'Ain't no one harder than you, one arm.'

Harry laughed, relieved to have awkwardly established he had some inner world beyond drinking, smuggling, drinking, fishing, drinking and killing people.

'What are we doing here?' asked the Laughtons and the Bradleys.

'I guess we've just the Haves with louche cameo roles sneering at the Have Nots,' said the Gordons. 'Look at that fat woman. No one could love her.' That woman, with plodding inevitability, was Marie.

Shots rang out as the Cubans robbed the bank. Bee Lips left his guts on the road. The others ran down to the quay. 'Get moving,' they yelled. The tall one pulled out a shotgun and wasted Albert.

'What you kill that loser Have Not for?' Harry gasped.

'It's a symbolic gesture.'

Harry reached for his machine gun and watched the Cubans' heads explode. He took a drink. A Cuban took a dying breath and blew a hole the size of a fist in Harry's stomach. 'One man aloan got no fuckin' chance,' he groaned.

Some other Haves enjoyed themselves in the marina as Harry's body was brought ashore.

'Some books Have It,' Marie sobbed, 'and some books Haven't.'

REBECCA

Daphne du Maurier

Last night I dreamed I went to Manderley again. I swear that the house was not an empty shell but lived and breathed as it lived before, but I awoke many hundreds of miles away in an alien land.

I wonder what my life would have been like today if Mrs Van Hopper had not been a snob. 'That's Max de Winter,' she whispered excitedly in the lobby of the Hotel Côte d'Azur. 'They say he's never got over the death of his wife. We must invite him to tea.'

'You have a very lovely and unusual name,' Mr de Winter said as we met alone after Mrs Van Hopper had conveniently caught influenza.

'It's so lovely and unusual,' I answered, 'that no one will ever once mention it in the book.'

'No matter,' he said, languidly smoking a cigarette. 'I shall call you "my child" and I shall sweep you off your young, impressionable feet with my aristocratic hauteur and studied melancholia.'

'Oh, thank you Daddy,' I said, my heart soaring with passion.

'You may call me Maxim,' he replied. 'My God, but you are different from all the others. Marry me, my child, and after we have honeymooned in Venice we shall return to Manderley.'

The staff lined up outside the front door as we motored down the rhododendron-lined drive. 'Good day, Mrs de Winter,' said the tall, unsmiling figure of Mrs Danvers.

'Don't worry about Danny, my poor lamb,' Maxim said. 'She was devoted to Rebecca. Now run along and make yourself at home. I've got some very urgent letters to write and cigarettes to smoke.'

How slowly that afternoon passed as Maxim attended to his important business and how greatly I felt the weight of Rebecca's presence as I tiptoed through the East Wing. How could I, a mere child, compare to that beautiful creature?

Later that evening we went walking in the grounds and Jasper the dog went missing along a secret path.

'Don't follow him,' Maxim shouted, his voice turning dark and queer.

I ignored him, making my way down to a beach hut further along the cove where a strange figure combed the beach.

'Get away from Ben the Idiot,' Maxim said. 'He's just an idiot.'

'Ooh air, theee oother woman was thair.'

'Is this where Rebecca drowned?'

'I knew we should never have got married,' Maxim said, his voice turning even darker and queerer. 'Now I shall have to go away to write some letters in London.'

The days felt endless without Maxim and the only interruption to my solitude was the unexpected arrival of a bounder. 'The name's Jack Favell,' he sneered. 'Rebecca's cousin. And if you'd like a bit of rough and tumble as well . . .'

'Don't ever mention Mr Favell to Mr de Winter,' Mrs Danvers said, brushing her fingers through Rebecca's perfumed underwear drawers. 'Just concentrate on making yourself look like that woman in the picture for the Manderley ball.'

'Get changed at once,' Maxim said darkly and queerly as I made my entrance.

I hid in my room sobbing, waiting for Maxim to join me. He never came. Why had I not realised that Mrs Danvers had dressed me to look like Rebecca? My marriage was over. I could never replace Rebecca in my husband's affections.

Two days later Maxim reappeared. Oh joy! 'Let's start again,' I pleaded. 'I'll be your boy if you don't want me to be your wife.'

'Everything's changed,' Maxim said. 'A storm has washed up a boat with Rebecca's body on board. The police will discover that I shot her. You see, I hated her. Everyone thought we had the most perfect marriage but she was a cruel woman who taunted me with her lovers and threatened to have their babies. And although I've always treated you like a child, you're the only woman I've ever loved, my child.'

'Oh Maxim,' I answered. 'I don't care if you killed your first wife. Anyone can make a silly mistake. Just kiss me hard and we can make it better.'

'It's all over,' said Maxim, writing yet another letter. 'The coroner's verdict was suicide.'

'That's what you think,' Favell slurred, helping himself to a whisky and soda. 'Rebecca was my lover and I've got proof you murdered her.'

My blood ran cold, yet I felt a strange elation. At least we would have another night together before Maxim was hung for murder.

'Show us your evidence then, you cad,' Maxim replied.

'Oooh air,' said Ben the Idiot.

'Rebecca didn't love anyone but me,' said Mrs Danvers, with a manic Sapphic intensity.

'Well, I don't think that proves anything very much,' said Colonel Julyan the magistrate. 'And as you are very upper-class like me, I'm inclined to believe in your innocence, Maxim. But we should go to London to check out Rebecca's mysterious doctor's appointment.'

'So, my child,' Maxim whispered as we drove back to Manderley. 'Rebecca not only had terminal cancer, she also had a deformed uterus. She was goading me to kill her all along.'

'Oh, darling,' I said. 'I always knew you were only a pretend wife murderer. And, look! Isn't that Manderley on fire in the distance? Silly old Mrs Danvers. I told her not to read *Jane Eyre*.'

THE BIG SLEEP

Raymond Chandler

I WAS NEAT and clean, everything the well-dressed private detective ought to be. I was calling on $4million. A door opened off the hall of the Sternwood place and a dame came in. It was Miss Carmen Sternwood; she was 20, but looked durable.

'Handsome aren't you?' she said. 'And I bet you know it.'

'You should wean her. She's old enough,' I told the butler as he took me through to the general. I struck a match on my thumbnail and lit a cigarette. The general eyed me from his wheelchair. 'What do you know, Marlowe?' he asked.

'You're a widower. Two daughters, fast and wild. One of them married to a bootlegger, Rusty Regan.'

'I liked Rusty,' he said. 'He's gone missing. But that's not why I called you in. I'm being blackmailed again.'

'Again?'

'I paid out $5,000 to Joe Brody a year back. This time it's a man called Geiger. I want you to mark him.'

'You need a Geiger counter.'

A flash of sheer stocking greeted me as I left the general's room. It was Carmen's sister, Mrs Regan. 'Will you find Rusty?'

'You've got swell legs, but don't try to interrogate me.'

'I loathe masterful men.'

'What are you afraid of, Mrs Regan?'

Geiger was in the smut book business. I tailed him back to his house. Three shots rang out. I ran in. Neither of the two people indoors paid me any attention, but only Geiger was dead. Carmen was naked, high on ether. There was no film in the camera. I took Carmen home; by the time I got back Geiger was gone too.

'Do you know him?' the DA asked, pulling a body out of the Packard.

'Sure. It's the Sternwood chauffeur. Someone sapped him before he drove off the pier.'

I headed back to Geiger's. The smut was getting shipped out to Joe Brody's. I went to his office. 'I'm being blackmailed over Carmen's photos,' said Mrs Regan. I could have wondered what she was doing there, but this was dime crime. Nothing made sense. So I said nothing.

'You're not a gusher,' she said, flashing a lot of leg. 'You can call me Vivian.'

'Another time, Mrs Regan.'

Carmen was laughing hysterically when I got back to Geiger's. I slapped her. I would have slapped her twice but she might have enjoyed it. The doorbell rang. It was Joe Brody. He was packing heat, but he wasn't a killer. The buzzer rang again. Brody answered and bit lead. I chased the shooter and pulled him down. It was Geiger's pansy. He thought Brody had killed his lover to take over the racket.

'Nobody thinks in noir,' I told him. 'You just turn the pages and count the body bags.' Turned out it was the chauffeur who had whacked Geiger, because he was in love with Carmen. Should have spotted the double-double-cross days ago.

I should have quit then. But this was two novellas bolted together. Out at Missing Persons I heard that Regan ran away with Eddie Mars's wife, Mona. Things were getting interesting again. Mars ran the casino where Mrs Regan liked to play roulette. I walked in to find Mrs High-Pockets winning $16,000. It was a lot of jack and she was tailed outside. I spooked her assailant and took his gun. I was collecting metal like it was going out of style.

It was all too obvious. Eddie didn't whack Rusty; jealousy was bad for business. Mrs Regan's attack was staged to make me think he wasn't involved with her. The double-double-cross had turned into double-double-double-cross. Back home I found Carmen naked in my bed. 'Hold me close, killer,' she purred.

'Learn the rules. Philip Marlowe never sleeps with the *femme fatale*.'

The dame called me a filthy name as I showed her the door.

It wasn't hard to nail the tail. It was Harry Jones, one of Brody's oufit. Said he had some info on Mona Mars. It was mine for 2Cs. It had better be good, I said. It will be. Mona hadn't run off with Rusty; Eddie had kept her quiet out of town so no one would think he'd killed Rusty. As Eddie's goon, Lash Canino, poisoned Jones, I could feel a classic double-double-double-double-cross coming on.

I got a flat on the way out to Realito. The man in the garage didn't know I had last seen him croaking Jones. Or maybe he did. I came round to find myself handcuffed next to Mona.

'You're a kick,' she said, untying me. 'Kiss me.' Her lips were like ice.

'No dice. The only game I play is no-spillikins,' I answered, plugging Camino full of lead.

Maybe it was just that we were nearing the end, but suddenly everything made sense. I nosed the Plymouth back to the Sternwoods' and gave Carmen back her gun. She pointed it at my head and pulled the trigger.

'Dames like her are trouble, Mrs Regan,' I said. 'She doesn't like it when men say no. She came on to Rusty like she came on to me, only Rusty hadn't emptied the chambers of her piece first. And you got Eddie to cover up the killing by hiding the body.'

I left the Sternwood house and went back to my $25-a-day life. The general would soon be joining Rusty and all the others in the big sleep. I was stepping into immortality.

BIGGLES IN THE BALTIC

Captain W. E. Johns

As the momentous words announcing that England was at war with Germany came over the radio, Major James Bigglesworth DSC turned to face his friends, Captain the Honourable Algernon Lacey MC and Ginger Hebblethwaite.

'Looks like we'll be in for a spot of war flying,' he smiled grimly. The telephone bell shrilled. 'And that, unless I'm very much mistaken, is Colonel Raymond of the Air Ministry with our orders.'

'Now listen here, men,' said Colonel Raymond. 'We've got a top secret mission for you. Just before the war began, Britain bought a small island, Bergen Ait, in the Baltic. It's an unremarkable piece of rock, but it's close to Jerry. Your job is to give the Boche a pounding. And if you're not careful, you might run into your old foe, Erich von Stalhein!'

'It's not going to be a piece of cake,' Biggles warned his comrades. 'So if either of you . . .'

'Count me in, sir,' yelped Ginger obsequiously.

'And me, old boy,' roared Algy. 'Wouldn't miss it for anything.'

'I knew I could rely on you,' Biggles grinned affectionately, 'and don't worry, we'll have two salt of the earth, strike a light cockneys, to do the cooking and mend the planes, so it'll be just like school.'

'This is spiffing,' Ginger gasped. 'I'm going to call my kite Dingo.'

'Then mine's Didgeree-du,' Algy pouted.

Biggles curled his lips suggestively. 'I'll call mine Willie-Willie.'

'Why?' asked Ginger and Algy, fingering the pleats of their trousers.

'You'd know if you ever run into one,' Biggles replied, repressing his homoerotic feelings manfully. 'Now, get some sleep. We're to bomb a fuel dump on the Kiel Canal tonight.'

'I've never known Archie like that before,' Ginger ejaculated, wiping the blood away from a deep cut on his face. 'That was some picnic.'

'Well done, chaps,' breezed Biggles. 'Now you get off to bed, Ginger. That graze looks nasty and you might have a slight temperature. Algy? How about some bacon and eggs?'

Just then Biggles heard a sound and froze. A U-boat was moored in the cove.

'That's a nuisance,' he muttered. Ten minutes later the flier was smiling again. He had captured the secret German code book and sunk the U-boat.

'Shame there were no survivors,' said Ginger.

Biggles shrugged. 'We don't have the facilities to look after any Huns, so it's probably for the best.'

Two days later, Biggles and Algy were forced to make an emergency landing out in open sea, after a daring raid to the German mainland to blow up a railway tunnel.

'Whato,' said Algy. 'Looks like a fishing boat has come to rescue us . . .'

'Not zo fast, Britischers,' sneered a tight-lipped German.

'I might have known we'd run into you sooner or later, von Stalhein,' Biggles rasped. 'And how typical that you Nazis should be so cowardly as to break the rules of war by using an unmarked boat.'

A plane flew overhead. It was Ginger. 'Tally ho,' said everyone as deadly tracer carved through the fabric of the boat.

'It looks like we'll have to swim the 10 miles back to base,' grinned Biggles.

'You haven't heard the last of me,' yelled von Stalhein, waving his fist at the fliers as he scrambled aboard the German luxury liner, *Leipzig*, that had come to his rescue.

Back at base, Biggles and Algy got back into their familar routine of joshing one another. Trying not to sulk, Ginger decided to explore the island by himself. Climbing higher and higher, and traversing an underground lake, he eventually found himself stuck on the summit of the island and unable to return to his chums. What a silly-billy I've been, he thought to himself, though maybe being stranded here will turn out to be useful later on.

Algy and Biggles watched their plane sink into a sandbank after yet another emergency landing. 'Nothing we can do about it,' said Biggles, 'so let's explore.'

'Hmm,' Algy whispered winsomely. 'That looks like a major supply depot for the Huns . . .'

'And that's a Dornier flying boat,' Biggles interjected. 'If we could help ourselves to supplies and steal the plane . . .'

Landing back at base, Biggles decided it was time for some shut-eye. 'I can trust you to bomb the depot and torpedo the *Leipzig*, can't I, big boy?' He smirked, tapping Algy lightly on the cheek.

'Und zo, ve meet again,' von Stalhein sneered unpleasantly. 'Und zis time I vill make no mistake. I will have you shot immediately.'

Biggles awoke to find his arch enemy's Luger pointing at his head and the base crawling with Nazis. He couldn't remember having ever been in such a pickle before.

Ginger was getting desperate. Biggles needed him, yet what could he do? He picked up the largest sub-machine gun he could find and sprayed a magazine towards the Hun.

'Thanks,' Biggles grinned, as he escaped to join Ginger. 'Now let's detonate a grenade and crush the entire German navy that has gathered below in a rock fall. And then we'll be home in time for tea.'

'Congratulations,' said Colonel Raymond curtly, as the three fliers met for a debriefing at the Air Ministry.

'I'm sorry we couldn't have done more, sir,' wept Biggles.

'So am I. If you'd carried on like that for another week the war would have been over. As it is, it will probably carry on for another five years.'

DARKNESS AT NOON

Arthur Koestler

THE DOOR TO Cell 404 slammed shut. Rubashov immediately fell into a deep sleep. An hour before he had been dreaming of being arrested when two men had knocked on the door of his apartment and driven him to the prison in a foreign car.

'How do these capitalist automobiles cope with our roads?' he had asked, trying to engage his captors in conversation.

'It's a Ford Escort. It would fall apart anywhere,' the short one had replied, signalling the discourse was at an end.

The sound of a bugle woke Rubashov from a contented, dreamless sleep. 'I suppose some might think it highly unnatural to have fallen asleep so easily at a time of great stress he thought to himself, yet as the whole purpose of this book is to framework the ruthless deterministic inevitability of a totalitarian regime, you will see there is no cause for anxiety when you know you will be shot on page 210.

He stretched out and surveyed his cell. A picture of No. 1 hung over his bed. The face looked at once familiar yet unfamiliar, Rubashov mused. In a certain light, it could have been mistaken for Stalin yet that could not be so for No. 1 was not merely a representation of a Soviet five year plan of upper-lip facial growth, but a symbol of the repressive nature of moustaches in general.

The recognition of this triggered a toothache of equal symbolism and Rubashov allowed the pain of memory to wash through him. As a younger Party apparatchik, had he not expediently expelled a young German called Richard from the Party whilst on one of his visits overseas, thereby condemning him to death?

And as his toothache worsened, had he also not been implicated in Little Loewy's suicide when he had forced him to break the year-long strike and allow Soviet weapons into Fascist Italy? Rubashov had done it unquestioningly for the good of the Party, but now as he allowed the grammatical fiction of the capitalist first person to penetrate his consciousness a stirring of bourgeois guilt emerged.

A tapping on the pipes disturbed the silence. It was No. 402 sending a message. A-R-S-E. Rubashov tapped back urgently. D-O-N-T Y-O-U M-E-A-N A-R-I-S-E? There was a moment's pause before the answer came back. T-H-E-R-E I-S N-O I I-N S-O-C-A-L-S-M Y-O-U A-R-S-E. Here is the dialectic flaw of vowellian Communist fiction, Rubashov thought. Since when was there an I in EGO?

The cell door opened and a guard led him down the corridor. Was this the moment of death? He was taken into a brightly lit room where his old Party colleague, Ivanov, was sat behind a desk.

'We have evidence that you have been engaged in counter-revolutionary activities and have been plotting the death of No. 1,' Ivanov said.

'You know that's nonsense,' Rubashov replied. 'I have always been a loyal member of the Party.'

'We have ways and means of dealing with false consciousness.' Ivanov smiled gently. 'But because you are my friend and to make the point that totalitarian regimes can also distort the truth without recourse to violence, we won't be torturing you.'

I am very worried you may not have noticed this is a serious critique of totalitarianism so in the guise of Rubashov's diary this chapter explores the moral relativism of authoritarianism whereby the ends always justifies the means.

The grammatical fiction of personal guilt prompted another toothache, in the course of which Rubashov recalled how he had betrayed Arlova, his mistress and librarian, when the First Secretary had decided her judgement was untrustworthy. Had he not effectively condemned her to the same fate he was about to suffer?

'Enough of this capitalist sophistry,' Ivanov declared at Rubashov's next interrogation. 'Surely you have worked out by now that none of this is personal. Totalitarianism can only survive in a climate of fear and mistrust, and for that we need an enemy from within as well as one without. Today it's your turn. You are muggins. Just confess to a lesser charge and you'll be out in five years.'

'OK, then,' Rubashov replied. 'But you didn't need to do anything so crude as to let my old friend Bogrov be shot outside my door to force my hand. Totalitarianism is so much more subtle than many believe, and I would have confessed anyway.'

'I'm sorry. That was the idea of Gletkin. He doesn't have the nous of us old Party members.'

I am still very worried you may not have noticed this is a serious critique of totalitarianism so in the guise of Rubashov's diary this chapter explores the moral relativism of authoritarianism whereby the ends always justifies the means.

Rubashov relaxed as the guard took him for his final interrogation session. Today he would shake Ivanov's hand and sign the deal that would save his life.

'I'm afraid we've had to shoot Ivanov for not being on message,' said Gletkin.

'Oh dear,' Ivanov sighed. 'I suppose that means we've got at least another 50 pages on the duplicity and amorality of repression and that you are going to present me with mountains of flimsy evidence and witnesses who have deliberately misunderstood my jokes which will conclusively prove my guilt, while maintaining that embryonic totalitarian regimes are not bound by the same legalistic niceties as mature democracies because the importance of their survival transcends an objective truth.'

'Indeed,' said Gletkin. 'And you will come to realise that you are definitely guilty of something – if not the crimes of which you are accused – and will decide you cannot avoid the totalitarian inevitability that it is better for you to accede to the state – thereby showing how triumphantly repressive it in fact is – than to risk damaging it with a futile challenge.'

'You are so right. I am guilty of everything.'

'In which case, for the charge of going on and on about the evil of authoritarianism long after everyone has got the point, this court sentences you to death.'

W-S-H-T W-A-S M-E, No. 402 tapped out.

I wish it was me too, thought the reader.

'Thank God it's me,' said Rubashov as a bullet shattered his skull.

THE OUTSIDER

Albert Camus

MOTHER DIED TODAY. Or maybe yesterday. *Bof*. Who cares? The old people's home is 50 miles from Algiers so I asked my boss for two days off. He didn't seem pleased. I caught the two o'clock bus. It was very hot. I slept most of the way.

'Mrs Meursault was happy here,' the warden said. 'She was bored living with you.' It was true. She cried a lot the first few days at the home. But that was only because she wasn't used to it. After a month she'd have cried if she'd been taken away. That's partly why I never went to see her. And also because it was too much effort.

The caretaker began to unscrew the coffin lid. I stopped him. 'Don't you want to see the body?' he asked. 'No,' I answered. 'Why not?' 'I'm not bovvered.'

The inmates came to join the vigil. I'd never before noticed what huge paunches old women can have. Their sobbing interrupted my sleep. The sun was already high in the sky as the procession moved off. 'Was she old?' the undertaker asked. I shrugged. 'Maybe.' At last her body was in the blood-red earth. I could go home and sleep for 12 hours.

I decided to go swimming the next day. In the water I met Marie Cordona, who used to be a typist in the office. I brushed against her and asked if she wanted to go to the cinema. She seemed surprised when I turned up in a black tie. I told her Mother had died. She wanted to know when. 'Whenever.' The film was pretty stupid. Afterwards she came back to my place. When I woke up the next morning, Marie had gone. I spent the day smoking cigarettes and staring out of the window.

It was hot in the office the next day and I walked home by the docks. On my way upstairs I bumped into old Salamano, my next-door neighbour, who was swearing at his mange-ridden dog. 'He's always here,' he said. 'Then why don't you get rid of it and get another one,' I suggested. Just then my other neighbour came in. Locals say he lives off women. He's always seemed fine to me. He's called Raymond. He invited me in for black pudding and told me he'd been in a fight with his Moorish girlfriend's brother. 'He was upset that I'd beaten her up,' he said. 'But she had been deceiving me. Is that not fair enough?' I'd been smoking Raymond's cigarettes so I said it did seem fair. He asked me to write a letter for him that would hurt and punish her. He was extremely pleased when I agreed.

Marie and I were disturbed by dull thuds and a woman's shrill voice. People gathered on the landing and banged on Raymond's door. 'He hit me,' the woman said. The plumber called a police-man. Raymond asked me to be a witness. He told me to say she had cheated on him. I agreed and he asked if I wanted to go to a brothel. I refused as it was far too tiring.

The following week Raymond phoned me. He said that a friend had invited me to stay at his chalet on Sunday. I asked if I could bring Marie. That evening Marie asked me if I wanted to marry her. 'If you want,' I replied. 'I ain't really bovvered.' Did I love her? *Bof*. Maybe yes, maybe no. Probably not. We walked in silence for a while. I asked her if she wanted to eat with me. She said she was doing something. She looked at me. 'Don't you want to know what?' I did, but I couldn't be bothered to ask.

The sun was very hot. We met up with Raymond and his friend, Masson, and went for a walk along the beach. We came across his former lover's brother sitting with a group of other Arabs. There was a fight. Masson got cut. The Arabs ran off. Later Raymond handed me his gun. I walked down the beach alone. I met the Arab. It was even hotter now. I shot him once. Then I shot him four times more.

'Why did you shoot him?' the magistrate asked me. 'It was too hot.' 'Do you miss your mother?' 'I'm not bovvered.' 'Do you believe in God?' 'I said I ain't bovvered.'

Marie came to visit me once. 'Would you have got married to anyone who had asked you?' she asked. 'Probably.' Apart from missing cigarettes, I quite enjoyed my 11 months in prison. And I even got used to not having cigarettes after a while.

My case came up the following summer. It was very hot in the court and I felt dizzy as the prosecuting lawyer questioned me. 'Did I love my mother?' 'Whateva.' 'Had I picked up a girl the day after the funeral?' 'Whateva.' 'Had I deliberately gone back to the beach to shoot the Arab?' 'Whateva.' It was very hot when the foreman of the jury read out the guilty verdict. The judge told me in a peculiar way that I would be decapitated in a public square in the name of the French people. Did I have anything to say? I thought it over. 'Not really,' I said. 'I ain't that bovvered.'

Three times I refused to see the chaplain. He'd looked at me sadly, begging me to hand my soul over to God. Eventually I grabbed his cassock in frustration. I'd lived in a certain way. I'd done some things and I hadn't done others. I realised that I'd been happy, that I was happy now. For the final consummation, all I needed was a crowd of spectators at my execution saying they weren't bovvered either.

CANDLEFORD GREEN

Flora Thompson

LAURA SAT UP beside her father on the cart and waved. 'Goodbye Laura,' the neighbours cried, while Dawn French bounced up and down, overacting in the background. Her leaving had caused quite a stir. It was an epic eight-mile journey from the sleepy hamlet of Lark Rise to the sleepy village of Candleford Green, and no one was quite sure if they would ever see Laura again.

After stopping for a fizzy orangeade along the way, they reached the Post Office where Laura was to start work as an assistant while Candleford Green was taking its afternoon nap. Yet their arrival did not go entirely unobserved, for the Postmistress, Miss Dorcas Lane, who was widely held to be as sharp as vinegar, which is more than can be said for this prose, had heard the clattering of hooves upon the cobbles and arose from her slumber to greet them.

'You must be exhausted,' Miss Lane declared. 'I shall get Zillah to make us tea and scones. I've been rushed off my feet myself, what with the Misses Pratt dropping by for three penny stamps and a gossip.'

Laura was unable to begin her arduous duties until she had been officially sworn in by Sir Timothy on the morrow, so she retired to her room to unpack her trunk and to recover from such a busy day.

The interview the next morning was not as terrifying as she had expected. Sir Timothy patronised her courteously, saying she appeared remarkably bright for a fourteen-year-old peasant girl, and Miss Lane commented appreciatively on the depth of her curtsey. Once dismissed from Sir Timothy's presence, Laura was introduced to the other postal workers.

'I have recently converted to Methodism,' said Mr Brown, 'and the surveyor tried to make me deliver the mail on a Sunday.'

'How very distressing for you,' Laura replied.

'Indeed it was, but luckily someone else agreed to do the deliveries in my place.'

'It was a very worrying hour of prime time television for all of us,' said Miss Lane. 'I need a slice of Victoria sponge and a lie-down just thinking about it.'

Over the following months Laura quickly mastered the half-penny and the penny stamps, but the five-shilling stamps always caused her grave anxiety from which she liked to recover by reading the sonnets of Shakespeare or – if she was feeling somewhat racy and was certain she was not being watched – Byron's *Don Juan*.

In Laura's time, Candleford Green was still a village and every member of the community knew his or her place, which made it the ideal Sunday-night feelgood costume drama. The poor, of course, would have liked an extra farthing a week to spend on dripping, but no one begrudged Sir Timothy and Lady Adelaide their palace as each year on Boxing Day they allowed the hunt to gather just outside their gates. What excitement this grand occasion merited, with all the women planning their wardrobes months ahead!

No English village in the nineties was without its idiot, and Candleford could lay claim to more than its fair share. Yet Lumey Joe, an unfortunate deaf mute, was the undisputed king of the idiots. How he used to chuckle as the children gaily threw stones at him and pushed him in the river! It was not all fun and frolics, though, for people did, from time to time, fall sick and die. Yet when they did, how the lower orders pulled together, swapping turnips and baking dainties for one another!

'Some folk might say Candleford is the kind of village that appears on chocolate boxes,' said Miss Lane, waking up from a deep post-prandial snooze. 'Which reminds me. Who ate all the toffees?'

Candleford was never short of entertainments, for twice a year a man would come to give public readings on the Green. It was at one such event that Laura, her hair cut into the Alexandra fringe that was all the rage at the time, was asked by a Godfrey Parrish, a young reporter on the *Candleford News*, if she would mind if he were to walk her home. She accepted and they arrived back at the Post Office two minutes later. The village talked about little else for years to come, though Laura and Godfrey never did meet again.

During this time Laura became acquainted with her neighbours, the two Misses Pratt, who ran the haberdashery store and whose father had mysteriously vanished for a year only to turn up in a hedge, yet she continued to throw herself into her work wholeheartedly. She learned to use the complicated telegraph machine and, when the delivery man was ill, she personally would walk twenty-five miles to make sure that Sir Timothy received his letters on time, and so fast was her stride she would still have time to press some wild flowers before tea.

'You're a good girl, Laura,' Miss Lane would say. 'Have a nice jam tart.'

It would be wrong to paint too idyllic a portrait of Candleford Green, for even then the village was beginning to show some signs of the changes that would see it become a monstrous suburb of Candleford, complete with its own Spar. Modern bicycles had begun to replace the penny-farthing and once a youth was caught trespassing in Sir Timothy's spinney. On such occasions, the Candleford folk would sigh 'Such is Life,' and return to the kitchen to make some nice quince jelly.

Laura would often find that the greatest excitements came in threes. First there was the great oak that fell, causing Sir Timothy's countenance to turn most grave; then there was 'Old Bob' who found a panel that fetched five pounds at a public auction; and last there was the anonymous Valentine inscribed with the rhyme 'U-G-L-Y, you ain't got no Alibi. You UGLY, You UGLY'. This last incident caused Laura much distress, until Miss Lane reminded her that such were the heady dramas around which Sunday night television schedules were based.

'I'd better have a biscuit and a cup of tea,' said Laura, before going back to the counter to dispense stamps to the four customers of the afternoon. Yet she too was changing. The pace of life in Candleford Green no longer left her quite as breathless as it once had. Some days she could even manage without a nap and then she longed to escape the gossamer threads that bound her. Yet the threads that tied her to a life of boredom were more enduring than gossamer. They were spun from cherished memories of endless repeat fees.

BRIDESHEAD REVISITED

Evelyn Waugh

'It's not a bad camp, sir,' said Hooper. 'A big, private house with two or three lakes. You never saw such a thing.'

'Yes I did,' I replied world-wearily. 'I've been here before.'

I had been there; first with Sebastian more than twenty years before on a cloudless day in June, when the ditches were creamy with meadowsweet and the sentences heavy with nostalgia.

We had met several months earlier when he had been amusingly sick in my Oxford rooms. He had begged my forgiveness and thereafter allowed me to be his friend.

'Jump in the boot, Charles,' he had said, placing his teddy-bear, Aloysius, on the front seat beside him. 'We're going to have champagne and strawberries with Nanny.'

'You d-d-do know that my s-s-stutter is to let you know I'm a p-p-proper homosexual,' drawled the aesthete Anthony Blanche some time later in the manner of the Wandering Jew, 'and to l-l-let the reader know yours and Sebastian's c-c-campness is p-p-purely p-p-platonic. And n-n-ow is as good a time as any to fill in the b-b-backstory of Sebastian's family. His father, Lord M-M-Marchmain, lives in Venice with his mistress, while L-L-Lady Marchmain remains at B-B-Brideshead. His eldest sister, L-L-Lady Julia, is rather aloof. The youngest, C-C-Cordelia, is a hoot.'

I returned home rudderless and without money that summer.

'I'm in Queer Street,' I told my father.

'Why don't you get a job then?' he replied.

Such common sentiments irked me greatly and it was with some relief that I received a telegram from Sebastian. *I'm bored and you're the only person I know desperate enough to drop everything and come immediately*, it read. That summer was very heaven as we lay sketching, drinking and being clever.

'Let's go to Venice to see Daddy,' Sebastian chirruped one day. 'I'll pay.'

'Welcome to the palazzo,' growled Lord Marchmain. 'Don't you hate Catholicism?'

Sebastian and I were inseparable the following year. Perhaps I should have noticed then that his sadness was giving way to sullenness and that he was becoming a drunkard but I was intoxicated with pleasure that I, a mere agnostic member of the middle classes, should be allowed such proximity to Catholic aristocrats.

'I want a drink,' Sebastian shouted.

'You have done a very bad un-Catholic thing by giving Sebastian whisky,' Lady Marchmain reprimanded me icily. 'I hereby banish you from Brideshead.'

Knowing my place in the world, I had no feelings whatsoever about losing my friendship with Sebastian. Not even a jejune irritation. It was not until sometime after, when I met Rex, Julia's arriviste Canadian fiancé, in Paris that I heard how Sebastian had escaped the clutches of Lady Marchmain's appointed chaperone, stolen money from Blanche in Constantinople and run off to Tangiers.

Rex and Julia's wedding was a quiet affair. I later learned their plans had had to be hastily changed.

'Rex has been previously married,' Lady Marchmain had shrilled.

'Why didn't you tell me?' Julia had wondered.

'Because if I had there would have been no last-minute Catholic hand-wringing,' Rex laughed.

I returned to London to observe the General Strike and

wondered why, if the lower orders really didn't want to work, they didn't do nothing in the first place, like me.

'Mummy is dying,' sobbed Julia. 'She wants to apologise for being so beastly to you.'

'I absolve ourselves of any wrongdoing,' Lady Marchmain whispered. 'Now run along to Tangiers and see how Sebastian is getting on.'

Sebastian lay bearded and unkempt, preyed on by a parasitical German. His upper-class charm still shone brightly, though his alcoholism was a bit of a problem. 'I'm staying here,' he slurred.

Ten years passed, years in which I did agreeably little. My theme is memory, that winged host. Unfortunately mine is not that good, because on my return to New York from sketching in Mexico, I was unable to remember the name of my son or that my wife had been pregnant when I left.

'Gosh. Really?' I said, when Celia told me the news.

The storm raged, divinely symbolic of my inner turmoil. I took Julia in my arms and kissed her hard.

'Thank God Celia was unfaithful first so I'm not a cad,' I murmured.

'And I thank the Almighty that Rex is having an affair as well.'

'Then let's get married once we're both divorced.'

The arrangements were proceeding amicably when Julia announced her father had returned to England to die.

'Come back to God,' the priest intoned.

Lord Marchmain made the Sign of the Cross and died.

'See how Daddy has returned to Catholicism,' Julia cried. 'Sebastian is working for a monastery, Cordelia is doing good works, so I too must embrace my Faith. We can't be wed after all.'

'I quite understand,' I said, deferential to the last.

Brideshead looked at peace as we marched through its gates. I made my way to the chapel and prostrated myself. I too could be a Catholic.

CRY, THE BELOVED COUNTRY

Alan Paton

THERE IS A LOVELY road that runs from Ixopo into the hills. There the grass is rich. Keep it, guard it; for it cares for you. But down in the valleys the soil is barren. The men and the children have left. The soil cannot keep them.

The Reverend Stephen Kumalo looked up.

– I bring you a letter, *umfundisi*, said the child.

– I can see that, my child.

It had been sent from Johannesburg. Kumalo was reluctant to open it, for once a letter has been opened it cannot be put back in the same envelope. He called to his wife.

– It could be from our son Absalom. Or perhaps your brother John.

She opened the letter. It was from the Reverend Msimangu, saying Stephen's sister Gertrude was ill and that he should come to Johannesburg.

– That is a hard letter.

– Indeed it is not an easy letter.

– That's just what I was saying.

Kumalo wearily left for Johannesburg. His wife sat back silently, with the patient suffering of black women.

The train creaked slowly past the gold mines, the mines from which South Africa's Europeans had grown rich, the mines in which the blacks had been ripped from their villages for but a few shillings' pay. Kumalo shook his head sadly. People should pray more to God, he thought.

– Johnannesburg is a big city, he said to Msimangu.

– Very big, *umfundisi*.

– There are some bad people here.

– Very bad, *umfundisi*.

– The Peace of God escapes them.

– There is no Peace of God, *umfundisi*.

– But there are one or two nice people. Even among the whites. So questions of racial tension are not as straightforward as you might think.

– Very unstraightforward, *umfundisi*.

Kumalo slept badly, oppressed by the hardness of his thoughts. The next day he was taken to see Gertude.

– So you are a prostitute who sells liquor.

– I am, *umfundisi*.

– That is a hard thing for a brother to bear.

– Very hard, *umfundisi*. But Johnannesburg is a very hard town.

Msimangu then led Stephen to meet his brother John.

– You have not written, he said

– Indeed I have not, *umfundisi*, John replied in his great bull voice.

– That is a hard thing for a brother to bear.

– Very hard, *umfundisi*. But Johnannesburg is a very hard town.

– You have become a political activist.

– I only want what is fair, *umfundisi*.

– Only God can tell what is truly fair.

– If you say so, *umfundisi*.

– I do say so. Or rather, Alan Paton does because he's a devout Christian. But even he realises things are not easy.

– Very uneasy, *umfundisi*.

Msimangu clasped Stephen to his bosom, the bosom that was Africa.

– Now we must look for your son, *umfundisi*.

– It will be hard.

– Very hard, *umfundisi*.

They walked to the prostitute's dwelling where Absalom was last seen.

– He has moved to the Shanty Town, *umfundisi*.

– The Shanty Town is a very dangerous place.

– A very, very dangerous place, *umfundisi*.

O Shanty Town. Where all roads lead if you are black. O Shanty Town. Where tribal folklore is crushed in the dust. O Shanty Town. Where poetry dies on the page.

– He stole from white people and was sent to the Reformatory, *umfundisi*, said the liquor woman. He is bad.

– It is a hard thing for a father to hear.

– Very hard, *umfundisi*.

They walked past the tin shelters where dreams died. They walked past the flowered gardens of the whites who lived in fear of native crime. They walked to the Reformatory.

– Actually Absalom was not that bad, said the young white man who was there to show that whites are not necessarily racist bastards.

– That is an easier thing for a father to hear.

– Much easier, *umfundisi*. We released him early to be with his pregnant teenaged girlfriend.

– That is not such an easy thing for a father to hear when his son is not married. God and Alan will be cross.

– Johannesburg is hard, *umfundisi*.

– Very hard. We must try to forgive.

They walked to the teenaged girl's hut. She was heavy with child.

– I have not seen him for several days, she said, with the resignation of the black woman who expects to be abandoned.

– It is a hard thing for a father to hear that his son has abandoned a girl he should not have got pregnant.

Cry, the Beloved Country for those who live in fear of hard things! Cry, the Beloved Country for those who read one of the worthiest books ever written!

They returned to Msimangu's house to wash off the dirt of poverty and moral ambivalence. Msimangu picked up the newspaper. *LIBERAL WHITE MAN MURDERED BY NATIVE.*

– If it was Absalom that killed him, it will be hard for a father to bear.

– Very hard, *umfundisi*, for it surely will have been Absalom. And it will be even harder now he has killed a liberal. If only he had murdered a racist!

– We must do what we must do. Johannesburg is hard.

– Very hard, *umfundisi*.

– It was a kaffir that killed your son.

Jarvis looked up and nodded. Yet he was greatly disturbed for he had read his son's writings and now realised that possibly the whites were partly to blame for the oppression of the blacks. If only they had been a bit nicer and prayed to God a bit more, South Africa could have been a happy country!

The judge placed the black cap on his head.

– Even though you have confessed it was an accident, I am going to let your accomplices go free to show that Justice is not straightforward, and hereby sentence you to death.

– That is a hard thing for a father to hear.

– Very hard, *umfundisi*. But imagine how hard it is for me, said Absalom.

– Still not as hard as it is for me. Know that I shall take your wife and child and raise them as my own.

– And I shall become a nun, *umfundisi*.

– That is an easy thing for a brother to hear.

– On second thoughts I won't, *umfundisi*.

– That is a hard thing for a brother to hear.

*

Stephen returned to the village of Ndotsheni with a heavy heart, for the crops were failing and the children were dying. High above the village amidst the fertile soils of his verdant pastures, Jarvis was much troubled and he rode on an ass into the village.

– It must be very hard for a father to bear having a son that killed my son, *umfundisi*.

– It must be very hard for a father to bear having a son being killed by my son, *umnumzana*.

– Then we must find redemption through forgiveness and God. I will build you a church and a dam so your fields will have water. And send along someone who can teach you to farm properly, *umfundisi*.

– Thank you, *umnumzana*.

– It will be hard, *umfundisi*. But somehow very easy.

– Very hard, *umnumzana*. Yet very easy.

And on the day of his son's execution, Stephen went into the mountains to sing *Nkosi Sikelel' iAfrika*.

– 1949 –

LOVE IN A COLD
CLIMATE

Nancy Mitford

I AM OBLIGED to begin this story by emphasising the fact that
the Hampton family was very grand as well as very rich. Not to
mention congenitally stupid, a trait perfectly illustrated by Lord
Montdore, my friend Polly Hampton's father, who contented
himself with a few bigoted grunts and a walk-on part in the book.
There again, maybe he wasn't quite as dim as he first appeared.

Lady Montdore – Sonia to her *intimes* and minor European
royalty – was another matter. Her shallowness was on display
throughout, something for which there were no mitigating
circumstances as she wasn't middle-class, American or even a
particularly funny character.

After my mother left my father, I went to live with my Aunt
Emily and Uncle Davey, who were neighbours of the Montdores,
and Polly and I became close friends until she left the country at
the age of thirteen when her father became Viceroy of India. They
returned five years later and so it was that I was invited to stay for a
weekend in the Season.

'Do watch out for my uncle, Boy Dougdale,' Polly warned me.
'He tries it on with all the girls. We wittily call him the Lecherous
Lecturer. He's been having an affair with my mother for years. It
drives my Aunt Patricia mad.'

'Ah, the Bolter's daughter has arrived,' said Lady Montdore,
fixing me with her steely gaze. 'I apologise in advance for the
Caravaggio and the Raphael in your bedroom; they are very

country-house paintings. Now do try and find yourself a husband.'

I spent most of the weekend being ignored by various Rorys and Rolys who were entranced by the ever-so-risqué conversation of Veronica Chaddesley-Corbett, and the only highlight was a delightful pre-breakfast walk with the Duc de Sauveterre.

Lady Montdore cornered me later. 'So, Bolter's daughter,' she cried. 'Are you in love yet?' I thought of Sauveterre's lilting accent and his well-turned ankles and nodded. 'Well, don't be. You don't marry for love, you marry for all this,' she added, gesturing expansively towards Hampton.

And so the rest of the summer passed in a few averagely diverting set pieces, with Lady Montdore beside herself that the ever-so-beautiful Polly had failed to secure a husband, my Uncle Davey furious because he was obliged to sit next to a German at dinner, and Boy Dougdale doing needlepoint.

At the time I supposed it might have been the most daring comedy of manners with readers curious to speculate just how autobiographical it was about the magnificent Mitfords, but in hindsight I am more persuaded that it was rather a one-joke book with no real plot of which to speak.

Towards the end of the summer, I met Alfred Wincham, a young Oxford theology don, whose feelings towards me corresponded to my own for him, and within days he had asked me to marry him.

'Only if you promise to be a complete doormat and never reappear,' I said.

'I'd be happy not to,' he replied wisely, and so it was we were wed just before Christmas.

I was staying with Aunt Emily a few months later when Lady Montdore's Bentley pulled up outside the house 'Has someone died?' Aunt Emily asked.

'It's much, much worse than that,' Lady Montdore shrilled. 'Who cares if Lady Patricia passed away yesterday? It's the fact that Polly has announced she's now getting married to Boy that bothers me. I shall cut her off without a penny. The estate shall go to Cousin Cedric from Nova Scotia if the marriage goes ahead.'

I was asked to intervene but Polly was adamant. 'I know this sounds too absurd even for this clueless farce, Fanny,' she said, 'but though I've never expressed the slightest interest in Boy, I've always had a pash for him and we shall live in penury in Sicily.'

The second part of the story saw me happily settled into my Oxford hovel when Lady Montdore summoned me to meet Cousin Cedric who had arrived on a visit from Nova Scotia. I'm not sure why but Lady Montdore found it extremely amusing to repeat the phrase 'Nova Scotia', so I shall do so now. Nova Scotia. How very provincial.

'Well hellooo,' Cedric minced, 'I just love the white piping around your jacket. Let's go get a seaweed wrap and a facial and have lots of parties.'

With that one sentence, Lady Montdore was completely won over and I managed to waste about 100 pages talking about how much fun she was having, how young she was looking and how devoted she was to Cedric, while nothing much else happened.

Towards the end of the year Polly returned to the country and we arranged to meet. 'I'm bored of Boy now,' she said, as capriciously as she had announced her desire for him. 'But at least I'm pregnant.'

'Just as well the baby died,' Lady Montdore said matter-of-factly, in an upper-class scene of reconciliation. 'Children are very expensive. And I'm having the time of my life with Cedric.'

'Oh don't worry,' Polly laughed. 'It was very young and I'd probably have got bored with it.'

'Mmmm, Boy and I are off for a quick rub down,' Cedric screamed.

'Good Lord!' everyone gasped. 'You're both a couple of poofters. Who would have thought it?'

NINETEEN EIGHTY–FOUR

George Orwell

THE CLOCKS WERE striking thirteen as Winston Smith entered his seventh-floor flat in Victory Mansions. The voice on the telescreen babbled away about the overfulfilment of the Ninth Three-Year Plan as he gazed out the window at the bleak landscape dominated by posters of a black-moustachio'd face, with the caption *BIG BROTHER IS WATCHING YOU*. This was London, chief city of Airstrip One, itself a province of Oceania.

He sat down in the alcove, hidden from the Thought Police. He picked up the book he had bought from a slummy shop that Party members were not supposed to frequent and felt a tremor pass through his bowels. The thing that he was about to start was a diary, an offence punishable by death or at least by 25 years' forced labour.

I am a real 39-year-old man with real feelings. I am not just a cog in a heavy-handed political satire on Soviet totalitarianism.

Winston stopped writing. What's the point? he thought. I am just a cipher. He drank a tumbler of Victory Gin and headed back to work at the Ministry of Truth. The face of Emmanuel Goldstein, Enemy of the People, flashed on to the telescreen during the Two Minute Hate followed by the familiar exhortation *WAR IS PEACE, FREEDOM IS SLAVERY, IGNORANCE IS STRENGTH.*

As the telescreen went blank, Winston looked up and spotted O'Brien, an Inner Party member whom he had seen perhaps a dozen times in as many years. Something about the man's face suggested that, like Winston himself, his political orthodoxy was not perfect.

A feeling of imminence overwhelmed him. Not much may have happened up till now as his every action had so far only served to illustrate a not altogether convincing dystopian world divided into three superpowers – Oceania, Eurasia and Eastasia – that were perpetually at war with one another. But as he took a ruminative stroll among the coarse, yet heavily sentimentalised, Proles, he realised a young woman from the Ministry of Truth had placed a note in his pocket.

Winston unwrapped the slip of paper. *I LOVE YOU*. Why would an attractive 26-year-old woman risk everything in a world where love and sex was forbidden between Party members, for a nondescript middle-aged man with varicose ulcers whom she had never spoken to before? Such inconsistencies did not detain him long. Or at all. His heart raced. At last the action had really started.

'I've done this hundreds of times before with lots of different men, you know,' said Julia affectionately, as they lay together in an Oxfordshire meadow enjoying the secret thrill of a post-coital Victory Cigarette.

'You do know that we are bound to get caught eventually,' Winston replied, anxious that no one should forget the determinist realities of a repressive regime. 'And that when we are, we shall both be vaporised.'

'I do and I don't care,' she murmured defiantly, apparently unaware that she had just said she'd got away with it loads of times before.

Their meetings were infrequent over the following weeks, furtively arranged half-hours between work and Party commitments. Yet even the terrifying scuttering of a rat in the church belfry could not unsettle Winston for long. His heart and mind were now free.

'We must go to O'Brien,' he announced one day. 'I am sure he's a powerful figure in the Brotherhood and we can enlist in the resistance movement.'

'That sounds like an extremely rash assumption,' Julia didn't reply.

'I'm very glad you both could come,' O'Brien said, sipping a glass of wine. 'I'm going to give you a copy of Goldstein's forbidden book to read.'

The war with Eurasia was over and Winston found himself working long into the night rewriting the Party history to portray Eastasia as the enemy. Julia and I need a bolthole among the Proles, he later thought. Somewhere we can make love to the sound of Cockneys saying 'Gor bless yer, guv'nor'.

Winston found a room above the slummy shop where he had bought the diary.

'It's perfect, darling,' Julia sighed, untidily applying some contraband make-up.

'You look so much more attractive when you are defying the conventions of Stalinist brutalism,' he cooed romantically. 'Now let me read you page after page of extremely dull extracts from Goldstein's book that repeat everything about the regime you already know.'

'Put your hands in the air and come out slowly,' said a voice from behind the telescreen. 'You have been caught just as you always knew you would be.'

'You are going to have to learn DoubleThink,' O'Brien observed kindly, as electrodes were fitted to Winston's body. 'The art of holding two contradictory beliefs at the same time.'

'OK, OK. I believe this is both a ponderous and didactic political allegory and the most brilliant critique of Soviet Russia. But I still love Julia.'

'Then it's Room 101 and the rats for you.'

Winston sat out in the square enjoying Big Brother's latest magnificent victory. Why had he struggled so hard against the Party? How great it was to be a cog in the wheels of satire!

THE SHELTERING SKY

Paul Bowles

He awoke. He was confused. He had had a dream that he could not remember.

At a table in the darkest corner of the café sat three Americans: two young men and a girl. The thin, wry man looked existentially exhausted; his wife was trying to hold back the map that had kept them moving for twelve years. They were travellers, not tourists. Of course. And the map had sent them to North Africa.

'Everything's grey,' said Kit.

'Another Pernod?' Tunner asked.

'I've remembered my dream,' Port whispered. 'It wasn't very interesting.'

'Why did you tell Tunner your dream?' asked Kit when she and Port had retired to their hotel. 'We've only known him five years.'

He rose meaningfully. Kit's words meant nothing to him. Or anybody else, for that matter. He walked in the dark streets. Who were these people? He was in a bad way.

'I'll introduce you to a girl,' the Arab said. 'She's a dancer.'

He idly wondered whether Tunner would get Kit, as he was led across the sand towards the girl's tent. The Sahara was full of sand. She was full of sand. He slept with her anyway. She tried to steal his wallet. He ran away.

Kit worried about the omens. It was yet another of those days when she would think about nothing but herself. She had an inkling that Port must be up to something. Why was his surname Moresby? Surely no one was named after the capital of Papua New Guinea?

'I haven't mentioned what you did last night.'

'You couldn't because you didn't know,' Port said.

'Port Said is in Egypt. We are in Algeria.'

'I am everywhere and nowhere, baby. That's where I'm at.'

He went down to the lobby. He met an English couple named Lyle, mother and son. 'The French are stupid,' said the man. 'Their blood is too thin. Would you like a lift?'

He went back to his room. 'They can't take Tunner.'

'I'll take the train with Tunner,' Kit said.

Why were they together? No one was quite sure. Tunner had an idea of it; Kit just liked ideas.

Port sat in the front with the Lyles as they discoursed on their distaste for the Arabs and the Jews.

'You're a darling,' Tunner said, as they shared a fourth-class carriage. Kit debated whether to be hysterical. She woke to find Tunner in bed beside her. She pushed him out.

Port gave a cry of metaphysical pain. Am I humanity? They rode bicycles, sharing the emptiness, resigned to their oppositionality.

'The sky is protecting us.'

'What from?' Kit asked.

'From whatever is behind it. We are too deep for this world.'

She sensed Port knew about her and Tunner even if he didn't know he knew.

They got a bus to Ain Krorfa and engaged three smelly rooms. Kit sensed Port wanted to get rid of Tunner at Bou Noura. He visited a garden. Mohammed introduced him to a prostitute. He overpaid and left in a shudder of self-pity.

'The Lyles sleep in the same bed,' Mohammed said.

'My passport has been stolen,' Port said. 'I think it was the Lyles.'

Tunner offered to retrieve it from Messad. Port organised a bus to El Ga'a. Kit let Port spirit her away from Tunner.

'I've got a chill.'

She tried not to let Port's illness interrupt her solipsistic hypochondria as she stared moodily into the distance. His pain was ambiguous. How exciting to be seeing Arabs in the Atomic Age!

'You can't stay here,' the woman in El Ga'a said. 'We are free from the meningitis epidemic.'

They took a truck to Sba. Port couldn't have meningitis. But perhaps she did. How dare he steal her illness?

He thought about how little he did. He had been a writer once, but thinking took up too much time. Everything seemed too trivial for his brilliance.

'He has typhoid,' the captain said.

'I'm not sure I can be bothered to recover,' Port replied. 'I long for beauty.'

He was a cloaca. He had loved her once, but now he was going.

Tunner reappeared. Kit longed yet did not long for him to take command. Tunner held her tight, smelling her deeply in the moonlight.

He had not died, for he would first have needed to be in some way alive. 'I shall not be hysterical again,' she declared, vanishing into the desert.

Tunner felt embarrassed by Port's death and Kit's disappearance. He had only ever pitied her. He returned to find Lyle stealing Port's belongings.

'Please hit me,' Lyle begged.

She knew where she was. She was in the inevitable, pointless stream of consciousness coda. She took a camel. Belqassim pulled her towards him roughly and she surrendered to his friendly carnality. The days got hotter and she disengaged further. She dressed as an Arab boy. The other wives whipped her bare breasts. She hated the food, the savagery, the prose. She had to get out. She took her valise.

'You've had a long journey,' said the sister, wondering, 250 pages too late, if Kit wasn't completely mad.

Tunner reluctantly appeared to take her home. Her face contorted. It was the end of the line.

And, thank God, the book.

THE THIEF'S JOURNAL

Jean Genet

FLOWERS BEDECK THE fragility of the convict and I garlanded myself, lovingly pursuing a journey through sweat, sperm and blood that led to prison. Without what people call my evil, I am castrated. *Un petit-bourgeois rien.* There was a moral vigour in the acceptance of my destiny. I was hot for crime.

I give the name violence to a noble boldness that hankers for danger, and I have seen it in many of the pimps and thieves I have worked with, men whose authority and beatific treachery bent me to their will. René, Stilitano, Guy . . . I could describe them, but I won't. I am too much of a literary outlaw for that. Instead, let me take you back to the Barrios in 1932, where I used to grease my prick with Vaseline, jerking myself off into a sperm-spotted handkerchief, while thinking of my mother.

Oui. I am my own *Dieu*, I fashion my vanity, delighting in the vicarious transgression that has fashionable artists like those fools Cocteau and Picasso, who have never dared to suck the leprotic erection of a geriatric vagabond or have been ground into the pillow by the rotting stump of Stilitano's amputated arm, fawning at my feet.

Is any of this true? Who cares? It is if I say it is, for I define my existential self. *Je suis* what I say *je suis*, I beat up queers and stole from churches; burglary became a religious rite, elevating me to poet of the underworld even as I willingly debased myself in *pissoirs*.

René jerked himself off in a café full of whores to calm himself down, before stabbing the gipsy boy through the heart for a few *sous*. In that moment of love and death, I caught sight of Stilitano looking on and knew I must drink in the beautiful odour of his never-washed prick. He was the Sacred Black Stone to which Heliogabalus offered up his wealth and I prostrated myself to his treachery and indifference.

I was born in Paris in 1910. My mother was a whore and I have my roots in the parched bones of the buggered children who were massacred by Gilles de Rais. There was no precise time I became a thief, just a metempsychosis of Uranus that saw me graduate from the Reformatory to the Foreign Legion and thence to the piss and shit of the sewers.

Stilitano and I travelled through Czechoslovakia, Poland, Italy and Germany, becoming spies and finding a purity of evil idealism in the SS. I longed to play with the cellulose grapes that hung from his cock while he pushed me away like the bitch I was. He hated queers, though he sometimes talked of fucking me, and I wanted him to beat me. I became his noble valet, reduced to even greater humiliations, and even now I am reduced to verbal automatism, in thrall to his deity.

Can you feel the degradation? Allow your hands to wander inside your uptight bourgeois pants and feel the excitement of my squalor. But don't stop there! I can give you so much more if only you will open your flies to me. Lose your suburban values and embrace the negative hell of the poet of the woebegone.

I dressed as a woman and went to Tangiers with Maurice and Robert, occasionally allowing myself to commit an act the gravity of which gave me consciousness. *Oui*, I was *ennuyé*. It is no boast to say I was a clever thief, but still I went to prison where I found security in a world that had rejected me, offering up my mobile buttocks to anyone who showed interest.

Michaelis wanted me to love him, yet I taunted him with abstinence when I met Java, a muscle-bound Stilitano. Java still liked to fuck whores, but occasionally he would let me thread my prick up his ass when he was asleep, crying out in anger when I made him come. I then met * – I cannot mention his name because he is still alive, though maybe only in the Sartrean sense in which *je suis* – and we pleasured one another as an SS guard told us of the joy he got when he could see tears in the eyes of the victims he was about to kill.

My work as writer is mere pleonasm. It passes the time as I pursue the rehabilitation of the purulent, the dark thrills of the *interdit*. I left Nazi Germany because it no longer interested me; there, stealing did not differentiate me from authority. Where was the liberation in that? My aesthetics of crime were self-creation and I went back to shack up with Stilitano. Carrying packages of opium for him gave me a sense of CAPITAL LETTERS, MY SUBSERVIENCE A PURPOSE.

This is the life I lived and these are the people with whom I was preoccupied between 1931 and 1942. *Bof*! But I can sense your erection fading. So let me tell you more about the pleasures of treachery, how I beat up queers whom I robbed, how I bit Lucien until he bled while his prick opened up like an anemone, how I sucked off Bernardini, the head of the Marseilles secret police. Was I guilty? Who knows? I just became that of which I was accused.

Voila. Vous are *encore dur*. What more can I say? This book is my ascesis. I wanted to rob cripples and queers, I wanted to reclaim the joy of tragedy. But most of all I wanted to glorify myself. Being a thief is banal but writing about it is magnificent, and with this exhibitionist act of tedious subversion I have recreated myself once more, as gullible European radicals reclaim me for their own.

THE CATCHER IN
THE RYE

J. D. Salinger

IF YOU REALLY want to hear about it, you'll probably want to know about where I was born, but I can't be bovvered with all that David Copperfield crap. So I'll just tell you about all this madman stuff that happened to me around last Christmas, just before I got run down and had to come out here and take it easy. I mean, that's all I told D. B., and he's my brother an' all, so I sure as hell can't be arsed to tell you. He's in Hollywood and writes movies. I hate movies. They're so phony. But then I hate everything, 'cos everything's boring, right?

Whatevva. The day I want to start telling you about is the day I left Pencey Prep. Pencey is this posh school out in Pennsylvania, which I guess makes me some kind of trustafarian, but I, like, like to think of myself as this deep working-class hero, rebel without a cause, alienated gangsta. Anyway, that day I got back to school early after leaving all the gym gear on the New York subway, an' all the fencing team were mad as hell but I wasn't that bovvered, 'cos what did I care?

Did I tell you I had just been thrown out for flunking four subjects? Nah, thought not, 'cos I'm also a cool, unreliable narrator dude. Anyways, I wasn't that bovvered 'cos I'd been kicked out of all my previous schools. I mean, working is just so not hip when you've got all this other teenage shit going through your head, like sex an' girls an' sex an' how no one really, like, understands you.

Anyways, there I was kicking my heels till term ended on

Wednesday, thinking I really wasn't that bovvered about how pissed my father was gonna be when he found out I'd been kicked out, when that sexy bastard Stradlater came in late after dating a girl that I fancied and I went mad an' got him in a head lock and then he called me 'you crumby sonofabitch, Caulfield' an' beat me up 'cos he's, like, much bigger than me, so I thought, yeah, like, whatevva, sod this for a game of soldiers, and decided to leave school there and then.

So I picked up my last few hundred dollars and went to the station. I met the mother of a right bastard at Pencey on the train and told her I had a brain tumour, how funny was that? An' when I got to Penn Station I thought about calling my mother, my 10-year-old sister Phoebe, an' a couple of girls I vaguely knew who I imagined might want to have sex with me as I was feeling horny as hell, but then I thought, nah, can't be bovvered. I'll smoke 20 cigarettes an' try an' get drunk and check into a divey hotel full of perverts.

The bastards in the kind of phony bar that would have made you puke wouldn't serve me a drink – said I was too young – so I chatted up some 30-year-old women from Seattle. Two of them were right mingers though the blonde was OK, but when they started laughing at me, I thought, I ain't bovvered, so I paid for their drinks an' headed back to the hotel.

The elevator guy asked me if I wanted a prostitute an' I thought, I ain't bovvered either way but I might as well as I was a bit lonesome, so I said yes an' then she came along an' she was cute an' all but I couldn't, y'know, do it, because it didn't feel right. Truth is, I'm a virgin, no kidding, an' I don't really get the sex thing, so I gave her $5 an' then she came back with the elevator guy an' demanded another $5 an' I said no way so he beat me up.

An' that's pretty much the story of the rest of the book. I thought about sex, I rang a few girls, went to the movies, visited some museums, thought about how crumby and phony everything was an', like, how no one really loves me. Occasionally, for a bit of pathos, I thought about my brother Allie who died of leukaemia a while back, an' then I went home to see Phoebe 'cos I was running out of cash an' she's the only one who understands me.

'Dad will kill you when he finds out, Holden!' she yelled at me. 'Why d'ya do it?' 'Because school's shit and everyone's a phony,' I replied. 'But you hate everything, so what's the difference?' She was right, of course, but I weren't that bovvered, so I just said, 'No one understands me,' borrowed $8.65, an' left to wallow in more repetitive existential angst and have deep thoughts about saving children from adulthood in the long rye grass.

I went to see an old teacher, Mr Antolini, but he turned out to be a pervert, so I went back to Phoebe's school to tell her I was heading west to work in a gas station. 'I'm coming with you,' she said. 'No way,' I replied, but she followed me to the funfair and we hung out together an' it wasn't too bad so I thought, whatevva. I wasn't that bovvered what I did, so I might as well go home.

An' that's it really. The psychoanalyst guy they've got here wonders if I'm going to apply myself when I start a new posh school in the fall, but in truth I doubt it. 'Cos at heart, I still ain't really bovvered.

A QUESTION OF
UPBRINGING

Anthony Powell

For some reason, a glimpse of the lower orders warming themselves at a brazier in the street made me think of the ancient world. These classical projections in turn suggested a Poussin scene, where Time gives shape to the steps of the dance that had hitherto felt unfamiliar. So where better to start my meandering epic than at the school – there is only one so I need not be so vulgar as to name it – where these classical allusions first started to become choate.

It was December 1921 and I was returning from the High Street when Widmerpool appeared on his daily solitary run. His status was not high so I did not acknowledge him, contenting myself with a dozen pages of snobbish asides that I hoped would be interpreted as witty irony, before arriving back at my rooms.

That term I was messing with Stringham and Templer. Templer had gone to London for the day so I was greeted by Stringham alone. We reflected with great humour on Widmerpool's paucity of social graces before our bantering reverie was interrupted by a knock.

It was my Uncle Giles. 'I am very worried about my share of the family Trust,' he said, while lighting a cigarette.

Quite why I've bothered to recall something quite so inconsequential I'm none too sure, save that many years later I have come to recognise the value of £180 per year, though it might have been better for all concerned if I had also learned the value of having an emotional interior world or anything approaching a personality.

Anyway, the upshot of Uncle Giles's visit was that our housemaster, Le Bas, accused us of smoking in our rooms and our cards were marked thereafter. Yet Stringham did get his own back after he phoned the police to accuse Le Bas of being a small-time conman. Heraclitus, how we laughed when Le Bas was arrested! I guess you had to have been there.

Some months later, Stringham invited me to spend the weekend with his mother and her new husband at Glimber. 'I wanted you to meet Mater before I go off to see Pater in Kenya, Jenkins,' he said languidly. 'I couldn't possibly have invited Templer as he's rather non-U.'

As usual, I had no thoughts of my own on the subject and continued my impression of a parasitic *tabula rasa*. I did, though, allow myself some very deep observations on aristocratic family life, a milieu in which I was entirely at home, and did eventually conclude that perhaps we had in some infinitesimal yet somehow important way become estranged from Templer.

After Stringham had departed for Kenya, Templer bade me visit him and strangely our estrangement was temporarily forgotten, while my days were filled with yet more important social nuances that helped define the way the educated elite comported themselves in the post-war era. The row between Templer's brother-in-law Stripling, the racing motorist, and Sunny Farebrother, who had had a good war, over starching collars made an indelible impression on me.

It was also here that I felt the first pangs of passion when Templer's sister Jean said a friendly goodbye to me after ignoring me for days. To some, this sign of affection may appear a bauble, but to someone of my great sensitivities – not to mention lack of charisma – this was a major life event.

The summer before I went up to university – there are only two – my father sent me to France to learn the language. There, to my great astonishment, I met Widmerpool, who was also learning French while training to be a solicitor. As Widmerpool was still of a lower social class we didn't converse much other than for me to express amusement at the hostilities that had erupted between the Norwegian and the Swede, who were also staying at the farmhouse, over a game of tennis.

Widmerpool proved to be unexpectedly capable in brokering a truce but I – like you, I suspect – had long since tired of such a dull episode and could scarcely remember why I had bothered to waste a chapter on such an uneventful time, the highlight of which was once again to imagine myself in love with a woman I had never spoken to, and I was not unduly upset when my time in France came to an end.

Much of university life centred around Professor Sillery's Sunday tea parties. Quite why I was considered interesting enough to be invited was never entirely clear, but it was there that I got to meet the fascinating Mark Members, a budding poet whose work had been published in *Public School Verse*, and the rather oikish Northerner, Quiggin.

'You live very close to each other,' Sillery said to Quiggin and Members, and Stringham and I silently enjoyed their discomfort that Quiggin had been revealed to be less working-class than he maintained, and Members less upper-class.

'Come on you chaps,' cried Templer, who had arrived unannounced. 'Let's go for a drive in my new car and pick up some gals.' The proximity of a girl's ankles again played profoundly on my heartstrings, but after Templer drove the car off the road I rather concluded that the estrangement between him and Stringham was now irreversible.

Later that term, Stringham announced he was disappointed in university life and was going to take up a job in the City that Sillery's influence had procured for him. For my part, I retired to my chaise longue, exhausted by the excitements of the first book. How ever would I cope with the next eleven!

CASINO ROYALE

Ian Fleming

Bond's eyes narrowed in ironical satisfaction as he casually palmed a tip to the casino *vestiaire* and returned to the Hotel Splendide. The concierge passed him a note. Ten million francs was on its way from M; it wasn't enough, but it would have to do. He checked his room for uninvited guests. The safe empty room sneered at him; Bond sneered back before lighting his 170th cigarette of the day. He placed his .38 Colt under the pillow and his brutal, ironical face on top.

Two weeks before, a memorandum about Le Chiffre had reached M. The 18-stone flagellant's brothels were losing business and there was a fifty-million-franc deficit in the union funds he controlled for SMERSH. There was only one man for the job.

Bond gave Moneypenny a passing glance on his way into M's office; she would have been desirable but for her eyes which were too quizzical, so she would have to cope without him. 'Here's the dope,' M said. 'Play Le Chiffre at baccarat and clean him out.'

'The odds are reasonable,' Bond replied evenly. 'I'll pose as a Jamaican plantocrat playing complicated progression systems.'

'Anything you say, Bond.' M yawned. 'Mathis will keep you covered.'

Some of this back story conveniently passed through Bond's mind over a breakfast of seven scrambled eggs and a side of bacon. He looked up to see Mathis by his side.

'You'll be pleased with your number two,' Mathis winked. 'Especially her protuberances.'

Bond groaned. What were they sending him a woman for? It

wasn't a bloody picnic. Damn it, women were for recreation. At least Felix Leiter, the CIA chap, was around. He went outside and fired up his 4.5-litre supercharged Bentley and took it for a spin before returning to the Negresco baroque of Casino Royale.

'This is Miss Vesper Lynd,' said Mathis.

Her bodice was lasciviously tight across her pert breasts and her ironical eyes looked at Bond with ironical disinterest. 'Maybe I will bring you luck, Double-o Jamms,' she whispered.

He would sleep with her later, he thought; once the job was done. He rose from the table and walked outside. An explosion sent him tumbling to the ground; he picked himself up, removing charred flesh from his pristine dinner jacket.

'Your cover is blown, Jamms,' Vesper said. 'The two Bulgars blew themselves up instead of you.'

'No matter,' Bond answered. 'Here's the plan.' Vesper listened with attentive obedience, upset that her feminine charms appeared to hold no allure for him.

Bond's nostrils flared as he spotted Le Chiffre's henchmen on the way to the baccarat table. A tall guy and a cripple: he could deal with them. He leaned back in his chair, instantly disabling them both. Let the game begin. Beads of sweat gathered on his forehead. He was finished. Le Chiffre smirked. 'Enough, Mr Bond.' A waiter passed Bond an envelope from Felix stuffed with thirty-two million francs. Marshall Aid from the US.

'I think not.' Bond smiled. '*Suivi.*' Two queens. Zero. It was desperate. Then a nine. 'Banco.' Le Chiffre was bankrupt. The job was over. Now for Vesper's cold and arrogant body. 'Oh, Jamms,' she cried. 'I want you, but first I must see Mathis. He sent me a note.'

The silly bitch, he thought, as he raced outside. Mathis would never have sent such a note and he gunned the Bentley in pursuit of the Citroën in which she had been abducted. He was up to 345mph and closing in when the tyres hit the tacks.

Bond awoke to find himself naked in a bare room under an

alabasterine ceiling light. Le Chiffre had cut out the cane seat of the chair and Bond's buttocks were pushed through the opening. 'Where's my money, dear boy?' he said, thrashing Bond's manhood with a paddle.

'Go to hell,' Bond gasped. He could take a chance on losing some of his cock. After all, he had a good eleven inches to play with.

'Shtop!' A tall Russian with a crag-like face entered the room. 'You have lost SMERSH's money, Le Chiffre. For that you must die.' A third eye appeared on Le Chiffre's face. 'I should kill you too, Mr Bond. But I only kill to order. Good day.'

Bond lay back in bed. The main action was over but there was still another 40 pages to go. He'd better find some way to fill them. Vesper had sent flowers, but he had sent them back; no one could get away with implying he was queer. Yet he was curious about her actions. And his cock.

'Oh Jamms,' she wept. 'It is still so swollen.'

'I am just very pleased to see you.'

As the days passed Bond was surprised to find he quite liked her curved buttocks and hard breasts, and briefly toyed with the idea of resigning and getting married. But then he recalled the franchise. His heart and cock hardened as he stroked his memories and other parts. On reflection, there was something queer about her.

He found the note beside her dead body. *Oh, Jamms, I could not live without you but I am a double agent. So I have killed myself.*

Silly bitch, he thought. But there was pussy galore to come.

JUNKY

William S. Burroughs

I WAS BORN in 1914 in a solid, three-storey house in the Mid West. My parents were comfortable and I went to one of the Big Three universities. Why does a man become a drug addict? The answer is usually that he wants to become as cool as me. I have never regretted my experience with drugs. An addict never stops growing. Stupider. Junk is not a kick. It is a way of life. Or, in my case, a career move.

I first took junk during the war. A hardworking thief called Norton the Nob had stolen a tommy gun and a box of syrettes of morphine tartrate. I'd been looking for a way in. My old mates Jack Kerouac and Allen Ginsberg had become the voice of the Beats and I was getting left behind. 'Hang with the sleazeballs,' they advised. 'But keep it cute. What the middle-class merry pranksters want is a hit of vicarious drug porn.'

Angle, a dive-bar on 42nd Street, was the hangout for hoodlums and queers. I hooked up with Roy the Runt and Jack the Lad and got wasted. Jack the Lad told us how he pulped some fag's skull with a three-foot pipe and the blood spurted ten feet every time his heart beat. You want pulp *fiction*, I give you pulp fiction.

My first hit, the M hit the back of the legs and I crumpled. I must have dozed off for 24 hours. Like you. If there's one thing duller than taking junk, it's reading about it. I woke up and vomited. I did this non-stop for a month and mysteriously found I'd developed a habit.

Junk-sick is something else. Your cells cry out for junk. People with cancer don't know they are born. That's why you won't find no pussies or queers doing junk. Though I am a queer from time to time, but I'm saving that for my second dose of scumbag-vérité. Junkies are street soldiers, street saints, street poets, lost in the darkness at the edge of town. And in the mythology of their own pain and cool.

I also took a load of Benzedrine and nembies, and once bought several tons of weed off Lizzie the Lesbian. Tea-heads are a real downer, wannabe hipsters too wimpy to jab a dirty spike into an ulcerated artery. Fuck's sake. Why would anyone bother with a drug you can't get addicted to?

On days when junk was short in the Bronx, I hit croakers for dodgy scripts. Some docs gave you goofballs. It wasn't M but it kept the turkeys away. Money was always tight so George the Greek and I worked the lushes, but the feds soon got my mark. Timmy the Turnip bailed me out, but New York was getting too hot. My veins were all shot and I was shooting in my eyeball just to stay straight. I headed out to Lexington for my first cure.

I jumped a freight train down to New Orleans – so much cooler than driving – and stayed straight for ten minutes before I met up with Pat the Pillock and Percy the Pimp. It takes a year to get your first habit; seven days to get your second. I was pissed it took that long. The junk was sweet and I wasted pages getting wasted, rushing on my run, feeling like Jesus's son. And wasting your time, too.

The feds busted the hotel where me and Dolly the Doormat, aka my wife whom I've never bothered to mention before, were staying. 'Why do you do junk, Bill?' they asked. 'Because once I've shovelled enough garbage into my body,' I replied, 'I'll get away with shovelling any old garbage into print. Take it from me, some suckers will one day call *Naked Lunch* a masterpiece.'

I came out the slammer determined to keep off junk. Chris the Cretin met me at the front desk and I shot a gram of H into my penis. 'You are a little bit dull when you're stoned,' said Dolly the Doormat. 'It's better than being a lot dull when I'm straight,' I snapped, picking up an RPG, several kilos of smack, and going for a last-chance power drive.

Across the border in Mexico I ran into Lupita the Loser, the 300-pound dealer. Mexico City was full of pigeons so you had to be careful, but I got myself on a government programme and months passed in a two-dimensional flurry of drugalogs, dedicated to my amazing street cool.

Ike the Idiot brought over some cocaine and we started doing speedballs. C is non-addictive and therefore a bit rubbish, but if you take it with a bit of H it becomes more interesting. Apparently. Anyway, I decided to take another cure, putting myself – and you – through the tedious hell of yet another junk-sickness. After ten days I was clean, though I had become a full-blown alcoholic, vomiting green bile and suffering from uraemic poisoning into the bargain.

I've been off junk for two months now, though I'm still very cool, as junkies remain cool all their lives. Dolly the Doormat has taken the kids, whom I haven't mentioned either, down to Acapulco for a break. Actually she hasn't. I shot her dead while I was pretending to be William Tell, but the publishers thought that might be a bit of a downer.

Anyway, I'd better go as I'm off to try some psychedelics. They're the new hit on the block. Allen says telepathy is a fact. And he's right. Because I know you think I'm a bit of a wanker.

LORD OF THE FLIES

William Golding

THE BOY WITH the fair hair wasn't in the least perturbed that the plane he'd been flying in had been shot down or that the adults had been killed while all the boys had survived without a scratch. Instead, he played contentedly on the golden beach in the Garden of Eden.

'I can't hardly move,' said a far-off voice.

Ralph looked up. 'Who are you?' he asked.

A fat boy with glasses clambered over some fallen tree trunks.

'I don't care as long as you don't call me Piggy like people done before.'

'Then I shall call you Piggy, too. Piggy, Piggy, Piggy.' Ralph shrieked with laughter. 'And you have ass-marr! How very lower-middleclass! Now as I am officer material, I shall be your leader. Let's try and round up the rest of the boys.'

'I found a conch. It's ever so symbolic as it's the only one on the island,' said Piggy. 'You can summon the boys by blowin' into it.'

An eerie sound boomed into the distance as Ralph pressed his lips to the shell and before long a large group of Bigguns, as the thirteen-year-olds liked to call themselves, and Littluns were gathered together amid the sweetly aromatic, brightly coloured foliage.

'We need a chief,' Ralph said.

'Then it had better be me,' exclaimed red-headed Jack. 'For I am in charge of the choir and head boy.'

'I think we need a vote,' Ralph replied. 'Oh, wizzo! I've been elected. Now let's build some shelters, light a fire so ships can see us and scout out the island.'

Jack flushed till his face was as red as his hair. 'Then the choir shall be the Hunters and I shall be their leader.'

Ralph, Jack and Simon, above whose head a halo could be seen, set off through the undergrowth. And, lo, a piglet appeared before them. Jack held his knife aloft, but could not strike for his soul was yet pure, and the piglet ran free. 'Let us eat of fruits,' said Ralph, as he used Piggy's glasses to light a fire on the mountain ridge, and all was well.

For several days the Bigguns gathered wood while the Littluns frolicked gaily in the azure lagoon, until one night the twins, Samneric, fell asleep and let the fire burn out.

'You have done a very bad thing,' Ralph said, before he was interrupted by the sound of a wailing Littlun.

'I have seen a snake-like Beastie!' cried Percival.

'A Snakie! A Snakie! We have bitten from the apple of Original Sin! We are doomed!' the Littluns chorused.

'The Beastie is the Beastie within us all,' Simon observed, polishing his halo. Yet no one listened unto Simon for a prophet is without honour in his own country.

'We'll search the island to prove there is no Beastie,' Ralph declared, holding the sacred conch aloft.

As the boys lay sleeping, a dead fighter pilot parachuted softly through the starlit night, coming to rest in a copse at the top of the mountain, where eddying zephyrs rocked it from side to side.

'There is a Beastie after all,' Ralph shouted. 'Man has Fallen.'

'Then let's go hunting.' Jack laughed maniacally, tying back his hair that had become long and unkempt overnight and painting his face in a mask of red dye. The boys cheered with orgiastic lust, bathing their hands in a squealing pig's bloody entrails.

'We must impale its head on a stick and make an offering to the Beastie,' Jack said.

And, lo, Simon walked alone to the mountain to converse with the pig's head that appeared unto him as The Lord of the Flies.

'There is no Beastie,' said The Lord of the Flies, and Simon observed that the Beastie was a dead airman and that it was good. He ran to spread the Good News, even as the airman was blown out to sea, never to be seen again. But the boys were crazed with the sins of the flesh and had abjured the Path of Righteousness, and when Simon crawled on to the beach they mistook him for the Beastie and clubbed him to death.

An ethereal phosphorescent glow surrounded Simon's body as he ascended into heaven and Ralph knew that he had done wrong.

'We must return to the way of Truth,' he said. But the hunters had seduced the Littluns with the lure of the Flesh and only Piggy and Samneric came back to the camp with him.

'You are still my chief,' Piggy cried as Jack led a raiding party to steal his glasses to light the fire.

'They must see reason,' said Ralph as he led his saintly band of disciples back to the hunters. Yet reason saw they not. Samneric were tortured into changing sides and sacrificial Piggy was dashed to the rocks by a falling boulder.

Ralph was alone. 'There can be no rescue from this darkness,' he wept as he sought to avoid the painted mob. Yet even as he despaired, the hunters set fire to the island to smoke him out and a passing ship heard his ululations.

'I would have expected better from British boys,' said the officer.

'We're sorry,' the boys replied, having brushed their hair and put on their starched school uniforms. 'We promise never to do it again.'

LUCKY JIM

Kingsley Amis

'I WAS WONDERING if you might care to join us for the weekend, Dixon,' said Professor Welch. 'My son Bertrand, the artist, will be down from London. We'll be putting on some shows. It should be tremendous fun.'

There was nothing that Jim would have liked less than to spend a weekend with the ghastly Welches, but he hadn't got off to the best of starts with his head of department at the university and he was concerned for his job.

'I should love to come.'

'Good,' said Welch. 'And one more thing. I'd like you to give the Open Lecture on "Merrie England".'

It had been several weeks since Margaret had taken an overdose of sleeping pills after Catchpole, a previous boyfriend, had left her and Jim was feeling guilty that he hadn't been to visit her before.

'Thank you for displaying such tact and giving me a bit of distance,' Margaret said, leaning towards him in an unconvincing display of romantic melancholy.

Jim felt a mild surge of panic. He was happy to skewer everyone else for their class-bound pretensions and emotional dishonesty, and yet he himself wasn't at all ready to tell Margaret the truth. So he allowed himself the usual contemptuous asides about her plainness that he passed off as comedy before telling her how much he was looking forward to seeing her at the Welches.

The evening had not gone well. His lack of culture had been

exposed in the plainsong, he had insulted the absurd, beret-wearing Bertrand, and mistaken Bertrand's new girlfriend, Christine Callaghan, for his previous one. To cap it all, someone had informed the Welches of his surreptitious trip to the pub. Still, it had had its moments of slapstick, and being inebriated had its recompenses.

He kissed Margaret and was surprised to feel a flicker of passion. His hand moved to her leg. 'How dare you, James?' she exclaimed. 'Who do you take me for?'

Dixon was alive again, a dusty thudding pounding in his head. Something was wrong. His sheets were charred. How unlucky I am, he said to himself, failing to make the connection between smoking in bed while drunk and the mess he was in.

'Yes, you are very unlucky,' said Christine who happened to be passing by his room and was also prone to confuse misfortune with self-pity. 'Let me help you tidy up. With any luck the Welches won't notice.'

'Oh, I get the picture,' said Margaret, who also happened to be passing by his room.

'But you don't,' Jim groaned. Though, on reflection, he did. He was in a farce, not a satire. So why should he bother with the fictional niceties of character development and the conceit of luck? Why didn't he just play the whole thing for laughs as the plot lurched from one comic set-piece to another?

'I trust you'll be joining us at the ball, Dixon,' Professor Welch enquired.

'Then I'd better get to work on the next set-up,' Jim said. 'That will mean a lot more drinking, and sneering at you behind your back, not to mention some complicated by-play in which I can use some of my legendary funny phone voices to persuade Bertrand, who is secretly having an unlikely affair with another lecturer, Carol Goldsmith, whom he was planning to take to the ball, to invite Christine instead because he's desperate to get a job with her influential Uncle Julius Gore-Urquhart.'

It was getting late. 'I'm suddenly bored of all this comedic social climbing,' Jim said to Christine. 'And I think you are too. Allow me to take you home in a taxi.'

'Oh James,' she said, kissing him hard. 'I can tell you have a pure and noble gentility. What I would give to be with you! And yet it cannot be so, for however brutish Bertrand may be, I have given him my word.'

'And my nobility prevents me from telling you that Bertrand is having an affair with Carol. In any case, I have a duty to remain with Margaret even though our relationship has been built on her romantic misreading of our friendship.'

'It's too bloody.'

'It's too, too bloody.'

Jim pinched himself to make sure he hadn't wandered into a pastiche of *Brief Encounter*. Apparently not, he said to himself, as his chippiness and levity returned. Perhaps it was time for another prank call to the Welches.

'You can only hope to pull off that kind of gag once in a book, Dixon,' Welch snapped.

'Ah well, I'd better cut to the lecture then.'

His head swam. That seventh whisky hadn't been a good idea. He'd meant to give a bland account of all the old cultural mores that Welch held dear, but once he'd seen Christine walk out with Carol, he hadn't been able to help himself and had ended by ridiculing his cosy pretensions.

'You're fired,' said Welch.

'And keep your hands off Christine,' Bertrand snarled. 'She's mine. She's far too good for an oik like you.'

Jim had started packing when the phone rang. 'It's Catchpole here,' the voice said. 'Margaret was lying about me and her attempted suicide.'

'Then I don't have an obligation to the dull ugly one anymore and I'm free to run off with the rich beautiful one.'

'And I'm going to offer you the job Bertrand wanted,' Gore-Urquhart said.

'And Carol told me about her affair with Bertrand so I am no longer pledged to him,' Christine whispered.

'So all the loose ends are conveniently tied up and I've fought off my bad luck to prove I really am the handsomest, cleverest and richest man in the world.'

'Dream on, Kingsley,' said his friends.

LOLITA

Vladimir Nabokov

*I*T HAS BEEN *my task to edit the pages left by 'Humbert Humbert' who died of a coronary thrombosis before his trial started. It should be noted that 'Mrs Schiller' died in childbirth. I would also like it to be known I in no way intend to glorify 'HH', though if others appear to do so do in their enthusiasm to place themselves within my artistic orbit, I won't complain.* John Ray, Jr, Ph.D.

Lolita. Light of my life. Lo. Li. Ta Very Much. Weep at this tangle of thorns. I was born in 1910 in Paris. My mother died when I was very *jeune* and if you wonder where my peculiar interests came from, I should have to say it started when I was 13 with Annabel Leigh, who died of typhus just as we were *sur le point de la jouissance*.

On the issue of my pedanterosis, I should stress it is not just any old 12-year-old girl that attracts me, but only 'nymphets' with a sexual awareness. And how Humbert Humbert tried to be *bon*. In Paris, I sought palliatives with prostitutes and even, naïve as only a pervert can be, married Valeria who betrayed me with a Slav.

I arrived alone in New York and joined an expedition to the Arctic. It was not easy to satisfy my tastes as Eskimo women were too fishy, so in 1947 I moved to New England to do what every literary hero is asked to do by a creator who cannot imagine a world sullied by the banalities of earning a living: I started work on a book that would never be written.

Oh, the conceit, reader! But forgive the chuckles of Humbug Humbug. My landlady was Charlotte Haze, a woman of unbearable drabness, with whom I would not have stayed had it not been for her 12-year-old daughter, Dolores. Dolly. Lo. L. My downy darling nymphet whom *j'aime* for *toujours et toujours*, amen.

How hard I tried to maintain her chastity. *Primo*: I sniffed her as I dandled her on my knee; *secundo*: I drugged her at night. And I mourned when she went out for fear she would be too old for me on her return. Imagine, then, how I felt when her mother declared herself in love with me. On the one *main*, it was normal as I am irresistible, *mais sur l'autre,* it put me in an impossible situation with *mon vrai amour.*

Reader, I married her. For a month I acted the *mari parfait* while Lo was away, but then Charlotte read my diary. Her rage was incandescent and she ran out to denounce *moi*. I was steeling myself for righteous fury when a neighbour told me she had been knocked down by a car. I had palpated Fate.

I collected L from school in my Humber Humber and took her to a hotel where Lolita, *aux yeux battus*, seduced me. 'I'm a derlickwent, Dad,' she replied. I was soon bored of her tales of Sapphism and her first sexual conquest, but was magnetised by her nymphaea. When I knew she had nowhere else to go, I told her about her mother.

Thus began our Baedeker travels through the States. Lo. Li. Ta Ti Tum. You may sense the book entering Flaubertian *longueurs* as I recount how I swore my pubescent concubine to secrecy while taking her to natatoria in between some sessions of gentle sodomy for which I bribed her with a nickel. But we were walking in a winter Humbertland, where critics would conflate the *belles lettres* of my transgression with artistic genius. Some would even go so far as to maintain my pederasty was a metaphor for Soviet Totalitarianism.

'Thass bollox,' Dolly laughed.

'I know,' I said, 'but *un écrivain* never looks a gift *cheval dans la bouche*.'

In truth, I found Lo's obsession with comics *ennuyant*, but *peut-être* she felt the same way about me *poivre*-ing mes sentences *avec Français*. We argued over a school production of a Clare Quilty play and my jealousy became obsessive as we took off again on another dull, nay tawdry, peregrination across *L'Amérique*.

Sometimes I imagined we were being followed and wondered why L didn't abandon me. Then she did. I had reluctantly given up thoughts of intercourse to take her to hospital, and when I returned I was told she had left with her uncle. My paranoia *avait été justifié* as I fruitlessly tracked her kidnapper in a cryptogrammic paperchase that would have *la rive gauche* laughing into their absinthes at my repeated gags about Arthur Rainbow.

For three years I suffered a Proustian and Procrustean fate as I sought traces of my Lolita in a boyish woman. I even wrote poems. *Oh my Lolita / I long to meet yer.* And then I got a letter from a Mrs Schiller. *Dear Dad, I am married and having a baby. Please send some money.*

Humpty Dumpty took his gun, ready to kill the man who had taken his darling. But Schiller was innocent; Lolo had conspired in her own kidnapping with Clare Quilty and had left him when he asked her to star in a pornographic movie.

In Quilty, I recognised a pentapod monster like myself and Chum the Gun and Engelbert Humperdinck staked out his house. 'She was really just a bit too repressed,' Quilty drawled. I wrestled with him, shooting him 52 times before he uttered his last words. 'Ooh, that hurts a bit.'

So now I sit here, wondering if I will be given the death sentence. And whether, for all its show-*bateau*ing, this *livre* isn't really a load of aurochs.

BREAKFAST AT TIFFANY'S

Truman Capote

HOLLY GOLIGHTLY HAD been a tenant in the apartment beneath mine. Joe Bell ran a bar round the corner that we had used to make telephone calls. He was a sour man and we weren't close except in as much as we were both a pair of losers, so when he called I knew it must be about Holly.

He showed me a photograph of a Negro holding a carving that was the spitting image of Holly that had been taken by Mr Yunioshi, the Jap who had lived in the studio above mine.

'He took this in Africa,' he said.

'She's probably never been near there,' I replied.

'Maybe. But she's been gone years now and it's the only sighting we've ever had.'

I'd been living in the apartment for a week when I noticed the card by her mailbox, Holiday Golightly, Travelling, but it was only late one night when she kept her promise not to ask Mr Yunioshi to let her in after she'd forgotten her key and started taking advantage of me instead, that we became friends.

Or rather, I became an authority on her, her cat and the male companions she brought home. My existence rather passed us both by but, as I was a doormat, I was content with what scraps she threw me. One evening, when I was reading one of my unpublished stories to help her get to sleep, she even talked to me.

'I've got to be up early tomorrow,' she said. 'Each week Sally Tomato's lawyer pays me $100 to pretend to be his niece and visit him in Sing-Sing. There's nothing funny. I'm not like a nurse who does tricks or anything. All I do is talk to him for an hour.'

'I get it,' I nodded eagerly. 'It's a public service. A bit like those nice men who pay you $50 to walk them to the john.'

Holly patted me on the knee. 'I'm going to call you Fred. After my brother. He's very stupid, too.'

We next met at a party, where she introduced me to her agent, O. J. Berman. 'She's a phoney,' he said. 'She was going to be a Hollywood star but ran away to New York.'

'I've got too much ego to be an actress,' she observed curiously. 'O. J. can help you with your writing career. But first I'd like you to meet the fat, sweaty, but very rich Rusty Trawler. He looks fierce but he's a quiet sodomite at heart. I'll become his third wife if I can't find a dyke to look after me.'

It was thrilling to be in so transgressive a book, but I couldn't help feeling that the story was quickly piling up a car crash of characters that were diverting but insubstantial grotesques.

'That's the whole point,' Holly groaned. 'Nobody connects with anyone. Least of all you – though that's no great surprise. You won't even realise you're infatuated with me till the book's nearly over, even though it's as clear as day to everyone else.

'Look, I haven't given my cat a name because I refuse to do so until I know we belong together, and the only place where I can really be myself is Tiffany's. It's that deep, get it?'

Even I had got the point by now and our lives reverted to a series of meaningfully meaningless encounters, where more lightly sketched caricatures would dance across the pages.

'I'm M-M-Mag W-W-Wildwood, the six-foot s-s-stuttering Amazonian model with the c-c-clap,' said Mag.

'And I'm José, her Brazilian fiancé,' José added.

'Well, now that's sorted, I'm going shoplifting at Woolworth and then Rusty and I will go on holiday with you both to Havana. Maybe we'll even meet a blue-movie star,' cried Holly.

That Christmas I gave her a St Christopher medal from

Tiffany's and she gave me a $350 bird cage I had always admired, on the proviso I kept it symbolically empty, but we fell out soon after when she told me O. J. thought my stories were like me: good but dull. So we didn't see each other for a while, until I sensed I was being stalked by a middle-aged stranger.

'I'm Holly's husband,' he said. 'Her real name is Lula Mae.'

'Oh, that doesn't count as I was only thirteen,' Holly answered.

'Don't worry,' he shrugged, 'I'll slip as quietly off the page as everyone else. There's no room for real feeling here.'

Holly and I became closer after that. She had a slight dip when she found out her brother had died in the war and that Mag and Rusty had got married, but quickly got over it by getting pregnant and was planning to live with José in Brazil. 'Let's go riding in Central Park,' she said.

'Thank you for saving my life after the Negroes made my horse bolt.'

'No time for that,' Holly replied. 'I've just been arrested on suspicion of running messages for Sally from prison. It's all lies, of course, though I did smoke marijuana. It's just that I'm hopeless at maths. I've taken countless men to the john but by my reckoning I've somehow slept with only eleven.'

'So what are you going to do?'

'All my friends have abandoned me and I've lost the baby, so I might as well skip bail. Just got to dump the cat and I'll be off.'

'You bitch.'

'You're right. I want the kitty after all. We do belong together.'

'Well, it's too late.'

I never saw her again, though I did later find the cat. It seemed much happier.

– 1958 –

SATURDAY NIGHT AND SUNDAY MORNING

Alan Sillitoe

With 33 pints of beer inside him, Arthur Seaton fell to the bottom of the stairs. It was Saturday night, the best and bingiest time of the week, a riotous preamble to the Sabbath, and Arthur picked himself up and drank another 9 pints while smoking 40 Woodbines before emptying the contents of his stomach over Brenda.

'C'mon,' said Brenda, 'me Jack's awa', so's you can coom back to mine and gi' us wun.' She kissed him like a tigress, picking out the carrots from between his teeth. 'Doan't wake the kids, mind.'

'Meake sum brekfass, love,' Arthur said the next morning, as Brenda's kids jumped on the bed. 'An noah goan' tellun yer da that I been shaggun' his missus.' Best be off now. Didn't want to risk Jack finding him.

'Ooota bed, Arthur,' his father shouted. 'It's half-pust fife and it's teem fer worek.' Arthur smoked 90 Woodbines and got up. It was a fine life if you didn't weaken. He'd been working at the bicycle factory since he was 15 and was now earning £14 a week, enough to keep him in beer, cigarettes and sharp suits. Some people thought he was a Red, but he couldn't be too bothered with politics. His main concern was to drink as much as possible and make sure Jack didn't find out he was doing his indoors.

'Wassup?' asked Arthur, as Brenda seemed unusually glum when he slipped his hand inside her brassiere.

'Ah've a bun in mer uffen,' she replied.

'Wassa point a doan a marrud wumman if you aff ter use a Frenchie? Gissa quickie and ahll go roon ter mer Aunt Ada's an get 'elp.'

'Yer've bean a bit careless, son,' Aunt Ada laughed, fighting off her 57 children who were tugging at her apron. 'Yer jest wanna give lass an' ot baff an a paint o' gin an sheall be fain.' Arthur thanked her cheerily while cheating 23 of her kids out of 15 shillings at poker.

'Ah've goat ther villige eejit, Em'ler, in ter help,' said Brenda. Arthur smiled. Maybe he could try giving her a kiss after he'd had another 123 pints. He dozed off while smoking 745 Woodbines, before waking to hear Jack's key turning in the lock.

'Heus meant ter be on naite shift,' Brenda giggled. 'Yer'd betta sneak hoam.'

Arthur jumped over the fence and walked to the pub. Wasn't that Brenda's sister Winnie sitting on her own? He bought 33 pints and sat next to her.

'Where us yer huzban?' he asked.

'Doan hus National Service.'

'Ah laike yer mooonds of mischief.'

'Thun you can cum some and gi' us wun laike you gi' me sister wun.'

Life was good, very good, if you didn't weaken.

'Ah gotta warn you,' said Jack, 'Winnie's huzzban noahs yer been shaggun' his missus and he's promised to get his swaddie friends to beat yers up. He also says yer been doan mi Bren, but ah doan belief un.'

Good. Jack really was as stupid as he looked. Arthur went back to the pub to drink 2,764 pints and smoke 346 packets of Woodbines. A car knocked him down on the way home. He swore loudly, pushed the car over a wall and reset his 17 broken bones. It was just a normal Saturday night.

'Hello, Arthur,' said Brenda. 'Unbelievably, Jack has said notten aboot yer shaggun meh un Winnie. Sos yer can carry un shaggun erse berth wheneva yer want.'

'Thass greet. Hoo boot noo un ther cornfield?'

'Noah, luv. Ah've oonly gert faive munits.'

'Thun we kun do ait twarce.'

Arthur laughed as the police failed to notice he had hidden the air rifle, with which he'd shot Mrs Bull, down his trousers. Life as an anti-hero was good if you didn't weaken. Those middle-class London writers could go fuck themselves. Who said you had to be a poncey French intellectual to be an existentialist?

He could tell Brenda had a new fancy man. No matter, he could still do Winnie an there was always that new bird Doreen.

'I'll taike yer ter Goose Fair on Thursday,' he told Doreen. 'I'm not takin' yer Satday as yer havena poot out yet and ah'll be goan' wiv Brenda an Winnie.'

The cold night air rushed past him as he hurtled down the helter-skelter, before landing in a heap at the bottom where two swaddies were waiting. The last thing he remembered before he fell unconscious was that he needed a drink.

'Wassup?' said Doreen.

'Not a lot,' Arthur said, nursing 91 major fractures and 136 stab wounds. 'Less go doon pub an haff 6,436 paints.'

'Bless,' his mother smiled. 'Kids these days, jus doan't noah how to handle ther drink.'

'Wot are yer doan here?' Arthur asked Sam, the black man.

'I dunno,' Sam said, 'I think I was parachuted in from another story to make a point about racism. But let's smoke 23,000 Woodbines anyway.'

'In which case, ah'd best git back ter Doreen.'

'Oooh, you are a wun, Arthur,' Doreen giggled. 'Bert me mum laikes yer an if yer promisss ter marry me, ah'll let yer feel ma tits.'

CIDER WITH ROSIE

Laurie Lee

M Y LIFE BEGAN at the age of three as the carrier's cart dropped me at the cottage in the summer of the last year of the Great War. I was lost amongst the June grass that towered poetically over me, swaying gently in the soft Cotswold zephyrs, and even my Mother was temporarily entranced by the bucolic idyll I am now trying too hard to recreate. The long days crowed and chirped and rang as we gorged ourselves on berries and feasted on scraps of stoat and fox.

Peace was here, but I could tell no difference. The countryside still marched to the relentless, inexorable beat of the seasons and the cottage still flooded when the winter rains swept down off the wooded hillside, bringing with them blackened cabbages and the pagan flesh of rotting badgers that we fell upon with glee. In the ample night I lay close to Mother, until one day I found my place in her bed had been taken by my younger brother Tony.

'Thee art a man now, me luvver,' she laughed, 'and it is time for thee to share a bed with your 17 elder brothers and sisters.'

I keened with the Oedipal betrayal, hardening myself against the merciless rejection of women, and turned my attention to the outside world where Jones's goat caused a commotion in the village for several months by breaking into Albert the Devil's parlour to devour a mountain of scrumped apples.

'You're stoppin' home no longer, Loll,' my sister Marjorie laughed, sweeping me up into her rustic linen apron. 'It's time thee started school.'

'Boo hoo,' I cried, but to no effect and my days of lazy plenty were over. The school itself was a small, roofless barn some eight miles' walk away and we strode out across the pitted, frozen lane before dawn.

'Sit here,' the teacher said, patting the upturned carcass of an otter, while nuzzling me close to her warm, capacious bosoms. How those bosoms filled my infant dreams for several years, before I was abruptly wrenched from her creamy embrace!

'You're now a grown boy,' the headmistress Crabby B said, beating my frost-hardened back with a rusty ploughshare she kept under her gnarled, oak desk, while watching a seemingly endless procession of unmarked coffins being carried to the windswept churchyard, as Nature exacted its cruel price on village life.

Death was never far away, for the Cotswold nights were as cold as Cotswold nights can be, yet we never complained or fussed o'er much. Death was part of the cycle in an existence that was raw and bloody, and whether it was the discovery of Miss Flynn's body lying naked in the mill pond or the murder of a loud New Zealander, the village closed ranks. Life was given and life was taken away, and we were answerable only to ourselves.

I had never known my father. He had abandoned my bounteous mother after four happy years, leaving her with 19 children, so I was brought up almost entirely by women. When my mother was out trudging the 27 miles along rutted tracks to gather the scrapings of mould from the bakery or to trap a diseased rat, Granny Trill or Granny Wallon would battle to drip-feed me their fermented turnips, hand-squeezed through their soiled muslin drawers.

Winter marched to its own beat. We would slide our bodies along the gleaming, frozen pond in almost sexual ecstasy, while around us everyone would die. First Granny Trill, then Granny Wallon in quick succession; then we heard my father had cranked his car into a wall in Morden and our mother faded away within minutes. It was like that in our valley; death was all around and it took whom it pleased in a heartbeat.

I too had been a sickly child and many was the time my mother thought I was not long for this world. Diphtheria, cholera, typhoid, tuberculosis, pneumonia, mad cow disease; there were few fatal illnesses that did not sink their predatory claws into my enfeebled body, yet each time I pulled through. Seventy-three of my brothers and sisters were not so lucky, for Death claimed many for itself in the russet countryside. Sometimes I wondered if they had died so that I might live, but at others I was content to frolic among the verdant pastures, snaring dogs with Cabbage-Stump Charlie and beating the local cripple with a stick.

The highlight of the village year was the Festival of the Burning Otter when we were all invited to the Squire's Hall to dress up in polecat pelts, offset with fern fronds, to partake in a day and night of orgiastic frivolity in which strangers would ritually be robbed of half a crown. It was on one such night, as I lay drinking cider with Rosie Burdock under the hay wagon, that she pulled me down into her wide valley to rock unseen together in the subaqueous grass.

It was the beginning of my awakening, yet the end of an era. The coming of charabancs to the village and the passing of the Squire meant that no more could we boys indulge in simple pleasures. Gone were the days of innocence, those bitter-cold winter days when we would roam the woody woods clubbing foxes, those hot, sultry endless days of summer when we would plan to rape the simpleton, Lizzie Berkeley.

The world was changing. My sisters found themselves husbands who wanted more than sex with man or beast, while my brothers left for the metropolis of Stroud. I was left alone to my world of nibbling squirrels and writing; a world that future generations would have lingering cause to regret.

– 1961 –

CALL FOR THE DEAD

John Le Carré

When Lady Ann ran away with a Cuban racing driver just two years after getting married, a part of George Smiley died. The part that survived was his profession, which was that of intelligence officer – a job that provided him with colleagues as unmemorably short, fat and badly dressed as himself. He had joined the Service in 1928 whilst up at Oxford reading the minor German poets and had spent much of the pre-war period at a German university assessing agent potential.

During the war he had grown a moustache, having acquired a talent for disguise, but now that he had entered middle age without ever being young, he found himself working for Maston, a career man in search of a K. He was too old to go abroad, which was how he came to find himself being summoned to Cambridge Circus one morning in January.

'Bad show, Smiley,' said Maston. 'That chap Sam Fennan you were asked to security check last week. He's committed suicide. There's got to be an enquiry, but don't rock the boat. We can't have a word of this leaked to the Press.'

He's showing too much cuff, Smiley observed as Maston left the room. His deliberations were interrupted by Peter Guillam. 'What did you make of Fennan?'

'A decent cove. A Jew obviously, but reasonable nonetheless. Whoever denounced him was right: he had been a member of the Party in the 1930s, but he's one of us now. I as good as told him there was nothing to worry about over one of those new-fangled espresso thingies that cost a shilling. So his suicide is very rum.'

Smiley walked slowly along Merridale Lane in Walliston before knocking at the door number 15. It was answered by Elsa Fennan. She, too, was obviously a Jew, a fierce woman in her fifties with her hair cut short and dyed the colour of nicotine.

'Come in,' she said, blankly. Smiley entered, his trademark lugubriousness etched on his face. 'I was out last night at the theatre and I came back to find my husband had shot himself, having left a suicide note.'

'That must have been distressing,' Smiley replied with typical understatement.

'Indeed, I couldn't sleep. But then, I am an insomniac.'

The phone rang. 'I'll get that,' Smiley said. 'It's probably for me, even though I don't live here.'

'It's the morning alarm call you requested,' said the operator.

'Oh, yes, I remember ordering that now,' Elsa smiled.

Smiley wandered even more slowly than usual towards the police station, aware that thanks to the fortuitously improbable piece of plotting of him answering the phone he had managed to expose a network of deceit. It was clear Elsa had not asked for the alarm call, so it could only have been Sam who had. Yet why would someone who was planning to commit suicide do that? He must have been murdered.

'There's a number of things that don't add up,' Smiley said to Sergeant Mendel.

'Well, you can count on me, sir,' Mendel replied. 'I'm the salt-of-the-earth copper who doesn't fall for the Establishment line. I've made some enquiries myself and found that Mrs Fennan always met another man at the theatre on the first Tuesday of the month.'

Smiley walked so slowly back to Mrs Fennan's that he barely appeared to be moving. 'I'm curious about that phone call,' he began.

'I thought you might be,' Mrs Fennan laughed nervously. 'I don't know why I lied to you about it. It wasn't an alarm call. It was to remind me to do something I've already forgotten about.'

In later books Smiley might have wondered why Elsa could

not have come up with a more convincing second explanation, having had so long to prepare one, but for now he sat back in the car and recited the poems of Herman Hesse while Mendel drove him to his Chelsea house. He noticed a light on in the hall and rang the bell. A strange man answered the door. 'Wrong number, I'm afraid,' said Smiley, making his excuses and leaving. He had been moments from being killed. He was a worried man. But not as worried as the reader who was wondering why on earth the assassin didn't just run after George and top him, rather than allowing him to walk away at a snail's pace.

He shuffled into the Circus to find Maston eager to ensure the suicide verdict was upheld. Suddenly, Smiley felt very tired from all his plodding. He sat down to write his resignation letter.

'It's alright, Guvnor,' Mendel smiled. 'I've traced the number plate of one of the cars outside your flat. It belonged to a local villain in Battersea. He's now been killed, but luckily he spilled the beans to me first. He had an arrangement to lend the car to the East German Trade delegation in Highgate.'

Smiley frowned. This could only mean that his old student Dieter Frey was involved. But why had he not left the country once he had killed Fennan? Surely Fennan's secrets would have died with him. As he was pondering these things, he was struck from behind by the butt of a pistol and lapsed into unconsciousness for three weeks. Still, at least his stay in hospital allowed him to recap the main elements of the plot, which even in a comparatively short book had already become hopelessly convoluted. There was Sam Fennan, Elsa Fennan . . .

There was a knock on the door and Guillam entered. 'It's a rum do,' he mused. 'It turns out the secrets Sam was handing over to Elsa to hand over to Dieter at the theatre weren't really classified secrets after all.'

Smiley crawled from his bed. 'It's possible we've been looking at this from the wrong angle all along,' he said, briefly stirring himself from a wistful reverie of Goethe and Lady Ann.

'You don't say,' Mendel muttered. 'Who would have thought it?'

'It's time for some tradecraft,' Smiley exclaimed while writing a message in a distinctive European script. 'That should bring the pigeons home to roost.'

Elsa and Dieter took their seats next to one another at the Hammersmith Palladium while Smiley, Mendel and Guillam observed them from above. 'They've just realised that neither of them set up this meeting,' Smiley said, as Elsa slumped in her seat. 'Quick, after Dieter! He's killed Elsa.'

His Zimmer frame in overdrive, Smiley sprinted after Dieter and cornered him by the Thames. 'So?' Smiley said. 'So?' Dieter replied, before allowing the much older, much weaker man to push him into the river.

Smiley sat down, exhausted and overwhelmed by a need to recap in case some readers still hadn't quite gathered what was going on. And this time he would make it even easier for them by writing them in bullet points. 1. It was Elsa who was the spy. 2. Sam had become suspicious and was going to denounce her. 3. Dieter . . .

'Well, I'm glad that's all cleared up without the Press being involved,' cried Maston cheerily. 'I take it we can tear up your resignation letter?'

On balance, Smiley thought he could. It was true there had been a number of rough edges. Some of the plotting had rather stretched credulity and the characterisation had been thinner than he'd hoped. But it was a more than decent start and his career as Alec Guinness was under way.

THE PRIME OF
MISS JEAN BRODIE

Muriel Spark

T HE GIRLS FORMED the Brodie set. That was what they had
been called by the headmistress when they arrived at the
Marcia Blaine School for Girls at the age of twelve. At that time
they had been instantly recognisable as Miss Brodie's pupils, being
well informed on Mussolini and Renaissance art, but unaware of
the rudiments of the curriculum.

Now aged sixteen, the girls were all hastily sketched out by a
single identifying feature. Monica was famous for mathematics;
Rose was famous for sex; Eunice was famous for gymnastics;
Sandy was famous for her piggy eyes, and Mary for being a silent
lump. In truth, none of them was particularly interesting and it
was only their arbitrary relationship with Miss Brodie that kept
anyone awake for very long.

'Miss Lockhart has suggested I apply for another post,' Miss
Brodie said, goose-stepping her way into the classroom. 'But the
headmistress shall not get rid of me, for I am in my prime. You are
my mini-mes.'

The Brodie set smiled. Rose who was famous for sex, though it
was never made clear what she had done to earn this notoriety,
thought back to when Miss Brodie had told them she had once
had a lover who had been felled in Flanders. 'Can you have sex if
you are in your prime?' asked Rose, who was to become even more
famous for sex six years later.

'Miss Brodie seems to have been in her prime for a long time,' replied Sandy, who was famous even then for her piggy eyes. 'That is one of the book's comic conceits,' said Monica, who was famous for maths, 'so we should all say the word "prime" as often as possible.'

'There are so many comic conceits going on here,' said Eunice, who was famous for gymnastics and hadn't even noticed all the arch time-shifts, 'that it's becoming a bit laboured. I'd better do a somersault before I get married to a doctor in ten years' time.'

'I'd better say "prime" too, I suppose,' said Mary, who was famous for being a silent lump, 'as I'm about to get burned to death in a hotel hell-fire of Calvinist indecision in fourteen years' time.'

'Indeed,' agreed Sandy, who was famous for her piggy eyes and would become Sister Helena of the Transfiguration.

'I find it so hard to think that one of you must have betrayed me,' said Miss Brodie on a rare visit to the nunnery in 1946, while she was dying of cancer.

It was I who betrayed this tiresome woman seven years ago, Sister Helena thought to herself. And now everyone but her knows, we should return to Miss Brodie in her prime.

1932 was the year sexuality first came to the girls.

'I saw Miss Brodie kissing Teddy Lloyd, the one-armed art teacher, in the staff room,' said Rose, who was to become famous for sex.

'Impossible,' Sandy, who was famous for her piggy eyes, replied. 'Mr Lloyd is married and Miss Brodie is a moral woman in her prime.'

'If only the trains ran on time,' Miss Brodie sighed tartly. 'Come now, gels; try to remember I'm in my prime.'

Yet the question of whether she had engaged in sexual intercourse with Mr Lloyd occupied the girls' minds for many years, even after Miss Brodie appeared to have become closely acquainted with Mr Lowther.

'Miss Brodie is a woman in her prime,' said Miss Lockhart, 'and you girls must determine whether her morality has been compromised with Mr Lowther. If so, she must be dismissed.'

'I was a woman in my prime,' Miss Brodie would later declare to Sister Helena, 'but my relationship with Mr Lowther was always chaste.'

'Mr Lloyd has asked Rose to be his model,' said Sandy, who was famous for her piggy eyes, in 1938, 'and yet every painting resembles you in your prime. You can tell by the jackboots.'

'That's as it should be,' Miss Brodie smiled. 'Mr Lloyd is a good Catholic man with seventeen children and it's proper he should have under-age sex with Rose, who is famous for sex. Having sex with Rose is the same as having sex with me. After all, you are all shaped in my image. My only regret is that I spoke so fondly of Mr Mussolini; on reflection, he seems rather lax compared to that Mr Hitler. More tea?'

'To be sure, Miss Brodie is in her prime,' said Mr Lloyd. 'But Rose is just my model.'

'In that case,' replied Sandy, who was famous for her piggy eyes, 'I shall have an affair with you instead.'

After a short while, Sandy, who was famous for her piggy eyes, grew tired of Mr Lloyd but not of his religion and became a nun, though not before she had first betrayed Miss Brodie for no particularly good reason.

'So Miss Brodie is a fascist in her prime,' cried Miss Lockhart. 'Who would have imagined it from her Nazi insignia and constant whistling of the "Horst-Wessel Song"? She must be dismissed.'

'Before she died, Miss Brodie did wonder whether it was you who had betrayed her,' said Eunice, who was famous for her gymnastics, sometime later in the 1950s. 'Was it the shame of that betrayal that made you become a nun?'

'No,' Sister Helena, who was still famous for her piggy eyes, replied. 'You can only betray those to whom you owe a debt of loyalty. It was the guilt of betraying the readers with such a rubbish ending that drove me to Holy Orders.'

A CLOCKWORK
ORANGE

Anthony Burgess

THERE WAS ME, that is Alex, and my three droogs, that is Pete, Georgie and Dim. Dim being well dim, like. We was in the milkbar, O my brothers, keeping out of the bastard chill and peeting the moloko with knives ready for the evening's ultra-violence.

'What's it going to be then, eh?' my droogs entreated me.

Where can your humble narrator begin? The horrorshow boots gave a reet kicking in the pot to some malenky scholar and then we razzezed his platties as we ripped his slovo books before spending some cutter chatting up baboochkas. Next we cracked a drunkie with a few choice tolchoks, battered young Billyboy and his five eunuch jelly droogs before doing a newsagent to puff lordly on the cancers.

No one viddied us as we jacked a car and drove out towards a cottage veschch. 'Pray what kind of place is this, O my brother?' I enquired in my choicest goloss. The man's gulliver was shaking and his rookers too. I saw he was writing a book – *A Clockwork Orange* – and I read out a malenky bit. 'The attempt to impose upon man, to ooze juicily at the last round the bearded lips of God, laws and conditions appropriate to a mechanical creation, against this I raise my sword-pen.'

'Have you finished with the clunky morality plot line?' my droogs enquired.

'For the time being, O my brothers.' So we smashed his

glazzies and made his litso dripping before taking turns doing the in and out with his baboochka.

In verity, by the time I woke up the next day I was fagged and fashed with the horrorshow ultraviolence, but Mr Burgess, he being a young writer, like, and not yet gifted with chepooka like subtlety of plot and character, made me go back for more.

'We could also have you listening to J. S. Bach, Wolfie Mozart and dear old Ludwig Van turned up to vol 11.'

'O my brother Tonio,' I replied. 'Can you not viddy that even though you think that sounds surreally dystopian, it's the artistic vision of a try-hard middle-class controversialist, not that of a self-respecting droog with a taste for the horrorshow ultra-v.'

'Tough, my little Clockwork Orange, thou art mine bitch,' said Tonio, so once more your humble narrator went back into the malenky fray, skiving off skolliwoll, giving it large to my pee and em and making chai for P. R. Deltoid, my corrective adviser.

'Are you done, O my brother?' I asked at last. He nodded his gulliver.

'Then I'll be off to the musica to pick up two totty psitas, feed them barbo moloko and do the rough in and out and climax with the "Ode to Joy". Perhaps then I'll take my unruly malchickiwicks for a mansize crasting in the widow's dacha.'

'Come along, come along, come along now, Alex,' said the millicents, beating my litso to an oily red pulp. 'It's the Staja for you.' Prison. May Bog help me. And me only 15, like.

So here I am. Clanged up. Number 6655321 in the grazhny hellhole being tolchocked by some bazoomy malchickiwicks. The man of Bog was my saviour, for he let me read the stories of the old Yahoodies and the nailing-in while listening to the aurals of Luddy Van B.

'Pray tell me of the new rehabilitation scheme,' I enquired in my best goloss gavoreeting.

'I've rather lotht the will to live with all thish nadsat delinquenthly and slang,' the malenky prietht repliued, for all preiths have satirical lithps. 'But all the same I advise you not to think of it. Such aversion measures contravene God's freewill.'

'But I am keen for I could be home within two weeks, O my brother.' And so it was when that chelloreck Dr Brodsky made me his slovo guinea pig, I was not to be found awanting.

First they spiked me with multivits, then they tied me platties to the chair and made me watch heads splitting open while Luddy V did his thing. 'Enough,' I cried. 'It is not Ludwig's fault.' Yet retch and retch and retch like bezomny I did.

'He is cured,' the dirty Brodsky said.

'But this is Satan,' the Minister replied. 'Good and evil mean nothing in the eyes of God without free will.'

I was going to point out that Mister Tonio had screwed up again and that it was me who had willingly renounced my freewillywilly but then Tonio made some chelloreck come to beat me up and taunt me with a naked baboochka with dangly bazooka, and I like made to pulp him and do the jiggy-jig but then I retched and retched and watched my gulliver get turned to pulp.

'See,' said Brodsky.

Only the stupidest fool wouldn't. Yet still there were seven malenky chapters left of symmetry. Time to be go back to my domey. Time to be rejected by my pee and em. Time to want to do the in and out with a baboochka, only to puke my pot. Time to want to top myself, only to puke my pot. Time for one malenky coincidence after another. Time to be crasted by Dim who was now a millicent.

Time to go back to the domey of the chelloreck nancy who was writing *A Clockwork Orange*. Time to be paraded in the gazeta as a victim of state fascism. Time to throw myself out the window. Time for the millies to find me and reverse the treatment. Time to meet Pete and have the most unlikely conversion of all.

'Great photo of your malenky kiddywiddies,' I said. 'I rather fancy one myself. Perhaps this ultraviolence is a bit boring.'

Time to confuse iconoclasm with fictive daring. Time to know better.

THE BELL JAR

Sylvia Plath

I T WAS THE summer they electrocuted the Rosenbergs. I couldn't stop wondering what it would be like to be burned alive. It was like the first time Buddy Willard showed me a cadaver; I felt as if I was carrying the head around with me on a string.

New York was bad enough. Just nineteen years old, a scholarship girl winning a prize to work on a fashion magazine, I was meant to be having the time of my life. Truth is I was just bored. I sat back with Doreen and let the world slip though my fingers.

We were meant to be going to a party, but our cab got stuck in traffic. Some guy said he was a DJ and chatted up Doreen. No one noticed me so I drank neat vodka and thought some more about how stupid Buddy Willard was. Doreen's breasts popped out of her dress, so I popped home and locked the door. She came back later and knocked on my door but I couldn't be bothered to get out of bed and open it.

I figured if I mentioned Buddy Willard a third time it might generate a curiosity in the reader I couldn't muster myself. Normally I wanted to write poems; now I just lay around with food poisoning, not thinking of much. I would have gone to the movies, but they were all Technicolor. I only liked shades of grey.

Everyone assumed I was going to marry Buddy Willard when he came out of the TB clinic in the Adirondacks. I'd adored him till I found he was a hypocrite. After he took me to watch him cut up cadavers and deliver babies at medical school, he took off his clothes. He invited me to get undressed too but I couldn't see the point. I asked if he had had an affair before. He said yes. I felt betrayed. I wasn't jealous; just unreasonable.

I thought of all the things I couldn't do. I couldn't cook. I couldn't drive. I couldn't emote. But I reckoned I could sleep with Constantin, a short, ugly interpreter for the UN to whom Mrs Willard had introduced me. 'Do you want to sleep with me?' I asked. 'No,' he replied. 'You're too much like hard work.'

Mr Willard took me to the sanatorium. Buddy showed me a poem he had written. It was awful. Just like some Ted Hughes doggerel. 'I'm not going to marry you,' I said. 'You made me ski straight down a hill and break my leg.' He thought I was being neurotic. Typical male bastard.

Someone called Hilda – I would explain who she was, if I remembered or cared – said she was glad the Rosenbergs had fried. I went on a date with Marco, a real woman-hater. You can always tell a woman-hater. They are every man I've ever met. I hit him. He called me a slut. Or maybe it was the other way round. I'm a little vague sometimes.

My mother told me I hadn't made it on to the writing course. Maybe you can see why. Buddy Willard wrote that he had an infatuation with his nurse and I started to write a novel. This might even be it. I decided I needed experience. I began reading *Finnegans Wake* and the doctor sent me to a psychiatrist. I didn't trust Dr Gordon. He was a man, smooth-talking, good-looking. You might be wondering by now if I had issues with men, as every man I met was a complete bastard. Don't. I was fine. This is a protean feminist novel; all men are bastards. Especially Ted.

Dr Gordon gave me some electric shock treatment. It didn't work so I went home and tried to hang myself. That didn't work either so I tried to shoot myself. Then drown myself. Eventually I took an overdose of sleeping pills and woke up in a private hospital where I was greeted by Buddy Willard's first girlfriend, Joan. 'I tried to kill myself just like you,' she said. 'But now I'm better.'

The bell jar was still stifling me as I was shunted from Dr

Pancreas to Dr Syphilis. I then found myself speaking to a kind and beautiful psychiatrist, Dr Nolan. 'I hate my mother,' I said, for the first and last time showing any insight or interest in my condition. 'You need some more ECT,' she replied, 'though my ECT will be a touchy-feely feminine ECT, not like the treatment that electrocuting male chauvinist bastard gave you.'

I could finally breathe. The bell jar had lifted, though you wouldn't have noticed it from my writing which was as lifeless and unself-aware as ever. 'I'm leaving to be a psychiatrist,' Joan told me. There's no chance of me seeing you, I thought charitably, as I made an appointment with a doctor to get myself fitted with a coil. I needed a world free from babies where I could have sex with the right kind of man. Even though the right kind of man obviously didn't exist.

'Ouch,' I said. Irwin had warned me losing my virginity might hurt; he had been right. What a bastard. I started haemorrhaging profusely and took a cab back to the hospital, where the nurse greeted me with the news that Joan had hanged herself.

I couldn't remember who Joan was till Buddy Willard asked me whether it was a coincidence that both his girlfriends had been depressed. I smiled enigmatically, told him not to worry as I wasn't going to see him again anyway, and then went round to hit that jerk Irwin for my $20 cab fare to the hospital. I wasn't going to see him again, either. I was no longer a blob. I had been reborn. Well, maybe.

HERZOG

Saul Bellow

IF I AM out of my mind, it's all right with me, thought Moses Herzog. He had fallen under the spell of writing letters that he never sent. He was alone in the big old house in the Berkshires, overcome by the need to explain, to clarify, to have it out in the kind of effortlessly superior, macho prose that would become the hallmark of his acolytes.

What was his character? Narcissistic, masochistic, too knowingly unself-aware. Well, that was Bellow. But what of him? He had been a bad husband, a bad father, a bad academic; he had failed at everything. His wife, his ex-wife, Madeleine had made him spend his $20,000 inheritance on moving from the Berkshires to Chicago and then she had left him for his friend, his ex-friend, Valentine. Why had he been the last to suspect their affair?

Dear Einstein, Why does everyone hate me? Dear Herzog, Because you are relatively annoying.

He had gone alone to Europe to save the marriage and had only the embarrassment of an infection from Wanda for his trouble. On his return, Madeleine had thrown him out for the one-legged charmer and Valentine had not even put up a fight to get custody of their daughter, Junie.

There was Ramona, of course, but she was merely his sexual reflex. True, she was extremely attractive, in her late thirties and gagging for his balding, unfit late-forties body in the way that balding, unfit late-forties male authors often like to imagine. But he was not ready to get married again.

It was hard to concentrate. You know the feeling.

Dear Martin Luther King, Dear Mr Shapiro, I hope you don't mind if I riff on civil rights, Romanticism and the nature of Soviet Communism. Dear Mr Bellow, Your erudition is exemplary but where exactly is this getting us?

The lawyer had told him he was a mensch, not an egghead. *You could have fooled me.* He was a good Jew; he was born to suffer. *But not inflict it on the rest of us.* He didn't want to die. He would sell up and come to New York, though first he would stay with an old girlfriend, Libbie. The journey would allow him a lot of time to think about death.

Dear Libbie, I have to go. I can't stand the kindness.

Herzog flew back to New York to find a letter from a former student, Geraldine Portnoy. *I was walking past the house and noticed Valentine had left Junie locked in the car.* Hmm, he thought. As a plot device this was distinctly average, but it was better than anything else on offer and it did allow him an uneasy segue into a lengthy rumination on his first wife Daisy and their son Marco and Madey's brief dalliance with Catholicism. Trust him to get involved with someone more fucked up than a Jew!

Dear Rousseau, I am crushed by science, polemics, modernism, and the Id. Dear Herzog, Don't forget the Diaspora, the Holocaust, the Cold War, Kierkegaard, Hegel, Marx, Kant and Spinoza.

Ramona invited him to flirt with the Orphic. Why was he here? A question he is not alone in asking by now. 'I belong to you,' Ramona said while making love. He was good in bed. Very good. They tried to make you think you were old, but you are youthful, Bellow reassured himself.

He dropped her at work and went to see his lawyer. A sense of melancholy swept over him at the court house as he saw a mother accused of killing her child. He had to go to Chicago to see Junie. He had to make sense of his own mother's death and the World as Will.

Dear Mr Nobel, I've tried to cover all the bases for The Great Novel. Je n'ai jamais ecrit en Français. *Rachatz. And Yiddish. Can I have the Prize now? Dear Mr Bellow, Just hang in there.*

His body was rotting from the inside. Why were his brothers successful and he was down to $600? Why had he let the bitch torture him? He stopped by Tante Taube's house to collect the old pistol with which his father had threatened to shoot him when he'd asked to borrow money. Reconciliation then death; from madhouse to mausoleum.

Herzog pulled up outside the bitch's house. He saw how tenderly Valentine bathed Junie. Firing the pistol was nothing but an idea of Bergsonian duration. He would take Junie to the aquarium instead. The brakes were stiff and the Falcon careered across the road. Herzog checked to see Junie was OK before remembering how he had crashed in the very road in which he had been sexually abused by a tramp when he was ten.

Dear Mr Bellow, There was no need to throw in the kitchen sink.

'What's with the pistol?' the two Negro cops asked.

'It was going to be a paperweight,' he replied.

'He was going to kill me,' said the Bitch, dripping Bitchness.

His brother posted the bail bond and dropped him at the house in the Berkshires. This had to end, Herzog thought. Enough solipsistic kvetching. *Too right.* He did not need happiness or meaning; History is cruelty; existence is meaning. His house may not be much, but it was enough.

There was just one letter left to write.

Dear Mr Disney, I've always admired your saccharine-sweet contrived endings.

'Hello,' said Ramona. 'How about we get married sometime?'

THE CRYING OF
LOT 49

Thomas Pynchon

Mrs Oedipa Maas came home from a Tupperware party to find that she had been named executor, or she supposed executrix, of the estate of her former lover, Pierce Inverarity, a California property mogul who once lost two million dollars in his spare time. The letter said her co-executor was to be a lawyer called Metzger from a firm called Lookat, Meimtrying, Toohard, Tobewacky.

As she mixed herself a whiskey sour and waited for her husband, Wendell 'Mucho' Maas, to return home from his shift on FUCK radio, Oedipa allowed herself some anarchic thoughts about Vivaldi's kazoo concerto and how Pierce used to call her in funny voices.

'You're too sensitive,' she said in an access of helplessness as Mucho detailed his latest defeat. 'I'm going to see my shrink.'

'Why are you not taking the pills?' Dr Hilarius asked. 'I need you for my LSD trials.'

'I'm hallucinating already,' Oedipa replied.

'So early in the book? Then you are cured.'

She felt the onset of revelation, an absence of intensity, a shimmer of mystic meaninglessness, and lowered her hair, Rapunzel-like, into the studied opacity of chapter two.

Oedipa drove south to San Narciso – less of a city, more a rather dull concept – that had been Pierce's domicile and checked in to the Echo Courts Motel. A drop-out called Miles appeared from behind an enormous statute of a nymphet with vermilion-tipped breasts.

'I'm lead singer with the Paranoids,' he said. 'I'm too old to Frug.'

'You can leave all the enigmatic shit to me,' said another man, who introduced himself as Metzger. 'I live inside my looks. I was once a child actor called Baby Igor. How about we play Strip Boticelli?'

Oedipa went to her room and put on several more layers of clothes. It could have been a good gag but she blew it and went to bed with him anyway. That was the problem with post-modernism. No self-will, no motivation, no character. She wondered if she should confess her infidelity to Mucho, but why bother when he might have been writing the story?

Things did not delay in becoming more curious when they came across Pierce's stamp collection, thousands of coloured windows into time and space, ex-rivals for her affections that would be broken into lots. Oedipa sensed a revelation as she drifted into a bar called Scope.

'Join the Peter Pinguid Society,' said Mike Fallopian, a right-wing nutcase. 'We communicate via a rebel mail service using the W.A.S.T.E. system.'

'What's that?'

'I could tell you but it still wouldn't make any sense and you wouldn't care anyway. Best to keep you guessing. That way you might think there's a point.'

'You're right,' Metzger agreed. 'We should go with the Paranoids to check out Pierce's investment at Fangoso Lagoons.'

'I'm your inverse,' said a man called Di Presso. 'I'm a lawyer turned actor. I've no idea what I'm doing here but a load of GI bones got turned into charcoal filters.'

'That's like a Jacobean tragedy that's playing at the Tank Theatre.'

They immersed themselves in *The Courier's Tragedy*, a play of incest, murder, the Thurn and Taxis mail system, and the mysterious breakaway Tristero postal sect. Nobody said an in-joke had to be funny.

'Where's the text?' Oedipa asked.

'There is no text,' the director Randolph Driblette answered. 'This is the text. I made it up.'

She longed for meaning. Maybe she could find it in Zapf's bookshop. Who were the Tristero assassins? Had she given them life? Had someone been smoking too much dope? She came across a man drawing the Tristero sign of the horn. Why? She visited John Nefastis, the man who postulated Maxwell's Demon with his perpetual motion machine.

'Entropy connects the laws of thermodynamics to information flow,' he said.

'You're so right-wing, you're left-wing.'

'There's a conspiracy theory,' Genghis Cohen, the stamp expert, explained. 'All Pierce's stamps are deliberate Tristero errors.'

Metzger was not that bothered by Oedipa's leaving, but then why should he be? He'd had enough and he had never existed without her. Besides, he had a fifteen-year-old nymphet to fuck. She looked at some deaf-mutes, went to a fag club and dropped in on Mucho. He had dropped out on acid. She went to see Dr Hilarius. 'I was a Nazi doctor who tortured the Jews at Buchenwald by making them read this kind of crap,' he laughed, firing a gun indiscriminately, before the police came for him.

Oedipa headed to Berkeley to meet Emory Bortz, a world expert on Jacobean tragedy. 'Driblette has committed suicide,' he said.

'Why does everyone leave me?'

'I can't imagine.'

'Now I'll never know the secrets of the Tristero. Did it really exist? Was it Pierce's last elaborate hoax? Am I mad? Or am I just stuck in a dated timewarp of empty counter-cultural allusions to which 1960s stoners and reviewers scared of being thought stupid will attach great depth and revelation?'

Self-absorbed with her own one-dimensionality, Oedipa never heard Pynchon laughing as he scammed the literati once again. Instead she waited for the crying of lot 49, to see who would bid for Pierce's stamps. Oh, look! It's you.

WIDE SARGASSO SEA

Jean Rhys

THEY SAY WHEN trouble comes, close ranks, and so the white people did. But we were not in their ranks. The negroes hated us too. 'You ain't nothing but white cockroach niggers,' the young Tia said, stealing my dress as I bathed alone in the lush sensuality of the biblical garden pond.

They were all the people in my life – my mother, my brother Pierre and my nurse Christophine – since old Cosway, my father, died five years back when all the slave-owners left. Some said it was drink, some said madness, but emancipation surely did us no good.

I was a bridesmaid when my mother married Mr Mason, but though he released us from the steamy undergrowth of our sweaty impoverishment, we could not escape the madness of the post-colonial reinterpretation of *Jane Eyre*.

'Why must I flit from one half-remembered scene to another?' I asked. 'Each more laden than the last with the heavy, humid symbolism of female oppression and neo-Marxist alienation.'

'Because you are a creole, Antoinette,' Christophine said, 'and I am an old Jamaican negro, steeped in the ways of obeah.'

Flames licked the bamboo walls of our home, a haunting prelude to the historical inevitability of my death. 'Black and white, they burn alike,' the mob chanted, as Mr Mason carried Pierre to safety. A stone struck me on the forehead and I lapsed into a month of yet more fevered modernist memories of charred parrots and poisoned horses.

'Is it true Pierre has died?' I asked on returning to a semi-lucid consciousness. 'I long for the release of death.'

'They are saying it is a blessing the cretin has passed,' Christophine replied, 'and your mother has been committed to an asylum. She does not recognise you.'

'Then they will say I too am touched with madness.'

'It is unavoidable,' Mr Mason added. 'Madness is indeed a deterministic inevitability of a patriarchal, imperialist regime. So let me hasten you towards your destiny by marrying you off to an impoverished English gentleman here to take refuge in sunshine and death.'

So this is Massacre. How did I come to honeymoon on the Windward Islands? Like so much else in my pitiful life, I too am now the victim of a proto-feminist Marxist plot to reinterpret Brontë's classic. See how I'm never given a name, yet you assume I must be Rochester! See how the action has been carried forward 30 years to resonate with the Emancipation Act! Truly economic determinism works in mysterious ways!

Yes, I married Antoinette to escape the shame and guilt of debt, but I was struck by the fevers of this oppressive, dream-like Carib jungle, and now that I am well, I find I do not love her. Like her? Yes. But, love her? No. My heart is the very essence of stone-cold, Victorian materialism steeped in the pig-iron of the industrial revolution: she is black, yet white, mad, yet sane, the very essence of the Hegelian dialectic.

'I beg you, Christophine,' I said. 'Give me an obeah potion to make him love me. For else I shall descend to madness.'

'It is a hard thing you ask,' she said. 'For black is white, night is day, and you cannot escape your ending.'

The jungle breathed in, its lungs full of fetid menace, as I ravished my reified Antoinette before falling into a stifling, tormented sleep. I awoke to find myself full of hatred for her. Yes, hatred for her, my mad creole bride. Hungry for revenge, I forced myself on the willing maid Amelie while Antoinette listened by the keyhole.

'Your cousin Daniel has written to say that all your family is mad and Amelie tells me you have kissed your nigger cousin,' I said. 'How do you answer that, my Antoinette, my Marionette, my Bertha?

'Why do you call me Bertha?'

'How else will everyone know you are the mad woman in the attic if I don't give you the same name, Bertha?' I sneered. 'And how better to objectify you than calling you that which you are not?'

'Then my alienation is complete. I am dead though I am not dead. I am but a post-colonial zombi,' she said, biting into my arm and drawing blood in a half-acknowledged homage to 1960s horror films.

'See what you have done,' cried Christophine Lee. 'Your male, petit-bourgeois, racist cruelty has carried her off into total madness. One day you will be made to atone for the collective guilt of your class and gender.'

'Did you think I wanted to be portrayed in such simplistic terms?' I replied. 'Did you think I liked being at the mercy of a woman who cannot write about men? Did you think I could escape my own determinism any more than she could? Enough! I am taking Bertha back to England.'

The candles guttered as I placed them carefully next to the muslin curtains. Come burn, flames. Arise, sister, you have nothing to lose but centuries of feminist oppression. And a few expensive fixtures and fittings.

COUPLES

John Updike

THE HANEMAS WERE undressing after the Thornes' party. 'You're not happy with me,' said Angela, revealing her surprisingly luxuriant pudenda. Piet did a handstand. 'How can I be when you won't sleep with me any more?' he replied.

Piet gave up trying to pleasure her and started toying with his hardening ivory rod instead. He thought of the other Tarbox women he would like to fuck. There was Carol, Bea . . . and that Foxy Whitman woman who had just moved into town.

'Shall we have some bad 1960s dinner party dialogue?' the repulsive Freddy Thorne had said with the easy intrusiveness of a man who believed himself attractive.

'That's *une bonne idée*,' Harold little-Smith had added with his irritating tic of inserting French words into his speech. 'And we could also talk about Cuba for context *historique*.'

'Oh don't be such bores,' Carol had squealed. 'Let's go back to flirting over charades and pretending we're clever and interesting while acting as if we don't know we're all shagging each other. Though with the utmost suburban decorum, of course.'

Georgene Thorne moistened her cleft as her breasts bobbed like Hansel and Gretel abandoned. 'You are so big,' she moaned as Piet thrust himself inside her. 'Welcome to the post-pill paradise.'

'Do you think I can get away with endless Bad Sex descriptions of the cunts I've fucked, if I try to disguise it as the poetry of sexually forensic literature?' Piet asked.

'No, because for all your feeble efforts at satirical detachment, you're obviously a pervy voyeur on the sly,' Georgene giggled, smearing her erect nipples with his glutinous ooze. 'But don't knock it. The middle classes looking for cheap thrills will love it.'

Piet felt the need to assert his literary credentials. He thought in short sentences. Try-hard language. Church. Dead pet symbolism. *Italics*. Roth. Shakespeare. Saffron-robed monks. Molecular. Photosynthesis. Cancer. But then he thought 'sod it,' and reverted to the low-tide smell of cunt.

For eighty pages, the conjoinings of the Applebys, the little-Smiths and other marginal characters pointlessly took centre stage in the cloistered world of anodyne counter-culturalism, but once Updike had shot his load, it was back to Piet and Foxy. And thus, in a typically grating arch sentence, the rift among the Tarbox couples began to unfold.

'How I despise Ken for not getting me pregnant sooner!' Foxy said, rubbing her swollen belly as Piet forced himself inside her. 'Nobody makes me feel like you do.'

'I wish I could make you come,' Piet gasped, frantically grinding against her swollen clitoris.

'Oh, don't worry about that. I'll sort myself out later. It is enough for me to be a bucket for your sperm.'

Piet choked with emotion. A woman had never declared her love to him so soulfully before. And Foxy's downy bush was a great deal more attractive and younger-looking than Angela's.

'I'd better go before Ken gets suspicious,' Piet said. He wiped himself clean before driving to see Georgene.

'I wish you hadn't dumped me for Foxy,' Georgene sobbed, sucking avidly at his giant phallus. 'How I adore you, my darling God-fearing orphan.'

Georgene swallowed the last drop of his shuddering orgasm. 'I'd better go before Ken gets suspicious,' Piet said. He wiped himself clean before driving to see Bea.

She undressed quickly, eager to feel her yearning cunt completed by his protean penis. 'I've had all the other men and you've had all the other women, so we might as well fuck each other.' Bea smiled.

'I've just been to church and now I'm going to put the kids to bed,' Piet said. 'That's nice,' Angela replied abstractedly. 'I've been to see a shrink. It's a shame Kennedy's been killed. Are you sure you're not sleeping with anyone else?'

Piet needed gravitas. A longer paragraph. His nights were riven by tortured nightmares. The church had burnt down. Symbolism was all around. He was tired of the party whirl. He had striven to maintain his distance from Foxy but he had succumbed two days after she had given birth, sliding between her sweaty thighs. She had wanted the baby but he had insisted she get rid of it. Only Freddy had been able to arrange the abortion and the price had been high.

'Freddy wants to sleep with you,' Piet told Angela.

'Fair enough,' said Angela, with the perfect logic of the middle-aged male novelist. 'If it makes you happy.'

Angela lazily opened her legs, willing Freddy to get on with it. 'I can't do it,' he sobbed theatrically. 'I think I'm gay. Do you mind going to sleep and I'll wank on your tits instead?'

The book was running out of control. Like Piet's bowels, which exploded in cathartic diarrhoea while he and Angela were talking in the bathroom.

'Ken has had a tantrum and wants a divorce from Foxy,' he said.

'How very un-Tarbox. Well, you know I'm a typical 1960s feminist so you can do what you want,' Angela replied. 'If you want to divorce me that's fine, and if you want to stay that's fine, too.'

'Thanks,' Piet nodded. 'I think I'll have 30 pages of dithering angst in which I'll tie up a loose end by fucking Carol . . .'

'Your end is never loose, big boy,' Carol's cunt purred.

'. . . and then I'll marry Foxy, though she's looking a bit old and flabby since she had the baby.'

'That's nice.'

THE FRENCH LIEUTENANT'S WOMAN

John Fowles

Looking out over Lyme Bay in 1867, a telescopist might have noticed a well-dressed couple walking along the Cobb and correctly inferred they were a well-to-do couple from out of town who were shortly to be wed. But he would have been at all at sea with the motionless woman standing at the end of the mole.

'I hope you haven't been talking about the silly ideas of Mr Darwin again,' Ernestina chided. 'Papa so hates the idea of being descended from an ape.'

Indeed Charles had been talking of just that, for what self-respecting, free-thinking man would have talked of anything else? Just as today such a man might talk of DNA, the Cold War and the right to self-determination.

Yet the reality is that Charles has no right to self-determination as he is but the construct of my imagination, so let us now make him catch sight of the woman at the end of the Cobb.

'Who, pray, is that?' he asks.

'They call her the French Lieutenant's Woman,' Ernestina replies. 'She fell in love with a shipwrecked captain who abandoned her. She is quite disgraced and is now a servant to Mrs Poulteney.'

'I wish you hadn't told me such a horrible story, but we must escort her back to Lyme for she is not safe here.'

Charles made to counsel the woman but her eyes warned

him off, eyes that betrayed a sorrow as deep as the sea.

But as this is my book, let's leave this introductory scene and make some wry observations about both the characters and their Victorian values. Charles Smithson, we may conclude, is a man of moderate virtue. Freed by a private income from the necessity of work, he is a lost soul of 32 years, passing his time before claiming the greater inheritance from his uncle by hunting for fossils, and tortured by memories of his liaisons with prostitutes.

His fiancée, Miss Ernestina Freeman, is what we would now in the 1960s call petit-bourgeois. In short, her father is in trade. But what trade! If you will excuse the overuse of exclamation marks! He owns department stores in London and is a man of considerable self-made wealth; his only daughter a worthy catch for a man, such as Charles, of greater class but fewer means. Ernestina's only drawback is that she is, as we would say in 2010, a bit of an airhead.

Miss Sarah Woodruff, or the French Lieutenant's Hoo-er as some Lyme Regis folk described her, we will come to shortly; the other minor characters need not detain us greatly. There is Mrs Poulteney, a widow who has taken in Miss Woodruff to offset her bigotry and increase her chances of entering the Kingdom of Heaven.

And then there's Sam and Mary. How sweet the lower orders are in love! And how little they appear to dissemble compared to the romantic vicissitudes of their betters! For Mary is maid to Ernestina's aunt and Sam is Charles's man. Such a useful contrast for the novelist! Yet do not underestimate the Crafty Cockney's ability to put one over on his master!

We could also spend many pages discussing Victorian society from a modern perspective, with recourse to such imagery as computers , but first I would like to talk again of me. It's tough being a novelist in the 1960s, unsure if your characters exist and wanting to pretend you aren't really controlling their story. Yawn.

Enough of this. Now to the Undercliff, that secret prehistoric world of vaginal fecundity where Miss Woodruff walks alone. And where Charles is searching for a fossil.

'Miss Woodruff,' he says.

'Mr Smithson,' she replies.

Dark passions begin to simmer.

'I worry for your health.'

'My health means nothing,' she declares. 'I know the French Lieutenant will never return, but the shame I bear defines me.'

Had he been born 100 years later, Charles might have recognised this as an expression of Sartrean existential angst. Instead, he felt a disconcerting swelling in his trousers and kissed her on the eyelid.

Miss Woodruff looked back, her long red curls swept from her alabaster forehead by the wind machine situated behind the director. 'If we are seen together I shall be expelled from Mrs Poulteney's service.'

I could make more of this rather slender, contrived courtship. I could discourse longer on Victorian science and religious hypocrisy. I could begin a sub-plot where Charles is left rudderless by his uncle's marriage to a fortune hunter, a union that diminishes his prospects yet leaves him with the opportunity to terminate his betrothal to Ernestina with a patina of probity. I could arrange further portentous encounters between Charles and Sarah, one of which could end by Sarah deliberately allowing herself to be observed and thus fulfil her Freudian need to be expelled from Mrs Poulteney's home.

Yet I prefer to cut to the chase, so let's take ourselves to Exeter where Sarah is staying at Endicott's Hotel. Here I have a dilemma, for I must maintain the artifice that my characters have their own lives and I don't know how the story ends. Daringly, then, I leave you to decide.

First we have Charles denying himself the fulfilment of a night with Sarah and returning to Ernestina, with whom he will live happily ever after for the next 173 years. But I don't want to do that. So let's also find Charles collapsing on Sarah's naked body after 17 seconds of intense copulation.

'My God, but you were a virgin!' he cries. 'So the French Lieutenant did not . . .'

'Indeed not, but I needed the world to imagine he had so as to explore my shame and loneliness and prepare myself for you.'

Had Charles read any modern psychology books he would have realised Sarah was a nutter in need of therapy. But as this was 1867 he merely says, 'I adore you.'

Oh dear. The complications increase. See how Sam fails to deliver Charles's letter to Sarah and their romance is snuffed out before it has barely begun. See how Charles is ostracised for ending his engagement and forced to wander the world like the Flying Dutchman, reading Tennyson, sleeping with prostitutes and mixing metaphors in his search for Sarah.

If only I'd known how messy it was going to get, how I was making myself write another 100 unnecessary pages, I might have stuck with the first ending. But I didn't. So now I must leave you another two as Charles finishes a love poem. *I weep and weep, I'm very deep / I yearn to sleep with Meryl Streep.*

He finds her two years later, living as Rosetti's muse. 'I cannot marry you. I still want to be alone. But we have a daughter,' Sarah says.

Or . . .

'I will marry you, but it's only Platonic.'

You'll probably choose the second. Readers always think the last more real. In truth they are the same. Either way, Charles and Sarah have ended up in a postmodern cul-de-sac.

PORTNOY'S COMPLAINT

Philip Roth

PORTNOY'S COMPLAINT *n*. (after Alexander Portnoy 1933–)
A disorder in which a fictional character the same age as the writer kvetches on sex, guilt, sex and Jewishness for 250 pages without pausing for breath.

She was so deeply embedded in my subconscious that for the first 13 years of my life, I truly believed my mother, Sophie, was everywhere. So I became honest. I had to be; she knew everything. How did my father take this? By having constant constipation. He'd stuff himself with bran and still only be able to manage a rabbit pellet on the toilet. So what do you make of that, Dr Spielvogel? Repression?

He'd go to work each day selling insurance in the slums, but no one cared. As far as the goyim and the schwartzes were concerned he was just some dreck Yid. It was my mother who did everything. She held my penis when I needed a wee – God help me, I still can't go unless she's around and I'm 33 now – and she tried to make me eat. 'How can you love me if you leave that bagel?' she would holler.

Then came adolescence. Half my daily life spent firing my wad down the toilet, into my fat elder sister's brassière, anywhere. 'Come and give me all you've got,' the neighbour's cat whispered. So I did. I battered my penis to a pulp. I tried to cut down to 17 sessions a day, to save it snapping off or getting cancer, but it had a life of its own. Especially at the thought of shikses. 'Get off the toilet,' my father screams. 'I need to go.' 'I've got diarrhoea,' I yell back. My mother starts yelling. 'He's doing something unspeakable.' She knows. I'm done for. She's going to cut off my penis. 'He's eating a hamburger. The shame!'

We moved to a Jewish neighbourhood in Newark when I was eight. Did that make a difference, doctor? Or was it my father shtupping the shiksa from work? Who knows? This, I suppose, is the material. You work it out. Would psychoanalysis even exist without the Jews? Every goddamn hang up, we Jews have worse than everyone else. You think I'm self-hating? Whew! Just wait to find out how many grievances I've really got. Judaism. All that pointless Rosh Hashannah nonsense. Why do Jews love that saga shit? My mother. Just give me a break from her constant 'Why don't you become a doctor, get married and give me grand-children?' My father. Castrated and servile.

Oy vey. You've heard all this Jewish angst shit dozens of times before from Bellow and Updike. Well, fuck them. I'm going to up the ante so far it's going to send the Jewish novel disappearing up its arse for years to come. Did diddums Saulie have a dose of Oedipal guilt when he heard his mama do a poopie? Well, get this. Did I tell you about the time I whacked off into my baseball mitt while I was on the bus? That's more like it. And then I shoved some tuna paste on my fingers and jerked off imagining they'd been in the Holy Sophie's cunt. Suck on that, Johnny.

I took the Monkey to Italy. Sorry, I haven't mentioned her before. She's the long-legged shiksa model who used to be married to the elderly rich goy who liked to shit on a glass table over a schwartze while she ate a banana. Hence Monkey. Her real name is Mary Jane Reed and she's a thinly disguised caricature of my alter ego's first wife. Put the id back into Yid. Revenge really is best served cold.

'You've made me as degraded as you,' she yelled after we'd just had a threesome with an Italian whore. I don't think so. You degraded yourself in your pointless search for love with a Jew. We don't do love. We just do guilt and shame. It was you who got the whore in and you who ate her pussy. Not saying I minded, I wasn't going to look a gift horse and all that. But I couldn't even get my shlong hard. Imagine it. You wait 33 years for a threesome and you can do zilch.

That's the story of my life. My friend Arnie took me to see this shiksa, Bubbles. We were 15 years old and were on to a sure thing. For the first time I was going to shoot my load into a wet cunt rather than my sister's cotton panties. 'I'll give you 50 strokes,' she says. 'Please go on,' I beg. 'No.' I take my shlong in my hand and think of my mother. My wad almost blinds me.

I wanted to do the right thing, I wanted to be good. I'm a goddam human rights attorney in New York city. But I'm ruled by pussy. I yearn for it, can't believe my luck at some of the glorious muff that comes my ugly, long-nosed way, but I treat it badly. I guess only my mother's would really do. 'I'm gonna kill myself if you don't marry me,' the Monkey says.

She can do what she likes, I thought, as I left Italy and headed for Israel. This was to be the start of my real life, a life among real Jews. I met Naomi, a six-foot commando in fatigues. I had to fuck her. What if I had caught syph from the whore and gave it to her? 'You Diasporic Jews are pathetic and impotent,' she says. 'I wouldn't let you fuck me even if you could get an erection. You can shove your psychoneurotic American Jewishness.'

'Your six hours are up, Mr Roth,' Dr Spielvogel said. 'I'll see you at the same time in your next book.'

FEAR AND LOATHING IN LAS VEGAS

Hunter S. Thompson

W<small>E WERE SOMEWHERE</small> on the edge of the desert when the drugs took hold. The sky was full of screaming bats and my attorney, the Samoan, was pouring beer on his chest. I hit the brakes on the Great Red Shark. 'You drive,' I said. No point mentioning the bats. The bastard would see them soon enough.

There was still 100 miles to go and we had to get to Vegas by 4pm to claim our press suite for the Mint 400. A New York magazine had taken care of the reservations and the editor had given me $300 in expenses which I'd already spent on two bags of grass, five sheets of acid, 75 hits of mescaline, a salt-shaker of cocaine, a galaxy of uppers, downers and screamers and a bottle of ether in LA before we left.

It was the Samoan who saw the hitchhiker and said: 'Let's give this Okie a lift.' The kid got in and started talking. 'What's the story?' he asked. I took a half dozen tabs mixed with a few black bombers and shot a gram of scag into my eyeball.

'What's the motherfuckin' story?' I laughed. 'There is no motherfuckin' story. We are the fuckin' story. This is gonzo, pal. We're chasing the American Dream. Right to the motherfuckin' end of the rainbow.'

The kid looked freaked and we dumped him on the edge of Vegas. The Samoan pulled out a .357 Magnum and put it to my head. 'As your attorney, I strongly advise you to drive to the hotel at top speed,' he yelled, pumping 27 amyls and a quart of tequila into his aorta. 'And don't even think of trying to outdo me on the narcs again.'

'What are your names?' the clerk inquired, as the Great Red Shark skidded to a halt by the front reception after smashing through the hotel's plate-glass doors.

'What's it matter?' I cried. 'Call me Mr Thompson. Call me Raoul Duke. Call me Dr Gonzo. Just give me the goddam room.'

We went upstairs and threw the bag full of drugs on the bed. I eyed up the Samoan, before pulling out a blade and chopping my arm off and ramming some mescaline and ether into the stump. 'I warned you,' my attorney said, amputating his leg and plunging a speedball into his femoral artery. We'd already been awake for three days, and hours and hours of catatonic despair lay ahead.

'We ain't gonna make the dune race,' the Samoan said, 'ain't got the Vincent Black Shadow and no one can see shit in that dustbowl anyway.'

The snakes were freaking me out. But not as much as the polar bears or the girls doing their Friends of Debbie Reynolds impressions by the slots. Maybe I needed to go easy on the psychedelics. I called Timothy Leary and Allen Ginsberg but they were too whacked out to answer, so I took a fistful of downers.

'Don't wimp out on me,' the Samoan yelled, turning 'Sympathy for the Devil' up to 11 on the radio and ripping open my guts to pump out the barbs. 'This is serious counter-cultural satire. This is the Seventies, man. The hippies have flaked and the reactionaries have won. There ain't no reality more twisted than Nixon's American Dream. So don't get real, get surreal. I'll see you when I've sodomised a teenager.'

My head started spinning and vomit seeped from my neck through a hole in the windpipe. I was fucked. The magazine was gonna kill me for not finding out who won the motherfuckin' race, the hotel was gonna have my ass for credit card fraud and the police were gonna bust me. I had to do a runner. I chopped off my head, blew a couple of quarts of nitrous oxide into my lungs and headed for the lobby.

'There's a telegram for you, Dr Gonzo,' the clerk said.

It was from the attorney. We had a new story. A story about a story. A story about a story about us covering the District Attorneys' narcotics convention at the Moonlight Hotel. Unlimited money. A brand new Caddy, the White Whale.

'So you made it?' said the Samoan, slicing open a live hobo and removing his adrenal gland. 'Fancy some adrenochrome?' Another five months of being insane. What the fuck. Why not? I took out the .357 Magnum and blew away an iguana before blowing a hole in my arm. 'Best way in,' I laughed.

This gonzo shit was wearing thin. Sure, we went to the DA's convention and found they knew jack shit about drugs. Everyone knows marijuana's just for stoner losers. Sure, we got the locals a bit pissed at us on the freeway. Sure, we kited some cheques and did more drugs. Sure, we fooled the chambermaid into thinking we were undercover cops. What better cover was there than a pair of drug fiends? Sure, I bought an ape. But it was all getting a bit tired, a bit predictable. I tried writing in a new format.

Duke: We're looking for the
American Dream.
Waitress: It's down by the Old
Psychiatrists' Club.

That didn't work either. The only people left reading were a few old *Rolling Stone* heads who still thought that sex 'n' drugs 'n' rock 'n' roll were gonna change the world. I had to get out of Vegas. I chopped off my remaining limbs, grinding the last of the drugs into the open wounds, bounced my torso into the front seat of the White Whale and raced a DC8 down the runway.

– 1973 –

CRASH

J. G. Ballard

V AUGHAN DIED YESTERDAY in his last car-crash. Driven on a
collision course towards the limousine of the film actress
Elizabeth Taylor with whom he had dreamed of dying for so long,
his car jumped the rails of the London Airport flyover and
plunged into a bus of tourists.

As I knelt over Vaughan's body, I remembered the vision he
had had of her death; compound fractures of the thighs impacted
on the handbrake mounting, wounds to the genitalia, her uterus
pierced by the heraldic beak of the manufacturer's marque.

Before his death, Vaughan had taken part in many crashes,
where blood had spilled from open wounds while semen jerked
from his mutilated penis and the seats were smeared with
excrement. For him the car-crash and his sexuality were fused into
a techno-erotic dystopia of twisted metal, punctured lungs and
natal clefts drenched in blood and rectal mucus. I guess you get
the picture.

I began to understand the sexual excitements of the car-crash
for myself when I first met Vaughan shortly after coming out of
hospital. I had been admitted with multiple fractures to my legs
after my car had hit the central reservation of the Western Avenue
and hit a saloon travelling in the opposite direction, instantly
propelling the driver through the windscreen and into the path of
a lorry which crushed his torso under its wheels, leaving his wife
catatonic by the wayside.

For many weeks I had lain in the empty ward that was
normally reserved for air-crash victims at Ashford Hospital,

squeezing the pus from my wounds and trying to stir my penis into life. From time to time my wife Catherine would visit. She worked at the airport and I could smell the rancid semen of the many airline pilots she would take as lovers on her fingers.

'Tell me about your encounters,' I would ask as she idly gave my penis a Chinese burn.

'I had 10 men penetrating me inside the silver phallic fuselage,' she would say, yawning, before tearing open my stitches. I bit off her nipples and my penis jerked into life, entering her natal cleft still sticky with the other men's stale ejaculate. We rutted a while, looking out of different windows, before petering out in a tired orgasm.

'This isn't working, James,' she said.

'I know,' I replied. 'But I'm only any good at creating dystopian worlds. I can't do character development so we're resigned to pretty much repeating the same kind of pointlessly shocking sexual behaviour for the next 150 pages.'

My head spun with graphic images of bowels opened by chromium tail-fins and clitorises severed on instrument binnacles etc, etc, in the days before I went home. 'There's some man watching me,' I said while Catherine lubricated my penis with engine coolant as I slit her perineum to make a single orifice in which to insert a carburettor.

'They sure as hell aren't reading you any more,' she replied, as pitiful globules of semen dripped from my glans.

Within days of getting home, I rented a car identical to the one in which I had nearly died. And once Catherine had left for the airport to have sex with 93 masked BOAC pilots, I took Renata, an assistant with whom I had been having an affair at the advertising agency where I worked, for a drive.

'Oh Mr Ballard, do you really think Elizabeth Taylor will appear in one of our car ads?' she enquired.

I smiled as I saw a look of bemused recognition cross the readers' faces as they realised that I was a meta-fictional persona of the author. Satisfied that I was now in a work of cutting-edge postmodernism rather than a one-dimensional X-rated piece of sci-fi, I gunned the accelerator and steered the car out of my suburban Shepperton semi on to the Western Avenue. As we reached the roundabout where I nearly died, I placed Renata's hand on my scarred thighs, while forcing my fist into her natal cleft, both of us juddering with excitement as we orgasmed simultaneously as the car sideswiped a cyclist.

'There you are, Mr Ballard,' said the man who had been following me. 'I'm Vaughan. I'd like your help in meeting Elizabeth Taylor.'

Vaughan took me to a yard full of tangled car wrecks. In one corner, with the help of a stunt driver named Seagrave and a crippled woman called Gabrielle, Vaughan had staged re-enactments of the crashes in which James Dean and Jayne Mansfield had been killed. All the car seats were coated with thick layers of semen and vaginal mucus. Also at the scene was Helen Rimington, the widow of the man I had killed. Wordlessly she got in my car, and as we approached the scene of an accident where five babies had been thrown through the windscreen with another impaled on the instrument binnacle, she allowed me to sodomise her vigorously, etc, etc.

I felt as if I was chained to treadmill. My prose had limited itself to merely repeating phrases, such as 'natal cleft', 'instrument binnacle', 'stale semen' and 'severed clitoris' as the plot stagnated in a pool of putrid bodily fluids, minatorily extruded through disfigured orifices.

'You seem to have forgotten you are a cog in a powerful exegesis on how normal sexual relations become alienated by the cold steel of technology,' Vaughan said.

I had to confess I hadn't been aware this was necessarily that interesting or valid an idea, but such was the spell under which Vaughan had put me that first I took Gabrielle for a drive, forcing my erect penis deep into the scar tissue on her legs as we ran over

12 pedestrians on a zebra crossing. And then, after I had told Vaughan that Elizabeth Taylor had withdrawn from negotiations for the advert, I allowed him to brutalise two airport whores in the back of my car before consenting to let him sodomise me as we drove on to the runway and ploughed into a jumbo jet.

Returning home with Vaughan's semen still flowing from my anus, I found Catherine in a state of trauma. Earlier that day Vaughan had strapped her to the bonnet of a sports car and repeatedly forced a pilot to penetrate her natal cleft with the nose cone of his aircraft, while he had sex with the decomposing bodies of women who had died in a multiple car crash the week before. On dropping Catherine home, he had stolen our car and tried to run her over.

I knew then he was in danger of losing his mind and it was no surprise to find him a week later, lying dead in a twisted heap of sheared metal and semen after his failed attempt to drive his car into Elizabeth Taylor's. But as I wiped his semen on to my own penis, I was already designing my own next car-crash. Of a novel.

THE MEMOIRS OF A SURVIVOR

Doris Lessing

We ALL REMEMBER the time. It was no different for me than it was for the others. Yet we tell each other over and over again the particularities of the things we shared. Usually in high-flown overwrought imagery. We learned about it, not from newscasts tainted with the Authority of They, but from casual conversations on the street. But I shall return to the it later.

I shall start before the it, in a time of generalised unease. I was living in a decaying block of flats – the vertical streets of the poor – where the walls were stained with urine. Most people had already left the city for the north and only a few of us remained; public services had stopped and only gangs of youngsters roamed the streets.

Days would pass with me staring at the walls, listening to the noises of my neighbours, until one day I realised I could no longer hear familiar sounds. I say realise, but it was more a dividing of the self brought on by immersion in the largely discredited works of R. D. Laing, and as my consciousness began to split so I discovered I could pass through walls to reveal dreary – yet oddly portentous – echoes of a childhood.

The first time I walked through a wall, I did not get very far. But as I got used to it I travelled further. Though to no great effect as I had acquired the knack of being both immensely forgetful and entirely incurious about my new paranormal powers.

The child was left with me in this way. I was in the kitchen smoking a cigarette when a man appeared with a 12-year-old girl. 'This is Emily Cartwright,' he said. 'Look after her.' With that he left. I suppose a rather more engaged character might have asked why on earth a stranger might think I would be pleased to have a girl live with me, but instead I chose to wander off through a few more walls.

She was still there when I got back and I noticed she was stroking an ugly dog with a cat's head. 'I'm afraid I've probably had too much acid, too,' Emily said sadly. 'His name is Hugo.'

Emily did nothing for the first few weeks she was living with me, save wash her clothes, do the ironing and tidy the flat. I had never met a more indolent child. From this you can infer I had in fact never met any children. Even on my many journeys through the walls. In many ways, however, it was an idyllic time. Though I knew we would have to leave the flat at some point soon, there had been no new gangs appearing from the south, the trees were heavy with blossom, and she and I would sit by the window, criticising everything we saw and shouting 'What a fuckin' liberty,' at every passer-by.

As I wandered through rooms meeting various children who could have been Emily or myself in a regressive state – I was never really interested enough to find out for certain – I noticed that Emily had made herself hugely fat by stuffing herself with sticky buns. It was at this time that Janet, our neighbour's daughter and her only companion – occasional at that – dumped her. I can't say I was surprised.

The seasons passed. Snow, rain, wind, we had them all, though I barely went out other than to buy a dead rat for my tea. After passing though many walls once more, I returned to find Hugo moping by the window: Emily had crossed the street to visit the commune run by an unprepossessing 22-year-old named Gerald.

She returned a few hours later, having lost all the weight she had gained. 'Come and meet my new friends, Hugo,' she said. The cat-dog wagged his tail enthusiastically, yet within minutes Emily had been forced to bring him home once more as the commune had laughed at his ugliness and had threatened to eat him.

For a while Emily chose to remain at home with Hugo as I continued to divide myself by passing through many walls to witness childhood scenes that made little impact on my expanding inner consciousness. Yet after one particularly strenuous trans-mural excursion that left me as emotionally dead as ever, I came back to find that Emily had spent the night with Gerald.

Again I suppose that perhaps I should have been more concerned that a now 13-year-old girl was having sex with a man in his 20s, yet as a dissociated proto-feminist I chose rather to rejoice in the liberation of her budding sexuality. However, her liaison was not entirely without its difficulties as Gerald proved to be of a philandering nature and was shagging every pre-pubescent that moved.

It is also time, I feel, to explain what the 'it' was that had reduced the country to a state of post-apocalyptic chaos. Yet try as I do, I still cannot put my finger on it. So just assume it was something like a world war, for above all this is a book of ideas. Or rather, one idea endlessly repeated. They – the rulers – always liked to tell us They were still in charge and from time to time the police would round up the passing stragglers, yet we all knew it was inevitable that everything went even more pear-shaped.

Within six months, a large group of feral teenagers had moved into our area and many of us were to afraid to go out. Emily and Gerald, though, made a point of befriending them and one afternoon Emily brought home a working-class 11-year-old called June. None of us had ever met a working-class girl before and she was not nearly as scary as we expected , though Emily was rather put out when Gerald started sleeping with June instead of her. For my part, I was too detached to care about the nature of the abuse: rather, I just assumed that June too must be a feminist.

During the time when Gerald and June were involved with one another, Emily came back to me and Hugo, and took us through the walls and upstairs to the rooms above. This was the first time I had ever left the Neanderthal reaches of my ground-floor consciousness where I had become both the Walrus and the Eggman and I was amazed to find the upper floors full of a better class of person buying fecund livestock and fresh produce from heavily laden market stalls. Though not as amazed as you, I'd guess.

It wasn't long before Gerald also tired of June, as he had set his heart on nurturing the lost children and making them part of his commune. Emily was happy to help him in this, though his pleasure was lessened by the fact that she had now reasserted her feminine superiority and was refusing to have sex with him again.

How strong she seemed in comparison with the pathetic Gerald! And how Hugo responded to her loyalty by curling his deformed cat-dog body into her lap. By now I had already lost sight of the physical Emily – not that I'd ever really noticed it anyway – and as the police led the feral children away and she took my hand and led me and Hugo through another hole in the wall, I was willing to relinquish my last tenuous grasp on reality and step out of the book for ever. To everyone's relief.

ZEN AND THE ART OF MOTORCYCLE MAINTENANCE

Robert M. Pirsig

E VEN AT 60 miles an hour the wind is warm as I weave the
bike along the roads less travelled towards the Dakota
mountains. I am channelling the universe, at one with my
megalomania, as my 12-year-old son, Chris, hangs on for grim
death.

'Why are we doing this?' he asks later that evening at the
campsite.

'To showcase my brilliance,' I reply.

'I'd rather go to Disneyworld.'

'That's because you are driven by your ego.'

I read a few pages of Thoreau out loud because it is so much
more important for Chris to hear something he does not
understand, before checking through my rucksack for the 17th
time that day and tinkering with the spark-plugs. John and Sylvia,
who arrived ahead of us, come over for a chat.

'My bike is making an odd noise,' he says.

'You need to adjust the tappets, novice,' I declare.

I am wasting my valuable breath, so I begin the first of what I
grandiosely call my Chautauquas – my philosophical digressions.
John and Sylvia are romantics, terrified of modern technology and
unwilling to engage with the dualism of the carburettor-points
split. While I tend towards the more rational classical position, I

have also learned to view the world through my all-seeing Middle Eye of the Buddha.

Sylvia nudges John awake and suggests we get something to eat.

'I don't feel well,' Chris says.

'You will never feel well until you subsume your egotism to mine,' I snap. 'Now sod off while I amaze myself with my genius.'

After he has made his way snivelling to his tent, I launch into yet another fascinating Chautauqua on the *a priori* presumption of a motorcycle before explaining to John that the doctor has diagnosed Chris with a severe mental illness.

'I'm not surprised with you as a dad,' John mutters.

'That's the typical response of the Unenlightened Romantic,' I reply, levitating with the self-congratulation of the logic of my Oneness. My Chautauquas accelerate with increasing intensity and depth as I expose the internal fallacies of Newtonian physics and pour scorn on the solipsistic abyss of the ramblings of Hegel and Hume.

I adjust the fuel-flow to harmonise the bike with the altitude and, as we pull into Bozeman, John and Sylvia inexplicably decide to head off on their own. I realise later I could have done more to flesh out their characters, but to have done so would have been to give them an existence independent of my own which, dialectically speaking, would have negated their reality as I alone am the Maker.

The ghost of Phaedrus hangs heavy but I take refuge in Mu, where existence and non-existence meet in Japanese Nothingness. I take Chris to meet DeWeese, a former colleague at the Bozeman campus where I taught.

'I'm bored,' Chris yawns.

'I'm doing this for the benefit of your ego,' I snap tetchily.

Who is Phaedrus? I hear you ask. He is my alter ego, the Searcher I once was before I was crushed by a world that was not ready for my IQ and was forced to undergo electro-convulsive therapy. The Spirit of Chautauqua strengthens as Aquarius aligns with Mars amid the acid casualties' Imagined Enlightenment and Phaedrus addresses his students.

'How can we know the Meaning of Quality?' he enquires rhetorically. 'Quality is of itself something we all intuitively know. So I'm going to stop marking your essays.'

'Isn't that a peculiarly narrow, US-centric view?' no one says. 'For is not the idea of Quality culturally relative?'

'You are too clever to teach at Bozeman,' the Dean declares. 'Grow a beard and go to Chicago.'

Exhausted by the originality of my latest Chautauqua, I race Chris to the summit of a desolate Montana peak.

'I'm scared,' he says.

'It's your ego that makes you such a wuss.'

Phaedrus distils the canon of western philosophical thought, showing up Plato, Aristotle, Locke, Nietzsche, Poincaré and the rest of them for the brainless halfwits they undoubtedly are as he tap-dances through the conundra of the substantive and methodological fields to emerge in the Elysian fields of Zen, where Quality is undefinable yet self-evident.

'But surely for something to be self-evident yet undefinable is a logical contradiction in terms,' Chris says, scratching his head, searching hopelessly for some self-evident Quality in the book.

'Your ego is still blinding you to the truth,' I say. 'Do you not realise that Phaedrus is Greek for Wolf?'

'Um, no, it isn't,' he answers.

'It is if I say it is. OK, buddy?'

I change the oil and tinker with the chain for several days before we complete our journey to the Pacific coast. I sense that memories of Phaedrus are tormenting Chris in his sleep and I long to merge our three selves in a Monist Trinity. We symbolically remove our helmets for the first time, high on the cliff overlooking the ocean.

The voice of Phaedrus weakens, the Socratic dialectic finally resolved in a half-arsed, pseudo-intellectual mish-mash of western and eastern philosophy.

I take Chris in my arms. 'Close your eyes, my son, and soar with me beyond the world of Kant.'

'You'll always be a Kant to me, Dad.'

THE HISTORY MAN

Malcolm Bradbury

RENEWED FIGHTING IN Vietnam, trouble on the Falls Road. Everywhere new developments, new indignities. In this uncertain climate, on the first day of term, the Kirks, a couple of the present, have decided to have a party. Not just any party; a party that is so genuinely unstructured, it needs its own five-year plan.

Howard is a sociologist at Watermouth University, a liberated consciousness-conscious Marxist with a wide intellectual constituency of Maoists, squatters and inconspicuous consumers. Barbara, too, is radical in her own way. She campaigns for teenaged girls to be given the Pill and sends food parcels to IRA hunger strikers.

But history has not been as kind to Barbara as it has to Howard. Since they met at Leeds University in the late 1950s, Howard has gone on to become the darling of the left after his book on the paternalistic dialectics of his own marriage – not that he or other academics would have defined its theoretical construct so narrowly – and, after writing a number of comment pieces for the *Guardian*, he has spent the summer on his own – apart from his regular Wednesday afternoon horizontal explorations of R. D. Laing's Marxist-Freudian theory of the sexual dynamics of female undergraduates – writing his latest book, *The Defeat of Privacy*.

After giving birth to two not entirely wanted children, Barbara has found her consciousness-raising activities somewhat curtailed. Yet after a number of affairs, which have seen their marriage revered as the iconic apotheosis of 1970s liberation, and by taking deliberately non-exploitative advantage of the childcare opportunities offered by Howard's bra-less Sandinistas – 'it would be wrong to dishonour their effort with a bourgeois financial transaction' – she has begun to spread her wings a little and, on occasion, she now goes to London for a 'wicked weekend' where she indulges in a little shopping at Biba and a lot of sex with drama students half her age.

The party is now in full swing. Howard toys with his Zapata moustache as he moves from room to room, nodding approvingly at the effortless rising of Kundalini amongst those smoking pot and having group sex. There is one woman he doesn't know, who introduces herself as Miss Callendar, a new member of the English faculty. 'Tell me,' he asks, 'where do you stand on the permanent revolution of existential thought?' 'I'm just a 19th-century liberal,' she says, 'who happens to be interested in story.'

Story is something that should occupy Howard more. He has already read enough of *The History Man* to understand that he is just a vehicle satire, a man of indefatigable false consciousness, and that as such his character will remain shallow and un-developed. But then, perhaps satire has its own historical inevitability and there is something to be said for starring in the definitive campus novel.

'I would like to show you my semiotics,' he purrs.

'I don't think so, Mr Kirk,' Miss Callender replies.

She leaves and he retires to his basement study, where a third-year student, Felicity Phee, is reading a manuscript of *The Defeat of Privacy*. 'You are invading my privacy,' he says. 'I'm no longer a lesbian,' she replies, and he reluctantly unzips his flies to release his means of production, looking up to the skylight to see Miss Callendar looking down. What he doesn't notice, because people like Howard never do, is the desperation of his old friend Henry Beamish, with whose wife Myra Howard once slept, as he puts his arm though the bathroom window.

The next morning Howard reasserts his feminist cultural

identity by leaving the washing up to Barbara and drives towards the campus, stopping en route at the flat of Flora Beniform, senior lecturer in developmental psychology, for an intellectual and fluid exchange.

'What did you make of Henry's injury?' she asks.

'It was an accident,' he says.

'For someone who believes in historical determinism, you can be remarkably stupid,' she answers, as he deterministically writhes on top of her. 'If you want to see me again, I have a half-hour diary slot on Thursday evening.'

The constant heavy-handed juxtaposition of theory and practice might have wearied some readers who have long since got the point, but the dialectics of satire are unforgiving, so now we must follow Howard to the social science faculty, where he is to be found furthering his own ends with a conspiracy about a proposed guest lecture by the racist geneticist, Professor Mangel, before rearranging the bourgeois furniture construct of teacher and taught for his first seminar of the term on normative theories of reductive consensus.

'You are an anal fascist,' he shouts at Mr Carmody, an unfortunate be-blazered student, who has dared to write out an essay – an essay laced with Weberian imperialist assumptions – in full. 'You have failed the course.'

Mr Carmody is unhappy about both his marks and this treatment, and complains to Professor Marvin, the head of department, and in due course Howard is summoned to his office to explain himself.

'Carmody is a neo-Nazi,' Howard says. 'He deserves to fail.'

'Yes, yes,' Marvin replies. 'He is an inadequate student, but I have read his papers and I feel he is a borderline pass.'

'Then that just shows the limitations of subjectivity.'

With the kind of relentless satirical determinism the reader has come to expect, the book follows its course through comedy and pathos, through departmental set-pieces and Barbara's unhappiness, to its inexorable conclusion with Carmody accusing Howard of gross moral turpitude for his relationship with Felicity.

Howard, of course, shrugs off such charges with his usual liberal panache. Partly this is because he knows that much as Bradbury mocks the emptiness of sociology, he also secretly admires it and himself longs for the applause of its self-congratulation. But mainly because he knows that Bradbury is an English academic and that there is nothing more historically inevitable in modern fiction than a psychologically unconvincing catharsis to bring about a desired conclusion.

'I'm aware I'm the only one who's stood as a mirror to your flawed radicalism throughout the novel,' says Miss Callendar. 'But for no apparent reason, I have now decided to sleep with you and defend you against dismissal from the university.'

So there we must leave Watermouth. Carmody's departure from the university goes unnoticed by all, while Howard continues to dazzle. But there is time for one more piece of historic inevitability, the fictive symmetery. So as the pages come to an end, we see the Kirks having yet another party. Only this time it's Barbara who puts her arm through the bathroom window.

QUARTET IN AUTUMN

Barbara Pym

T HAT DAY THE four of them went to the library at different times. Edwin had come to look through *Crockford*'s, Norman to be nearer to the British Museum, and Marcia, now that she, like the others, was nearing retirement, to find out whether she was eligible for free chiropody. Letty was the only one among them who actually enjoyed reading, but she had chosen to go later so that she could eat her lunch in silence and avoid contact with people. Not that the other three would have spoken amongst themselves, but it was simpler to avoid the embarrassment of avoiding one another.

'Did you have a dull luncheon break?' asked Edwin, when the others returned to the office.

'Yes, thank you,' they replied. 'We did absolutely nothing of any interest.'

'How most satisfactory. Shall we have tea and biscuits while we wait for the delivery of paperclips?'

They drifted into companionable silence with Edwin contemplating how he was going to broach the tricky subject of the unfortunate choice of hymns at last night's evensong with Father G. and Marcia wondering what Mr Strong, the nice consultant who had performed her mastectomy last year, would be wearing for her next appointment. Letty vaguely wondered what Norman was thinking and was on the point of asking him when she decided she couldn't be bothered. It was probably as well, for Norman was, as ever, thinking of nothing.

'Do you think we can go through this entire book in a state of complete ironic detachment from one another?' asked Letty several weeks later. None of the others replied, for to do so would have implied a level of emotional commitment they were unwilling to make. Instead, Marcia announced she was going home because she had heard there might be someone run over by a car in her street.

How most unfortunate that poor soul was not instantly killed, thought Marcia, as she entered her semi-detached south London home. She checked to make sure her prized collection of plastic carrier bags and empty milk bottles was in good order before the sound of the doorbell interrupted her.

'Hello,' said a fresh-faced young woman. 'I'm Janice, a social worker. I'm here to make sure that mad old bats like you are feeding themselves properly.' 'Yes,' Marcia replied, before slamming the door and adding, 'What a fucking liberty.'

Edwin had spent the weekend busy-bodying himself in church affairs, congratulating himself on his effortless superiority over the other three, while Norman had sat in his bedsit waiting for his son to call him on the telephone. At five o' clock precisely the phone had indeed rung, as it did at that time every Sunday and, just as he always did, Norman ignored it and went for a walk near the children's playground. Letty had visited her old friend Marjorie.

'I'm afraid you won't be able to live with me when you retire,' Marjorie had said, 'because I'm going to marry the vicar.' Letty said nothing in reply because there was nothing to say. Though inwardly she was not greatly upset by this turn of events.

'And what did you, Marcia?' Letty asked, as they shared a Rich Tea biscuit after a gruelling morning doing nothing very much in the office. Marcia pretended not to hear and carried on eating in silence.

'The two girls are retiring next week,' Edwin said to Norman. 'I suppose we had better organise a bottle of Cyprus Sherry and some plastic flowers.'

Letty and Marcia had been overwhelmed by the generosity of

their send-off and looked forward to their first day of retirement. Letty had initially forgotten she was no longer required to sit in an office stacking pencils and had got up early and taken the train into the centre of London before realising her mistake. What a silly billy I am, she thought. By the time she got back her house had been bought by a colourful Nigerian vicar.

Oh, dear, she thought, I fear he will be a little too Nigerian and colourful for me.

Janice had decided she ought to look in on Marcia again as she had looked a bit frail and had not changed her clothes in months. She rang the doorbell. Marcia saw her from the window and ignored her. 'What a fucking liberty,' she said to herself before checking her milk bottle collection once more. She was outraged to find an odd bottle from the Unigate dairy. It must have been the one that Letty had left. What a fucking liberty, she thought.

'I suppose we should arrange a reunion lunch for the girls,' Edwin said to Norman. 'I guess so,' Norman replied. 'As long as they pay.' The lunch at the Rendezvous Greasy Spoon was not an unmitigated success. Marcia had thrust the empty milk bottle into Letty's hands and refused to eat anything. Yet there had been an upside. Edwin had realised the vicar might be a little too Nigerian and colourful for Letty and had arranged for her to stay in the downstairs toilet of Mrs Pope, an acquaintance of his from the Parochial Church Council.

Norman had noticed Marcia was looking thin and had vaguely wondered if her cancer had returned. He even took the underground to visit her but once he reached her street he decided he couldn't really be bothered. Marcia had spotted him hanging around outside her house and was grateful he hadn't knocked as it saved her the effort of not answering.

'It's a shame we're stuck in a novel of deterministic, alienated old age,' Norman said to Edwin, 'as it might have been more interesting had we been allowed to develop as characters.' Edwin did not reply as he had fallen asleep.

Janice was perturbed she could not hear the sounds of Marcia ignoring her knocking. She pushed open the door to find Marcia unconscious. In the ambulance, Marcia thought it was shame she hadn't died, but fortunately death did not detain her for too long and she passed away in hospital a few days later.

'That was a nice funeral,' said Edwin. 'It's wonderful to see a service so sparsely attended.'

'I'm amazed that Marcia left me her house,' Norman replied. The others said nothing, for this was indeed one of the most unlikely pieces of plotting they could have imagined. 'But I imagine I will sell it because it's a bit rubbish and I prefer my bed-sit.'

'Marjorie's vicar has called off the engagement and she's invited me to live with her,' Letty said. 'But I don't think I will.'

They sat back in the hearse in silence, each one thinking of a future suddenly fecund with possibilities, where anything might happen. But almost certainly wouldn't.

STAYING ON

Paul Scott

WHEN TUSKER SMALLEY died of a massive coronary on the last Monday in April 1972, his wife Lucy was having her blue-rinse set by Susy in the Seraglio Room on the ground floor of the Shiraz, Pankot's new five-star hotel. His body might have lain unnoticed for longer than half-an-hour had not his dog's howling disturbed Mrs Lila Bhoolabhoy, the owner of Smith's, the hill station's rather older hotel in whose lodge the Smalleys resided. Unable to deal with the situation, due both to her great status and vast size, she despatched her husband to complain.

Mr Francis Bhoolabhoy had been running the hotel for several years before Mrs Bhoolabhoy decided to make him her third husband. Though delighted at this unexpected conferring of wealth, and occasionally heartened to be summoned to his wife's bedroom to arouse her passion, his greatest pleasure was reserved for Monday nights when he and his good friend Tusker met over a bottle at the hotel.

Yet Billy Boy, as Tusker chose to call him, was not looking forward to this evening's encounter after his wife had earlier forced him to write a letter terminating the Smalleys' lease, a missive that the servant Ibrahim had delivered, and his wife's latest command merely brought forward that awkward situation.

Tusker had first been taken seriously ill some months earlier, but had refused to go to hospital with a swift 'bugger bed', choosing instead to tackle head on the débâcle of the uncut grass.

'Day Barkle? Night Barkle? Yes, Sahib,' muttered Ibrahim, uncomfortably aware that many of the Indian characters seemed to have been lifted off the set of *It Ain't Half Hot Mum*, yet unable to stop himself.

For her part, Lucy wondered whether she and Tusker had not also been set up as comedic expat stereotypes, he the old Colonel unable to utter much more than a laconic 'Ha!' and she his put-upon wife, but for the moment her mind was on other things. She recognised Tusker was on borrowed time and was keen both to save him distress and to make sure their affairs were in order.

'See if you can get us another *mali* to cut the grass,' she ordered Ibrahim. 'But don't let Tusker know I'm paying for it.'

'Harrumph! Things aren't what they used to be,' Tusker grumbled. 'Make me a poached egg before I have a snifter with Billy Boy, Luce old girl!'

'Oh look, Tusker, I've had a nice letter from the Laytons in England harking back to events in *The Raj Quartet*,' said Lucy, 'and they've asked if we can have a good friend of theirs, a Mr Turner, to stay. He's interested in talking to people who stayed on.'

'Bugger Britain! Bugger *The Raj Quartet*!'

Lucy allowed Tusker to continue expleting to himself, for Mr Turner's imminent arrival allowed her time to tell the story of her relationship with her husband and to develop her own stream of consciousness technique whereby she would imagine herself to be having a conversation with Mr Turner while only delivering the bare minimum by way of punctuation and paragraphing. So, Mr Turner, since you mention it, I would have liked to have come back to England after the war but Tusker scuppered that choosing instead to become a box wallah in Bombay, holding back like he always had done, especially that time he denied me the opportunity to perform as an understudy, but that's not the worst of it though I can't mention what the worst of it was because I'm holding that back for nearer the end.

'Enough of that muttering to yourself, old girl!' Tusker growled. 'Isn't it time for our big set-piece?'

'You've held me back all your life, never even thinking about how the other wives looked down on me for knowing shorthand, and we're both getting on now so I need to know how I will be provided for if you go before me. Worst of all, we don't even know any white people as all your friends are black.'

'You're pissed, Luce old girl.'

Mr Bhoolabhoy had watched enviously as Lucy's character developed from Mrs Tufton Bufton to something more tragic in the space of 40 pages. Yet even though he too was now to be allowed his moment in the sun, he understood his role was to remain a figure of fun.

'You may service me tonight, Management,' Mrs Bhoolabhoy had said, unpinning her sari to reveal her sweaty rolls of flesh.

'Very well, Ownership,' he had replied, surprised to find he had the stirrings of an erection.

'That's all. You may go now,' she said distractedly once he had finished. 'I have to meet my accountant to finalise the deal to join the Shiraz Consortium.'

Mr Bhoolabhoy should have been pleased to have been released from this humiliating encounter, but as he made his way to the churchyard he realised there was to be no respite even in introspection as Scott turned his thoughts to visions of Susy's bottom as she played the organ and Kama Sutric memories of his night of passion with a good-time dancer in Ranpur. The guilt, the guilt! And now the guilt of knowing his wife was planning to throw the Colonel Sahib and Mrs Smalley out of their home to develop the Shiraz.

'You quite surprised me in the churchyard,' said Lucy, resuming the mantle of narration. 'You see, Mr Turner, I was a vicar's daughter working for a law firm in London when I first met Tusker, he was visiting from India and he seemed so exotic and accomplished and I envisioned a proper military wedding but it was not to be and I've since come to realise he is a man quite without ambition and after he retired from his box-wallah job in Bombay ten years ago, we returned to Pankot where we've been hanging on ever since.

Lucy returned to the lodge to find a letter from Tusker.

Dear Old Girl, you asked me about your prospects, well, you will have a pension of £1,500 and there's £2,000 in the bank so you will be able to return to England if you want. I know you wanted to return but I always felt we didn't have enough money and I was too old to do anything new and too young to retire. You've been a good wife. Love, Tusker.

So Lucy held this, her only love letter from Tusker, to her bosom, just as Tusker had held the letter from Mr Bhoolabhoy to his as he fell to the ground.

Lucy's upper lip remained stiff as Tusker was interred. She thought back to the unmentionable thing that he had done, how he had spent the money that might have taken them home on gambling, drink and the fancy woman with the mildly racist name of Mrs Poppadoum. She thought too that it might be quite nice if she was to invite a coloured person to dinner for the first time. And then she thought she'd probably go back to Blighty.

PRAXIS

Fay Weldon

Praxis Duveen, at the age of five, sitting on Brighton beach. Her sullen sister, Hypatia, silent beside her. 'Nice kids,' said Henry Whitechapel, a First World War veteran, turned photographer, who would probably abuse them within 50 pages. 'We gave them Greek names,' said their mother, Lucy. 'Praxis means orgasm; Hypatia means erectile dysfunction.'

'We're stuck in a late-1970s feminist paradigm, you slut whore,' Ben Duveen shouted, clubbing Lucy before raping her. She lay inert, her legs spread wide. 'Go on then,' she yelled. 'Objectify me, Jew boy.' They parted soon after.

Here I am. Lost in paragraphs separated by double spacing. A lonely old woman. Condemned by the deterministic inevitability of my gender. Condemned by New Woman who flaunts her braless breasts. A murderess. And not just of literature.

Ben moved out. Henry Whitechapel moved in as a lodger. Sometimes he slept with Lucy when he and she were a bit bored. Sometimes he didn't. Sometimes he hit Praxis when he had trouble dealing with his patriarchal anger management issues. Sometimes he didn't. Sometimes he slept with the maid, Judith. Partly as an expression of class solidarity. Partly because he was a man. Lucy went into a mental hospital. Neither need really detain us again.

Praxis and Hypatia were looked after by the local vicar who exposed his erect penis to them. 'We should change their names to Pattie and Hilda,' said his wife. 'Except when we still call them Praxis and Hypatia.' Hilda was very clever. She bullied a lot of girls as head girl and went to Oxford. Pattie thought about becoming a lesbian with Laura.

I'm still very miserable. And an ex-con. Written off by a society that denigrates women. A society that makes old women invisible. That shoe-horns me into teaser chapters as a substitute for a dramatic narrative. I adjust my incontinence pads. I want to know if I am alive. I'm certainly not on the page.

'Come along to a party, you Dirty Jew, you Daughter of David.' Anti-Semitism wasn't a big deal then; certainly not as big a deal as anti-feminist feeling. So Praxis was happy to accept Irma's invitation. They were both at university, though Irma was more attractive. Willy got Praxis very drunk and invited her back to his unheated basement. His friend Phillip impaled her first. Praxis thought she loved him. Then he left her and Willy impaled her for the next three months. Willy was two years above her at university and when he graduated she decided to leave as well, because she had no control over her destiny.

Willy was actually very boring but Praxis didn't seem to mind. Or notice. She became very good at cooking and visiting her mother in the mental hospital. She did so out of duty, not love. Willy was very frugal and would sometimes call Praxis a whore. One day Praxis decided to become a whore though she didn't always remember to ask the men for money. Though she did usually remember to make them wear a French letter. Praxis had some very strict rules. Anyone could have sex with her providing she did not have an orgasm. One man did make her have an orgasm. He turned out to be her father. Praxis wondered if this was a bit weird but wasn't overly concerned. Willy got very angry when he found out she had been turning tricks. So she consulted the star, Betelgeuse, and left him.

It's me again. My kids hate me. I hate me. I hate the way I'm forced into writing sentence after banal dissociated sentence to sledgehammer home the mind-body split of the subjugated woman. You probably hate me too. If only you knew how much.

Irma had wanted to marry somebody famous. Instead she married Phillip who now made documentaries for the BBC that were acclaimed as politically correct even though they invariably featured pendulous naked breasts. Praxis stayed with them for a while before she married another dreary man called Ivor who worked in advertising. They went to live on a dreary suburban housing estate and had two dreary children. Praxis didn't much care for the house or the children. Or Ivor for that matter. That's because she was so alienated from her femininity. She did the washing and the cooking, though, and when necessary had abortions. As you did.

Dull inevitability had its limitations. But none of the characters seemed to have realised this. So Hypatia broke off from her virginal introspection and sent Ivor a letter saying Pattie had been a whore. Ivor was very upset to have got this letter the morning after they had ticked yet another of the symbolically sexist boxes of the 1960s by attending a swingers' party and asked Praxis if this was true. Having spent the night being used as a sex object by aspirant marketing executives, Praxis wasn't that bothered. So she left her husband and kids.

I'm not a fit mother. I'm not a fit or credible lead character. But I'm strangely happy. I bet you wish you were.

Praxis moved back to London and had sex with Phillip. Irma was a bit put out, so she cut her hair and moved into a women's refuge. Praxis moved in with Phillip and was as distant with his kids as she was with her own. She preferred to chat to Betelgeuse. Betelgeuse was surprisingly talkative. Praxis got a job in advertising and made a lot of money. Phillip still made films with naked breasts. Praxis would often allow men to touch her up or have sex with her. Sometimes she knew them, sometimes she didn't. Sometimes she worried about VD and unwanted pregnancies; sometimes she didn't. Sometimes, when she was feeling especially docile, she allowed herself to be buggered. She also continued to do the washing and cooking and told herself she loved Phillip. Until she found him in bed with Serena and he threw her out.

'Life is unfair,' Praxis said. 'No it isn't,' Irma replied. 'You've been a bitch all your life and now Phillip's been a bitch to you. If you really want to escape your pitiful subjugated life, you have to join the Women's Movement.'

Praxis went to the hospital where a young mother was facing a lifetime of misery having given birth to a mongoloid child. 'There,' Praxis said with great satisfaction, having smothered the semi-vegetable to death. 'You can now pursue your ambitions, having been freed of the need to conform to matriarchal stereotypes by wasting your life at home with the retard.'

That's it. That's the great crime I've been alluding to since the start. I hope you think the journey was worth it. I don't. But I do feel a sense of freedom, a sense of relief that the end is nigh. You should certainly be able to identify with that.

THE SEA, THE SEA

Iris Murdoch

THE SEA WHICH lies before me as I write glows rather than sparkles in the bland May sunshine. I had written this sentence, destined to be the opening line of my memoirs, when something happened that was so horrible I cannot bring myself to describe it. I spoke of memoir, but I have no time for fine writing. I had intended to take myself away from the world and write a cookery book.

How overwrought this opening now seems! How knowing the artifice! But this was the 1970s, a decade when myth and Freudian allusion were sweeping through Bohemia, so perhaps I can be forgiven. And if my remarks about fine writing were too contrived even then – how happy I was to pick up the Booker Prize for my efforts – then do remember I was Prospero, desperate to abjure the magic of theatre for my hermitage by the sea, the sea.

Today I have been swimming naked in the blessed Northern sea, the sea, diving from the cliff into the gentle waves, my body growing scales like a merman's as I sported like a dolphin, before easing myself out of the mysterious deep, my fingers clawing at the rocks for purchase. I'm sorry. I'm doing it again. I don't seem to be able to help myself. Melodrama and opportunist symbolism have been my trade for so long, it is hard to loosen their bonds.

Perhaps I should make myself known as I make myself a ploughman's lunch, ploughman's lunch. My name is Charles Arrowby. You probably recognise the name. In my time I have been a famous actor, playwright and theatre director, but now I am in my sixties I tire of the egotism of the stage and have left London to live alone in Shruff End, a remote dwelling perched on the edge of land, o'erlooking the sea, the sea, that sometimes has the still calm of mill-ponds past and at others crashes tumultuously in frothy whirlpools of anguished darkness.

It is night and as I lie within the inner room – the house itself must be allowed its own Freudian symbolism – I feel the time is right to mention the thing that was too horrible to describe in the first paragraph. For as I looked down into the sea, the sea, the wild waters opened to reveal a vast grey monster from the deep. What sort of animal it was I cannot say! Though if you choose to see it as my subconscious staring back at me, you won't be far off.

Two days have passed since I wrote that, days in which I have immersed myself naked in the sea, the sea and I feel the time is right to introduce more characters. Clement was my first mistress. She was much older than me, an actress who took me under her wing and launched my career. I will promise more of her, but such is my unreliability, no more will be forthcoming. Then there is Lizzie. She is younger than me, a lesser actress, but hopelessly devoted to me. She now shares a house with Gilbert, a sweet, ineffectual gay thespian. Neither must we forget Rosina whom I stole away from Peregrine, only to discard her. Nor James, the Buddhist, my cosmic cousin, *doppelgänger*, alter ego, rival; call him what you will. So there we have them: Clement, Lizzie, Gilbert, Rosina, Peregrine and James. All names redolent of a certain class. But that's the way literature was back them.

That was the prehistory. Now we reach the history. The time when letters and characters began serendipitously to arrive as if by magic – that word again. First came Lizzie, pleading with me to love her, to let her be my object. It was tempting, but no. Next a letter from James that I read while lying naked after swimming once more in the turbulent sea, the sea. He too will come to visit. And now a car appears. It is Perry – he does so hate being called Perry – and Rosina. I am so very grateful to Perry for having been so adult about my elopement with Rosina, a level of maturity not since reciprocated by his wife.

'I'll kill you,' she snarled, 'if you take up with Lizzie again. You are mine.'

A more developed character might have wondered why it was that even though I was well into my sixties women could not resist throwing themselves at my feet, but I confess my limitations got the better of me and I preferred to dwell on the possibility of the supernatural.

'I am not in a relationship with Lizzie,' I declared. Rosina did not believe me and drove off angrily into the night. And in her headlights, I saw her. Hartley.

Once more I find I have been economical with the truth, but this time I shall tell all. I promise. Hartley was my childhood love. We were inseparable. A working-class Romeo and Juliet. And then she left me when I went to drama school. No reason, no explanation. She left me heart-broken. Perhaps it was because of her I became the thespian I am, but that's another story. And here she was again, mysteriously turning up after 50 years, living in the very same village as me.

What follows is the essence of tragedy. Though you may read it as pure farce, as coincidence piles upon coincidence and everyone starts behaving in still more unbelievable ways.

I followed Hartley to her home. 'You may now be old, fat and ugly,' I observed, 'but I have always loved you, darling Hartley.'

'Be still,' she begged, 'for I must remain unhappily married to the violent Ben, and together we must mourn the disappearance of our adopted son, Titus.'

If I hadn't been so busy swimming naked in the sea, the sea, I might have wondered if I was now in a bad Thomas Hardy novel, and as I emerged from the deep another car drew up. It was the meditative James with an unknown youth.

'I suppose you must be Titus,' I said. 'I am very much in love with your mother and would like to adopt you.'

'That sounds fun,' he replied. 'I'll stay for a while.'

My memory gets a little blurred at this point because people come and go from the house with extraordinary speed and little explanation, and now I find myself surrounded by Lizzie, Gilbert, Peregrine, Rosina, James and Titus.

'I'm going to kidnap Hartley and make her marry me,' I said.

Rather than, as lesser mortals may have done, seeing such action as delusional idiocy requiring the attention of a doctor if not the police, the others recognised it for what it was: an important expression of the futility of egotism. So they helped me enact my plan.

'I'm not that happy about it,' Hartley said. 'But I'm not so bothered I'm going to try and escape.'

A few days later we were out by the boiling sea, the sea. The next thing I remember is waking in my bed. Someone had tried to murder me! But who could it be?

'It was me,' said Peregrine. 'I've always hated you for taking Rosina away from me.'

'Phew,' we all replied. 'As long as it was only you, we don't need to call the police.'

'I think perhaps it might be time to take Hartley home, though,' James said sagely. Reluctantly, I agreed, though only once Titus had promised to stay, and we set off by car back to Hartley's hovel.

'Who is throwing stones down on the car?' we yelled as the windscreen shattered.

'It's only me,' Rosina laughed.

'Phew,' we all replied.

We made our way back to my house where we stripped off naked and plunged into the churning sea, the sea. A shriek rent the air. It was Lizzie. 'Titus has drowned.'

'Perhaps then Hartley will now be free to live with me?' I wondered out loud, before lapsing into a week-long fever during which I remembered that I had seen the sea monster again during my attempted murder and it had been a Buddha-like James, walking on water, who had rescued me.

I woke to find some letters. Hartley and Ben had emigrated to Australia; James had willed himself to death in a Tibetan trance; Perry and Rosina were going to Ireland, and Gilbert and Lizzie were doing something else. I swam naked in the calm waters of the sea, the sea – the monster replaced by seals.

There the history ends. Or rather it should have. Because I've just had a letter from a 17-year-old girl asking me to impregnate her. Will the absurdity never end?

SUCCESS

Martin Amis

J ANUARY
(1) 'Terry speaking,' I said. 'I'm afraid Gregory isn't here, Miranda.'

Gregory was in fact sitting next door. 'Success?' he called. 'It's so tiring when everyone demands you fuck their amber jewel.'

No one wants to fuck me any more. Not even the dwarf with big ears. What a bitch.

Greg is my foster brother. He's six foot one, elegantly handsome, with brilliant white teeth and a bit queer; I'm an ugly, five-foot-nothing ginger. You could say we're both caricatures, but who really cares when our sole purpose is to shock? Did I mention I was so desperate I'd even fuck a granny?

(2) So you've met Terence, my plebeian foster brother? My father took pity on him after his father murdered his mother and sister. It's a ridiculous idea, I know, but it's all I could come up with at three in the morning after a tough night out, and if Mart doesn't get Terence and me sharing my London bachelor pad then the whole conceit is fucked. Loosen up. It's the late 1970s. Suck on the panache of the unpleasant.

'Do wash the effluvia from the palatinate dome of my immense cock,' I said after yet another bout of sexual gymnastics.

April
(1) Guess what? I fucked a beautiful woman. April Fool! I bet you weren't expecting that. Oh, you were. So what can I tell you? Well, I work in some kind of sales job but I'm not sure quite what as

Mart doesn't know anything about proley jobs himself other than that sales is a proley job which is why I have it. And I'm worried about going broke. There's a rumour going round that some of us will be sacked and Mr Veale, the union rep, wants me to get everyone to join. Not sure I can be bothered, though, as I'd rather spend the book worrying if my cock is going to fall off.

'Hello, yobbo.'

That was Ursula, my foster sister. She's even more tonto than me. And even less of a rounded character, if that's possible. I think Greg may have fucked her once. I'm hoping to get a look at her tits.

Things may be looking up. There's a girl at work called Jan who doesn't seem to be put off when we go out for a drink and I end the evening voiding huge quantities of vomit over her enormous breasts. I'm hoping to take her home and fuck her this evening.

(2) Oh dear. I seem to have rather blotted my copybook. Terence had arrived back with a common-looking girl, June I think she was called, when the police rang to say Ursula had slit her wrists. There was obviously no point in both of us going to the hospital, so I stayed behind with Jean and buggered her till she bled – not just a Shock Jock but a Shock Cock too! – then booted her out. And, well, Terence wasn't best pleased.

Still, the good news is that Ursula has been staying with me since she got out of hospital and I'm idly wondering if we will resume fucking again or whether her downy orifices will no longer hold their former attraction for me. Come, come, don't get all petit bourgeois with me about incest. Let me tell you, it's a great deal worse being forced to service the ghastly couple Odette and Jason whose art gallery I deign to work in. The required tumescence is such an effort.

September

(1) You're getting the hang of this now, aren't you? I mean, come on, you'd need to be a dummy not to see where this is heading. OK,

I know I said things were looking up last time, but this time they really are. Sure, it was a blow that Greg fucked Jan and I'll admit I moped about the flat for a couple of weeks afterwards, but she left work and I didn't have to see her again and, so, onwards and upwards. Just like my cock.

The good thing about Ursula trying to kill herself is that it's meant she's come to live with us. You may have realised by now that Greg is a liar – no shit! A tricksy unreliable narrator! – and he might say he's out a lot but he spends most of his time alone, and as I've now, thanks to Veale, got loads of money, Ursula is all mine. Maybe sex is easy after all. You just insist. I point her to my cock and she sucks it.

(2) I haven't been altogether truthful. I only had sex with Jason and Odette in the hope they wouldn't fire me. But they did anyway, and I'm broke, getting panic attacks and shitting in my pants. Is that extreme enough? I need Ursula. I go to Terence's room to find her passively fucking him.

'You're mine,' I cry. 'I want you to fuck me.'

'I hate you,' she says.

'You can't do that. What will become of us?'

Why is it always the psychological clichés that make you weep?

December
(1) I suppose I ought to feel guilty that Ursula killed herself after that, but I don't.

Then my attempts at pathos when I described my father killing my sister didn't work either. So here I am. I've got loads of money. I've got a hydraulic erection and I'm fucking a lot of women. I even met Jan who told me Greg never fucked her because he couldn't get a hard-on. I'm doing all right.

(2) Ursula's dead. My father's dead. Everything's a mess and the proles are taking over. I should have been a writer. Like Mart.

MIDNIGHT'S CHILDREN

Salman Rushdie

I WAS BORN in the city of Bombay on August 15th 1947. No, that will not do. The time is important. It was at the stroke of midnight, the precise instant of India's arrival at independence. I, Saleem Sinai, later variously called Snotface, Baldy and Too Pleased With My Own Brilliance, had my destiny tied to my country's. Now my time is running out and I have so many stories – too many you may think – to tell, to save myself from crumbling into dust. But I am the Arabian Knight and you must put up with it.

The story starts in 1915. My grandfather, Aadam Aziz, fell on a tussock while praying and lost his faith. Blood fell from his not inconsiderable nose and solidified into rubies and diamonds, and I could already feel the Booker Prize in my hands. I had the critics by their guilt-ridden, post-colonial balls. Imagine! A book so laden with historical self-importance that no one could admit they had never finished it. Suck on that for magical realism, Ganesh, you with your elephant ears.

But back to my grandfather. He trained as a doctor and Mr Ghani asked him to treat his daughter, Naseem. 'But you may only examine her through a hole in a white sheet,' he says. Once more I explode with pleasure at the cleverness of my allusion. See how the partitioning of Naseem is a metaphor for the greater partition that is to come. Ah! You do. Then I will continue, Padma.

I see I have forgotten to explain my Padma, my chubby dung-lotus. She is the woman who plans to marry me, despite my having less lead in the pencil in my *kurta* – I cannot lie, my penis no longer works – than in the pencil in my hand.

'Do I have to go on listening to all your stories?' she yawns.

'Of course you do, you fool,' I reply. 'Otherwise my modern allegory of the 1001 nights is ruined.'

Aadam finally saw the whole of Naseem on Armistice Day 1918 – how these dates pile up felicitously – and they married. In time the Reverend Mother, for that is how Naseem shall be known from now on, gave birth to three daughters, Alia, Mumtaz and Emerald, and two sons, Mustapha and Hanif. The stories I could tell. And will. At length. How Aadam fell in with an anti-partitionist activist and hid his assistant Nadir in the cellar. How Mumtaz fell in love with Nadir and lived with him in the cellar for many years, though their marriage was unconsummated. How Emerald fell in love with Major Zulfikar, forcing Nadir – such an appropriate name – to abandon Mumtaz. Above all, stories of blood, mercurochrome, snot, thunderboxes and scatology.

'Do go on,' says Padma, painting her nails.

I fear I may be lapsing into repetition, yet what is life save a series of repetitions, and what is a Salman Rushdie book save a few good pages, overwritten and overwritten with the verbosity of an insecure intellect? But enough of Salman for now – though don't you dare forget him. Aadam has moved to Bombay, Mumtaz has changed her name to Amina and married my father Ahmed Sinai. At last, I hear you say . . .

'I was asleep actually,' Padma mutters

. . . my time and India's has come. Tick-tock. But not quite for my father has moved to the Methwold Estate in Bombay and my pregnant mother has visited a fortune-teller who says her unborn son will have two heads. Tick-tock. The midnight hour struck and I was forced screaming into the world. Yet my mother was not Amina. She was Vanita, the poorest of the poor on the Estate, who had an affair with Methwold himself, and gave birth at the same time. And the nurse Mary, toying with destiny at this most auspicious of times, switched the babies to give me the blessings of the world.

'Really?' Padma snored.

'I must continue. I can feel myself disintegrating into a thousand pieces.'

'Don't confuse yourself with the plot,' Padma replied, awake once more.

So I grew up, inheriting the enormous nose of my grandfather. What's this? I hear you say. How can you have inherited the enormous nose if you were not Amina's child? Hush, I say, for you understand not the possibilities of a Salman's leap of the imagination. How I was bullied for my nose and took to hiding in my mother's laundry basket. From there I heard her arranging to meet her lover while my father slept off the djinns. Her lover did not live another 24 hours, such were my powers.

My mother refused to speak to me and my sister, the Brass Monkey, was no help so I dwelt in silence. And then I began to hear the voices of the 1001 – that number again! – children born at the same time as me. I convened a Midnight's Children Conference with Parvati-the-Witch and my nemesis Shiva, the child with whom I was swapped, and our destinies criss-crossed the ether.

'That's nice,' said Padma.

There came a time after I had lost a finger that my parents discovered I was not their son. The future of India hung in the balance, but the Reverend Mother bade my parents love me and we moved to Pakistan to live with Emerald and General Zulfikar.

'Come and sit on my knee, nose boy,' the General said.

And so I sat on his knee and moved around some pepperpots and unwittingly put in place the coup that led to the military dictatorship. The pressures from Shiva and Parvati-the-Witch and India's war with China meant we moved back to Bombay once more and my nose succumbed to snot. I came round from my operation to find my telepathic powers had gone, to be replaced by a heightened sense of smell that could sniff out bullshit anywhere it was to be found.

'Except your own,' Padma pointed out.

The war with China had been lost and we returned to Pakistan where the Brass Monkey morphed into the veiled – let's hear it for Partition once more – Jamila the Singer, while my grandfather's silver spittoon, caked with snot, crashed on to my head at the very moment when West Pakistan went to war against the East, and my memory was erased.

'So how do you know what happened next?' asked Padma.

Questions, questions. 1001 literal questions. Reduced to a Buddha Dog, I roamed the jungle, quelling the independence movement in the East. The atrocities. The horror, the horror. I fled to the jungle. There I retreated to the snake-charmer's cave and lived with Parvati-the Witch while Bangladesh emerged from the ashes.

Parvati-the-Witch fell pregnant with Shiva's child and the villagers rejected her until I married her. My nose twitched with the stench of Indira Gandhi's corruption as her gladiator, Shiva, slew Parvati-the-Witch and herded me into the vasectomy camp. The 1001 Midnight's Children had been neutered; the magic had been destroyed.

India was in a pickle. So with a heavy heart and an even more heavy-handed metaphor, I, Saleem, went to work in a pickle factory. There, Holy Vishnu, I met you, Padma. And now my story is at an end. Here in the 31st year of my life, in the 31st year of my country, I feel myself disintegrating into dust, trampled by the stampede of the multitudes to come.

'Not a moment too soon,' said Padma.

BRIGHT LIGHTS, BIG CITY

Jay McInerney

Y OU ARE NOT the kind of guy who would be at a place like this at this time of the morning. How did you get here? It was your friend Tad Allagash. Your brain is rushing with Brazilian marching powder. You are talking to a girl with a shaved head. You want to meet the kind of girl who isn't going to be here. You want to read the kind of fiction this isn't. You give the girl some powder. She still doesn't want you. Things were fine once. Then you got married.

Monday arrives on schedule. You are late for work. You buy the *Post* and read the Coma Baby story. Are you the Coma Baby? Of course you are. It's just a fucking metaphor. You reach the lobby of the famous New York magazine for which you work, take the elevator to the Department of Factual Verification and say hi to Megan. You hope your boss Ms Clara Tillinghast, aka The Clinger, doesn't want the French piece as they'll find out you lied about your fluency in your resumé. You want to be a writer, not a fact checker.

'We want the French piece today,' says The Clinger with awesome inevitability. Your sinuses are hurting. You go for a walk and buy a fake Cartier. It falls apart. Even you can't escape the symbolism. You forget to buy Megan her Tab. Likewise. Your career is going nowhere. Pretty much like this book.

You get home to your apartment on West 12th Street. It's a wreck. Like you. No kidding. You wonder if Amanda will ever explain her desertion. She was a model and she thought you were rich. You never spotted she was an airhead. So what does that make you?

Tad turns up, looking ridiculous in a pair of red Brooks Brothers trousers. 'Got any drugs, had any sympathy fucks?' he asks. You notice you've written *Dead Amanda* instead of *Dear Amanda* on a letter. Deep. You go to Odeon with Tad and meet Elaine from Amanda's agency. You get some toot and lie about your importance. Everyone ignores you. Are you surprised?

You read in the paper that Amanda is in town. You look at some mannequins she modelled. They have more personality than both of you combined. You're in luck. The Clinger has called in sick. You could do some more work on the French piece and save your ass. But you can't really be bothered. You'd rather forget to buy Megan a bagel and nearly buy a ferret.

You think of Coma Baby. You think of Amanda. You met her when you were a reporter in Kansas City. She liked your Ivy League preppiness. You liked it that she never thought she was beautiful. You told her she could become a model. You hoped she could be cool and ironic. She couldn't. Then neither could you. She called you from Paris, said she was leaving you, had found another man, a photographer. You thought all photographers were fags. You haven't told your family or anyone at work she's left you. You get back to the office. The proofs have gone.

They're being too nice to you in the office. You're screwed. You buy some cocaine and get ripped off. You take the bus home. You've forgotten your keys but get in anyway. Tad gives you some flake and asks you to meet his cousin Vicky instead of him. You don't want to, but you do. She's reading Spinoza. That makes her interesting. Apparently. 'Tad's an ass,' she says. You agree. You kiss goodnight. Could this be intimacy? Duh.

The Clinger calls you in. 'I guess I'm fired,' you say. She doesn't reply that for once you've got something right. That might have been almost funny. You leave the office. You see your brother Michael and run away. You do some drugs. Yawn. You meet up with Tad. Yawn. You go back to the magazine at night, let loose a ferret and stumble on the office drunk. You are the American Dream. Hysterical.

You gatecrash Amanda's fashion show. You get drunk. Yawn. You steal a briefcase and pretend to have a bomb. You stand up and ask Amanda why she left you. No one gives a rat's arse. Security escort you out. You go back to the magazine and forget to take Megan out to lunch. You give her some powder. You're all heart. She invites you to dinner. She tells you about her son. She asks about Amanda. You tell her she's a fictional character. 'How achingly hip,' she laughs. You steal some valium, you make a pass, you pass out.

Coma Baby lives. Is this a sign? Yes. You see your brother Michael again. This time you tell him how you've been struggling since Mum died and that Amanda has left. He looks at you. 'You're not planning to undermine what little satire there was with a schmaltzy ending?' he asks. It looks that way.

You think some more about your mum. You take some lines. They don't work. You go to Odeon with Tad. Amanda is there. She says, 'How's it going?' You walk out. You need cash. The dispenser isn't working. You phone Vicky. 'I think my mum's a missing person,' you tell her. She sounds interested. She shouldn't be. Your nose starts bleeding. You pass a bakery, smell Mum's home-made apple-pie, smell redemption. You'll have to start again. Thank fuck we won't.

HOTEL DU LAC

Anita Brookner

THERE WAS A greyness of emblematic significance to the prose as Edith Hope, writer of romantic fiction under a more thrusting name, began her afternoon walk of excruciating dullness around the lake. Am I not to be allowed my lapse? she thought. And why should I be? I am a serious woman; many people have commented on my resemblance to Anita Brookner and, though I have bored others, I was not to be allowed to bore myself.

Exhausted, both by the exertion of her passivity and by the habitual use of extended parentheses, she returned to the hotel and began writing a letter.

My dearest David, After I did that dreadful thing which I won't mention now because I want to maintain some kind of interest, Penelope told me I had to leave the country for a month to let things calm down, so I have come to the Hotel du Lac in Switzerland, a location every bit as dull as me.

Edith dressed for dinner in her dowdiest Liberty print dress. It was nearly the end of the season and the restaurant was empty, apart from a sad-looking woman with an eating disorder and a dog that made a puddle on the floor, and an equally sad-looking pair who appeared to be mother and daughter. 'Please join us,' said the older woman, introducing herself as Iris Pusey. 'You seem to be as sad and dull as us. Meet my daughter Jennifer.'

As was her custom, Edith was content to remain silent while Mrs Pusey droned on about how rich she was, how good her husband had been to her before his early death and how she loved shopping, thinking only of how old Mrs Pusey might be. She must be in her 50s, she decided, which would make Jennifer in her late 20s.

Fatigued once more by the strain of having devoted so many pages to so little, Edith retired to her room, both to dwell on the unhappiness of her relationship with her mother and to commence another letter.

My dearest David, You never knew how I longed for your visits, but then how could you when I was replete with the repression of the lonely spinster? I would only present my cheerful self to you as it seemed unfair to burden you with my sadness when you could only escape the treadmill of the auction house and your wife once a month. Oh David, David.

'You quite remind me of someone,' Mrs Pusey said two days later after another action-packed chapter.

'Virginia Woolf?' Edith offered hopefully.

'Anita Brookner. Now I do declare that Mr Neville over there, who has just arrived, has quite taken a shine to you. He's trade, of course, but beggars can't be choosers.'

Edith considered replying, but thought better of it, concentrating instead on the lines on Mrs Pusey's face that showed up in the pale autumn twilight. Perhaps Mrs Pusey was in her 60s and the pallid Jennifer in her 30s after all! The excitement of such a thought brought an onset of the vapours and Edith excused herself to write yet another letter that would allow her to fill in still more of the back story.

My dearest David, None of my friends ever suspected our affair and Penelope became insistent on me dating an acquaintance of hers called Geoffrey. He was a man, unhealthily close to his mother, given to even greater flights of dullness than myself, and yet it seemed impolite to turn down his offer of marriage. Yet when the day came, I could not go through with it and all my friends were jolly cross. And that's my big sin. I warned you it wasn't very interesting.

'You quite remind me of someone,' Mr Neville said, escorting Edith on her 15-minute perambulation by the lake.

'Virginia Woolf?' Edith asked hopefully, for she was nothing if not consistent.

'Anita Brookner,' he smiled stiffly. 'Now look here, old gal. I'm as absurd and unconvincing as every other man in this book, so what say we get married even though we don't know each other? I was miffed when my wife left me, but you seem so boring and so detached my centrality will not be affected.'

Edith was not alone in her bewilderment at the use of the word 'centrality', but it would have been *déclassée* not to reply to such an invitation, so she contented herself with a question of her own. 'Will we be able to arrange the antimacassars together?'

The hotel was pulsing with activity on their return as Mrs Pusey awoke from her afternoon rest to declare it was her birthday. 'I'm 179 today,' she croaked as a cobwebbed retainer brought in a slice of Victoria sponge cake.

Then Jennifer must be 139, Edith thought. The same age as me. Now she understood why everyone appeared to observe the shocked, petit-bourgeois morality of the Victorians when it was actually the 1980s. Her eyelids heavy with a tiredness brought on by the pace of the action, she lay down on the chaise-longue to write a letter she would actually send.

Dear David, I'm going to marry Mr Neville. I don't love him but it would be impertinent to refuse.

Edith awoke refreshed and, donning her peignoir, let herself into the corridor where she espied Mr Neville quietly letting himself out of Jennifer's bedroom. A burst of unrepressed feminism coursed through her frozen veins. She would not marry Mr Neville after all. Why settle for being a doormat for someone she didn't love when she could be one for a man she did? She plucked up her quill.

Dearest David, I am returning.

THE UNBEARABLE LIGHTNESS OF BEING

Milan Kundera

Nietzsche's idea of eternal return has perplexed many philosophers. You, though, will find my eternal returning to the idea of eternal return over the coming pages merely annoying. But is not annoyance the heaviest of human burdens? Yet does not the absence of annoyance, the lightness, confer the unbearable burden of insignificance?

Parmenides would have posed this question in the sixth century had he been an East European intellectual intent on grinding his readers' noses into the superficiality of his thought. Which then shall we choose? Lightness or heaviness? Probably neither, for even the stupidest person can see this is a false dichotomy, that both ideas are equally invalid. If something only happens once, could not that make it more, not less, significant? But these counter-revolutionary thoughts have no place in the Prague Spring of 1968, so let's continue with the novel.

I have been thinking about Tomas, the Czech surgeon, for some years but only in the light of these reflections did I see him clearly. He had first met Tereza in a small town three weeks earlier. They had met for an hour. Ten days later she visited him in Prague. They made love and she came down with flu for 10 days. Then she went home again. In his inordinately deep way, Tomas was perplexed to find himself feeling something more for her than just a physical desire of objectification, so he said to himself, as we all do at such times, *Einmal ist Keinmal*, what happens once might as well never have happened.

One day Tereza returned again with a copy of *Anna Karenina* and Tomas saw her as a child in a bulrush and himself as Oedipus. Unperturbed by such pretentious imagery, he slept with her again and when he awoke to find her holding his hand in a transgressive act of dissent against Soviet alienation, felt obliged to marry her. Tomas had been married before and had a son whom we shall call, for argument's sake, Simon. Tomas had decided to have no contact with Simon – a decision that appeared to have given him few qualms and will go unquestioned by everyone throughout the novel.

Instead he chose to indulge his solipsism by shagging as many women as possible, arguing that love and sex were incompatible, and in Sabina, an artist who liked to fuck in a bowler hat and with as ridiculous a line in symbolism as himself, he found the perfect mistress. This being the work of a middle-aged male novelist, Tereza naturally came to accept Tomas's dissociative state as the natural order, though she was given to the occasional intensely symbolic dream herself as she photographed Russians in the streets of Prague.

For his part, Tomas's narcissism was startled to imagine that Tereza might once have slept with another man, so he suggested they move to Zurich so he could be nearer to Sabina. Tereza went along with this for a bit, but after Tomas had also shagged half of Switzerland, she got a bit fed up and went back to Prague. Initially, Tomas felt an incredible lightness that his wife of seven years had left him. But then he thought of Sophocles and Beethoven and the heaviness returned. So he went back to Prague and Tereza was quite pleased.

Tereza had had a difficult life and, were this novelist not quite so keen to be taken seriously, he might have said that Tomas had abused her as much as had her mother. But he didn't, so there we are. She too was very interested in the artificial split between lightness and heaviness and, after shacking up with Tomas for very different reasons to his, accepted she was a metaphor for Dubček's weakness and sadly patted her dog, Karenin.

Franz was Sabina's other Swiss lover, a man of less depth and substance than Tomas, though no less absurd. Unwilling to have sex with her in the same town in which he lived with his wife, Franz, unlike Tomas, failed to understand the importance of the neo-Marxist, post-Freudian bowler hat. With Franz the bowler hat was no longer a comic connection to her father and grandfather, it was a symbol of violence and public rape. Apparently. So she ridiculed his puppy-like nuzzling of her breasts in coitus. Such is the existential ennui of the *mittel*-European. A world of missed connections between Franz and Sabina, Tomas and Tereza. The misunderstanding between lightness and heaviness, between a book of substance and a load of bollocks.

Tereza took a job as a waitress after the Russians occupied the city. She regularly smelled other women's vaginal juices on Tomas's hair, but shrugged it off and went about her day pondering the lightness or heaviness of the Cartesian mind-body split. Was her body part of herself? She still wasn't sure after she had been fucked by an engineer who may or may not have been a Communist spy in the toilet. And certainly no one else cared. She wandered up to Petrin Hill in a dream and watched herself get shot by a firing squad while Tomas looked on. Either I'm a prostitute or I'm in love.

Meanwhile I was a little worried Tomas had forgotten he was also supposed to be an allegory for Soviet repression, so he began taking a previously well-concealed interest in Czech politics. His Sophoclean musings had led him to write a letter of dissent on the nature of passive complicity to a radical newspaper, and he now found himself being asked for a retraction by a Man from the Ministry. Caught in the balance between lightness and heaviness, between Beethoven's *Muss Es Sein?* and *Es Muss Sein!*, and between his existential Parmenidean obsession for finding the millionth part of difference in a woman and just being the figment of a dirty old man's mind, he refused.

Tomas was forced to resign from his job as a surgeon and became a window-cleaner in Prague, where his main duties were having sex with 37 women a day, all of whom unaccountably desired to surrender their anus, his favourite part of the female anatomy, to him. After a year or so, a radical editor who had admired his Sophoclean musings invited him to a meeting at which his son Simon was present. Naturally, the cause of modernist magical realism was best served by them not discussing the 20-year hiatus in their relationship, so instead the conversation centred on whether Tomas would agree to sign a petition protesting at the Russian occupation.

So why did he not sign? For one thing, the split between lightness and heaviness had been blurred in the editing of his Oedipal fixation and he did not hold the position ascribed to him. Yet more importantly, he did not sign because I did not let him for this is the moment in which the post-modern authorial intervention reminds you the characters are all my own invention and therefore facets of my own character. So rather Tomas thought of the ineffability of lightness and heaviness, the ineffability of unbearable tosh.

Tomas was surprised to discover that Tereza had detected vaginal juices on his hair, having believed a good wash of his body was all that was required, and in her own proto-Nietzschean way Tereza came to realise her duality was best resolved by being a doormat until Tomas's tragically light-heavy descent from being the finest surgeon in Prague was completed by his intractable attachment to being a complete Kant and they were obliged to become farmers.

Sabina moved to New York where she continued to wear a bowler hat and fuck anything that moved, and it was here she heard that Tomas and Tereza had died in a car crash. Franz had gone to Cambodia, bizarrely believing that his own lightness/heaviness situation with Sabina would somehow be resolved if he joined a protest. There he was hit over the head and died later in hospital, his wife believing that he did in fact love her after all. Tomas and Tereza lived their life refracted through their dog, Karenin, whom they believed had learned to smile. It was, though, a rictus as she had cancer. The only smile was on my face, having passed off the unbearable lightness of drivel as work of great heaviness.

BLOOD MERIDIAN

Cormac McCarthy

SEE THE CHILD. The mother dead at his birthing. At 14 he runs away. A year later he is shot in the back in New Orleans. So what? He walks. He walks. He is divested of all that he has been. He sees a parricide, the body hanging while urine darkens the trousers. In the spring of 1849 he rides into Nacogdoches.

The Reverend Green had been playing to a full house daily when a seven foot giant entered the tent.

The impostor had congress with young girls and a goat before he came to preach here, said the Judge. The teamster pulled out a knife and killed the reverend, with 79 other members of the congregation trampled in the affray. The kid looked on eagerly.

How dya know he was an impostor? the kid asked.

I didnt. I just made it up.

It had been raining for three months and the kid was sitting in the hotel with Toadvine, when a man asked him to get out the way. The kid pulled out a gun and blew his head off, the arterial blood spraying the walls.

Wed better get out of here, cried the Judge and Toadvine.

Sure, said the kid. But how come we got no speech marks or apostrophes?

Cos punctuation is for pussies.

They met a hermit who hated niggers. Even worse than Mexers, he said. We gotta get to Californy, they answered, disembowelling the barman and treading his intestines into the floorboards. Wed better join the irregulars and get us some mules.

For two long weeks they rode through the arid burnt pumice

of the desert sucking on antelope bones, dying of starvation. They passed a solitary divelling, the inhabitants all multilated save an old man pissing himself, before they were caught in a hail of Commanche arrows. Only eight survived. The rest were burnt in a bush on which hung the carcasses of dead babies scalped by the heathen.

Dying of thirst in the *terra damnata*, they were taken prisoner in Chihuauha and walked the gauntlet of flung offal. Let us go, said Glanton, and well kill you injuns and get Gomez. They drank mescal, stove in the skull of a crippled woman, said nigger a lot and left town. Nine days out they got ambushed by Apaches. The Judge laughed, plucking the arrows from his side before pulping the Indians against the rocks.

Whats he the Judge of? asked the kid.

Hes the Judge of American history, the expriest replied. The blood depravity and lawlessness thats been airbrushed by the victors.

So this is like a XXX-rated Spaghetti Western?

Clint Eastwood is a Disney shithead.

So its an anomic existential tale with no character development or revelation. We just gotta find new ways to kill or be killed in ever more remorseless graphic detail.

They rode back into the white heat of the desert, killing indiscriminately. The kid shot a man from 25 miles, watching his head explode in a ball of carmine, while the Judge and Toadvine drank the menstrual blood of scalped women and slit the bellies of pregnant horses.

They returned as heroes in harlequin hats to Chihuahua, dragging a half-mile chain of scalps behind them. They drank, they whored, they peeled skulls like polyps bluely wet, they pulled a dead man from a coffin and hacked him in pieces, knowing the desert would salt their bones back to nothingness.

The Judge pissed in the sulphur, fashioning gunpowder from the earth, and the sand ran crimson with the blood of 7,000 Mexers.

Who we killing now? asked the expriest.

We aint bothered. We killing everyone, the Judge spat. There is a purity in violence. War is the truest form of divination.

Dya reckon that kind of quasi-mysticism will have some critics falling for a highbrow Gnostic interpretation of all this killin? the kid spat back.

The Lord moves in mysterious ways. Might also help if we put the odd bit of Spanish in somewhere, the expriest muttered spitting further than anyone.

Eres mozo del caballado?

They resumed their massacres, bathing their arms in scarlet torrents of exsanguinations, boiling brains in their skulls, filleting infants and throwing their livers to the wolves. They double-crossed the Yuma at the river crossing and the Indians came after them, spearing Glanton through the throat till his tongue appeared out of his chest. The kid and Tobin escaped by mule, the kid taking an arrow in the leg, Tobin a bullet in the neck.

You gotta shoot the Judge, cried the expriest. The kid shot once and missed. The Judge laughed. Aint no one that can shoot me, he spat. They travelled on through the cold of the desert night, passing pile upon pile of desiccated corpses, the charred coagulate of preterite lives.

The kid made it to San Diego in time to see Toadvine swing, his leg dripping with urine as he breathed his last from the noose. He had lost all sense of who he was, who he was killing, as he was put in prison for his crimes. The Judge had him sent away, but the kid got released when he promised his jailers gold.

For seven long years, the kid travelled back east through the desert where bison carcasses lay rotting in their millions stopping only to plug innocent bystanders with lead in their rancid pelvises.

The kid entered a bar in Texas to find the judge, wearing the blackened ears of Mexers as a necklace and making a cross out of an imbeciles femur while crushing 1,129 children between his thighs.

You a disappointment to me, kid, he said. Before remembering to spit. You just don't enjoy killing quite as much as me. You at times shown an indecent humanity to the heathen.

The kid spat back. It was the first he'd heard of it. He looked on disinterestedly as the dancing bear's head was ripped off, before absent-mindedly whoring and butchering the penitents and the pilgrim in a final attempt to add meaning by using the language of faith. The Judge towered over him.

You don't wanna go in there, said one bloke having a piss in the latrines to another. Indoors the Judge was dancing. Fame, he spat. I'm gonna live for ever.

LOVE IN THE TIME OF CHOLERA

Gabriel García Márquez

ONCE THE STORMY years of his early struggles were over, Dr Juvenal Urbino had achieved a respectability at eighty-one years of age that had no equal in the province. Such was his routine that his wife, Fermina Daza, who was seventy-two years old and had lost the doe's gait of her younger years, always knew his whereabouts. He was the first man she had heard urinate and, as the years had weakened his stallion's stream to a trickle, she had come to treat him as a baby.

Juvenal Urbino took his afternoon siesta, feeling the weight of his hermetic pancreas, only to be awoken by a parrot in the mango tree. The ladder slipped from beneath him as he caught the bird and he realised he had died without Communion on the Feast of Pentecost. It was a memorable death, for Dr Juvenal Urbino had become known in his country for the drastic measures he used to ward off the last cholera epidemic, and its news soon reached Florentino Ariza.

'I have waited for this opportunity to repeat my vow of eternal fidelity and love,' said Florentino Ariza. 'Get out of here,' Fermina Daza replied. Until that moment, she had never been fully conscious of the drama she had provoked when she was not yet eighteen, but as she fell asleep, weeping with solitude and rage, she found she was thinking more of Florentino Ariza than her dead husband.

On the other hand, Florentino Ariza had not stopped thinking of her for a single moment since she had rejected him out of hand fifty-five years, five months and four days, three hours and two minutes previously – a period of time he would endeavour to make the reader experience in its entirety. He had been a serious young man, enhanced by constipation, when he had first noticed Ferrmina Daza as a thirteen-year-old girl, and had wooed her assiduously by sending her daily letters of devastating love and eating gardenias to better know her taste, before she had agreed to marry him on the condition she was not made to eat eggplant.

Her father disapproved and took her to the Andes for two years, but the lovers maintained their secret correspondence until they met once more by chance, when Florentino Ariza was eating roses in the market. 'This is not the place for a crowned goddess,' he said. Fermina Daza felt an abyss of disappointment. 'What is between us is nothing but illusion,' she said. 'Our devastating love is over.'

At twenty-eight years old, Dr Juvenal Urbino had been the most desirable of bachelors and had always attributed his falling for the plebeian charms of Fermina Daza as a clinical error, after she was incorrectly diagnosed with cholera. For her part, she was not quite sure why she had accepted his proposal when she had refused Florentino Ariza, yet after observing how ugly his penis was, she had resolved to be a faithful wife. Neither loved the other, but neither had they made a mistake.

Florentino Ariza devoted all his waking hours to thinking about Fermina Daza, which meant he spent almost his entire life asleep as he requited his devastating love in six hundred and twenty two long-term liaisons and countless fleeting sexual adventures. Gringas, mulattas, gentlewomen and widows; all were won over by his furtive hunting and explosive enemas. Most he only remembered as names in his notebooks, yet he did occasionally think guiltily of Olimpia Zuleta whose husband had slit her throat after he had discovered 'This pussy is mine' written on her pubis. But it was a noble guilt, born of concern that Fermina Daza should discover his infidelity.

Fermina Daza could admit there had been bad years. She had been forced to ask Juvenal Urbino to move out for two years after she discovered his affair with a mulatta, but at the time of his death she prided herself on being almost content now that their marriage was sexless and her husband's orifices were prone to leaking.

At this same point of time, the steady torrent of lovers passing through Florentino Ariza's bed had slowed to just one. América Vicuña had been just thirteen years old when her parents had entrusted her to his care and, after a period of steady grooming with no suggestion of paedophilia – for this was a South American novel where it was quite usual for a beautiful teenager to fall devastatingly in love with a decrepit, loose-bowelled septuagenarian – had become quite devoted to him. And he to her, though once he heard of Dr Juvenal Urbino's death, he started to give her the cold shoulder and she committed suicide.

Fermina Daza would have been shocked to discover that Florentino Ariza had interpreted her latest rejection as an act of love. But then neither she, nor anyone else for that matter, had ever understood how unpleasant he really was. He determined to seduce her again, this time with maundering musings on the nature of love and ageing, and after one abortive meeting in which his bowels dribbled with diarrhoea, Fermina Daza understandably found her resistance weakening.

'This book has gone on way too long as it is,' Fermina Daza told her children, explaining her decision to take a river cruise with Florentino Ariza. 'If I don't give in now, we could be in for another three hundred pages.'

'Your breasts are sagging, I am a virgin and my cock is dead,' said Florentino Ariza. 'But at least you can give me an enema.'

'Do you think we could pass this off as a love story if we spend the rest of our lives going up and down the river, pretending to be in quarantine for cholera?'

'When you've won the Nobel Prize you can get away with almost anything,' said Florentino Ariza.

ORANGES ARE NOT THE ONLY FRUIT

Jeanette Winterson

My MOTHER HAD never heard of mixed feelings. There were friends and there were enemies. Enemies were the Devil, Next Door and Sex. Friends were God and That's It.

She was Old Testament through and through and deeply resentful Mary had beaten her to a Virgin birth. So she did the next best thing and had a foundling. Me. Oh, Little Town of Manchester, how still we see thee lie. My father? You can forget about him. He's a man.

Once upon a time there was a beautiful princess who liked to interpolate her story with myth because she did not trust the readers to understand the metafiction. This was a mistake. No one was very interested in the fairytales.

My mother was Treasurer of the Society for the Lost. Every day we went to the Mission to hear the Pastor purge us of our demons; at night I read the Bible. One day a letter arrived. 'The Devil is in our midst,' my mother declared. 'I have to send you to school.'

Once I went deaf for three months, but no one noticed. My mother assumed I was in a state of rapture. I still didn't let my father say a word so who knows what he thought? My mother went out and I wrote a note to Miss Jewsbury, telling her I couldn't hear. She took me to hospital where the doctors took out my adenoids. My mother brought me an orange. 'They are the only fruit, Jeanette,' she said, portentously.

Once upon a time there was a beautiful princess who was

worried people would not realise she was a cutting-edge postmodernist. As if we could forget.

I got into a lot of trouble at school because the heathen did not understand they were possessed by the Devil. I was also upset not to win a prize for my tableau of the Second Coming made from a wilting daffodil. At the Mission I won prizes for handing out Bibles to converts, though a gypsy told me I would never marry. 'Good,' said my mother, ramming another orange down my throat.

Once upon a time there was a beautiful princess who wrote a story in which the prince chopped off the princess's head. I think she had issues with men.

There was a woman in the street who said she had married a pig.

Once upon a time there was a princess who took the fable of Beauty and the Beast wilfully literally.

'All men are the Devil,' my mother said. 'Have an orange.' My father was about to say something, but I couldn't be bothered to listen. I'll fall in love one day, I thought. Eventually I did.

I first noticed Melanie working on the fish stall but it was some weeks before I plucked up the courage to invite her to come to hear Pastor Finch preach. My mother didn't trust love after she once mistook it for an ulcer. 'Don't let anyone touch you down there,' she warned. 'Have an orange instead.' But I did let Melanie. 'Do you think this is an unnatural passion?' I asked.

Once upon a time there was a princess who was still not that certain that readers would understand her blurring of time and fiction, so she wrote a chapter called Deuteronomy that everyone skipped.

One day my real mother turned up at the door but my mother sent her away. I heard every word but I'm not going to repeat it here. I expect you wonder why. I haven't had a real feeling all through the book. Real feelings aren't trendily postmodern.

After I told Mother about Melanie, she took me to church. 'They are possessed by Satan,' the Pastor chanted. 'Repent, repent.'

'Hello,' said the orange demon.

'Hello,' I replied, 'I'm never gonna give you up.'

'Nor is Rick Astley.'

Melanie told me she was going to go to university when I visited her later. 'You don't look well,' she said. 'You have the humours,' my mother added. 'You need a good shagging,' said Miss Jewsbury. So we spent the night together, though I didn't really enjoy it.

My mother gave me more oranges and I pretended to change my ways. It made me popular at church and I managed to convert a great many heathens, including Katy, who worked in a shop. We quickly became lovers.

Once upon a time there was a beautiful princess who also chose to weave in the allegorical quests of Winnet Stonejar and Perceval with Jeanette's metaphysical journey, but no one was very interested in those bits.

'She is possessed again,' my mother sobbed, burying me in a crate of oranges. My father didn't say a word. Perhaps he had died. He might as well have done.

'I'm leaving home,' I said. I missed God but I didn't miss the church. I got a job selling ice-creams at Testifying Elsie's funeral before I left Wigan for the City of the Godless, as my mother called it.

'I expect you'll be eating fancy apples down south,' she said.

I came back to Wigan once. I saw Melanie with a baby in the street. She looked bovine. That's what happens when you turn hetty.

My mother had given up being Treasurer after someone had embezzled the funds. 'We've got a coloured pastor now,' she said. 'I feed him pineapples.' I left. I'd got the point of fruit-coded bigotry long ago.

BELOVED

Toni Morrison

1 24 BLUESTONE WAS full of spite. Sethe and her daughter Denver lived there all alone. Too scared to go out. Sethe's mother-in-law, Baby Suggs, had lived with them for 18 years but she had wisely chosen to die before the book had started. She had suffered enough already.

The sideboard started playing up again. Singing 'How much is that doggy in the window?' 'Why can't you learn some Bob Dylan?' Sethe implored her poltergeist. 'Freedom's just another word for nothing left to lose'. 'No one expects the unexpected'. Polty smiled.

Paul D came in from nowhere. Sethe hadn't seen him in 25 years when they were living in Sweet Home, Alabama. He had been one of those mad niggers fucking cows as a badge of slavery while waiting for a woman to come across.

'We have a ghost here,' Sethe said. 'It's Beloved. My daughter whose throat was cut when she was two years old.'

'I can see that,' Paul D replied, ducking as a table was hurled towards his head.

'And I've got a chokecherry tree growing out my back,' Sethe murmured.

'Of course you have.' Paul D nodded. 'Every slave with poetry in her soul and post-modernism in her heart is similarly oppressed.' He took her in his arms. He remembered how Sixo had walked for 17 days just for one hour with a woman. Paul D had walked for 25 years and had come in 12 seconds. And he didn't even much like her breasts.

But these were the magical realisms he had to live with: the lyrical and the supernatural locked in a battle of forgetting and re-memories that made the juxtaposition of year-long rape and subjugation still more shocking. The noise and violence of Beloved's Polty moods subsided the longer Paul D stayed; Sethe dared to remember how a white woman named Amy had saved her and Beloved in childbirth, while Denver just thought about an antelope's head that must have meant something to someone once. Even if it was only to Toni.

Slavery, though, dances to its own beat, a beat of pain and guilt, so no one questioned what the hell Toni was on about when, just as Paul D had persuaded Sethe and Denver to go outdoors for the first time in 18 years, a mysterious figure rose out of the river and joined them at 124.

'How did you get here?' Denver asked.

'With great baptismal symbolism,' the woman said, for Lo! She was the very resurrection of Beloved.

Sethe's eyes opened wide. She was overwhelmed by memories of how her husband Halle had disappeared and she'd been raped for three years straight in a barn by a white man and his son when they'd been chased off the Garner land.

'Jesus, Mum,' Denver shouted. 'Now you've got snakes and bears hiding in that tree on your back.'

Paul D was consumed by his own degradation. The bit in the mouth, the beatings, the chain gangs. In his dehumanisation only the supernatural was real, and he succumbed to Beloved's advances.

'I'm feeling rather frisky,' Beloved said, flashing her robes coquettishly. 'People always assume that ghosts are either angry or sad. Well, I am horny too. Come to me, Big Boy.'

'Get thee behind me,' Paul D cried, retreating to sleep in the grass among the snakes. Beloved was not to be resisted. She taunted Sethe, accusing her of slitting her throat, while Denver sobbed as she learned her mother was a murderer, and though

Paul D longed to impregnate Sethe, her siren voice lured him inside her cavity. But very tastefully.

'White men are all bad. Slavery is evil,' Paul D sobbed as he left 124 for good.

Stamp Paid suggested the only reason Denver was still alive was because Sethe had killed Beloved. 'There's a twisted logic,' he said. 'She killed her to outhurt the hurters. Death was the better option.'

'So why did she let me live?' Denver asked.

'Um, I guess she didn't give so much of a toss about you. She just didn't get round to having you whacked.'

'And who are you exactly?'

'Just another person who pops up from time to time with a different reality. By the way, it's just possible that the woman in the water isn't Beloved but some other girl who was topped a while back.'

'And why do you mention that now?'

'To confuse you as much as possible, and to underline the point that slavery has not one but many truths.'

'I see. Well, I still think she's my sister.'

'And I think she's my daughter,' Sethe added.

Many moons passed as the narrative grew ever more complex. Time frames merged. Reality slipped. Memories became re-memories as slaves were tortured, freed, recaptured. As Halle watched Sethe be raped non-stop for three years in the barn while he hid under a hay bale. As one by one they all suffered. As Baby Suggs died. And was reborn. And died again. As Denver toiled among the snakes and unicorns.

The arguments between Sethe and Beloved grew worse. The imagery ever wilder and more intense. Yet ever heartfelt. Insults were thrown, objects hurled. The gaps between the sentences became profoundly wide. Perhaps even unbridgeable. Though Toni was keeping shtoom. It was always so much more satisfactory for the readers to lynch themselves in nooses of their own pretension.

The gaps grew thin once more and so did Sethe, wasting away, saving her scraps for Beloved. Beloved's belly grew ever larger, bloated with her pride and fertility. There was no room for Denver. She stepped off the edge of the world to meet her death. Yet did not die. To Lady Jones she went, work requesting, and came there back the women of the village, their love and food the ghost exorcising.

Till peace once more befell 124 and Paul D returned to find a house of quietude. For Beloved was no more. But then, had she ever been? For in this kind of novel, it's always handy to keep your options open.

THE BONFIRE OF THE VANITIES

Tom Wolfe

Two WINGS: ONE for the WASPs who lived there, one for the help. Sherman McCoy scoped his $3 million Park Avenue apartment. He was the man, Master of the Universe, the highest earning trader at Pierce & Pierce. 'I'm just taking Marshall for a walk,' he yelled to his wife, Judy.

McCoy dragged the dog out into the rain and headed to a call box. Dialled some numbers. 'Can I speak to Maria?' he asked. Shit! It was Judy. He'd rung home by mistake. He slammed the phone down. Got through to Maria instead. Judy was pushing 40; Maria was young, foxy and married to the octogenarian billionaire Arthur Ruskin. Fuck it. McCoy was Master of the Universe. He deserved that kind of pussy.

Assistant District Attorney Lawrence Kramer was having a bad day. The preacher Reverend Richard Bacon was getting the blacks all fired up, the Jewish mayor was coming up for re-election and his approval ratings were through the floor, and the Bronx Court House was teeming with the usual scumbags.

Tom was feeling good. He was going to pull it off. The big New York novel, the zeitgeist of the 1980s. He was the Master of the Novelverse.

The Giscard deal was coming good, Maria was looking better in the front seat of his $50,000 Mercedes. In half an hour they'd be back from the airport. His Master's cock stirred.

'Shuhman,' Maria whined in her South Carolina drawl. 'Ya missed da turrrnin.'

Jesus. They were off the freeway and in the Bronx. In among the trash. Fuck. Two black guys blocking the road. What the fuck they want? A jackin'? He stopped the roadster and got out. A squeal of tyres. Shit. Maria was at the wheel. 'Geddin,' she shouted. She reversed hard. A bump.

'Fuck sakes, you hit one of them,' Sherman cried.

'It's a jungle,' Maria laughed. 'Them and us. They was tryin' to rob us. 'Sides, I hardly touched him.'

Not a dent on the car, nothing in the papers, the Wall Street shoeshine buffing his hand-tooled brogues to a mirror; Maria was right. The trash couldn't touch the Master of the Universe. Shit. The Giscard deal was blown. Couldn't be. He'd hedged it. Fuck. He was down $6 million.

Tom was sweating. He'd done all this research, he just couldn't bring himself to leave any of it out. Cram it in. Cram it in. He was Master of the Novelverse. Fuck it. Just like Sherman, he was headin' outta control.

'We gadda problem,' said Weiss, the Bronx DA. 'The Reverend Bacon says this good kid called Lamb got hit by a car, went to hospital with a broken arm and is now in a coma. Remembered the first two letters of the Merc's reg before he went sparko.'

'That's all a piece-a crap,' the Irish-American Detective Martin replied. 'We ain't got nuthin'.'

'Sure it is, but we got da blacks up in arms moanin' about there being one justice for the blacks and one for the WASPs. So get your asses outta here.'

Peter Fallow downed a Mojito. Like all Brit hacks in New York, he was out of money and out of his depth. He hadn't had a story in weeks and was too posh to look for one. 'This Lamb case gonna be big,' said one of the Reverend Bacon's sidekicks. 'There'll be riots. Do as I say an' you'll get the exclusive for City Lights.'

Tom was in deep shit. He'd done the blacks, the Jews, the

Italians, the Irish, the WASPs, the kikes and the expats, but New York was just getting away from him. It was too big to nail down. Cram it in. Cram it in. But where were the fucking Chinks and Mozzers? He was losing. Losing readers. Losing the plot. He needed a set-piece.

That dinner party at the Bavardages' had got him out of a hole temporarily. Name-dropping, brand-checks, satire in overdrive. But then, boom. More pages, more this, more that, too many fucking sub-plots, too much shit no one cared about, too much going over the same stuff. Fuck it, we got it the first time. Hell, he was doing it for New York, but New York didn't give a . . . The Master of the Novelverse was hanging on by his fingernails.

So was Sherman. Maria had gone to Italy, he'd as good as lost his job. Fuck it, he had been almost broke on $2 million when he had one. Now Martin had nailed him, taken him down the Bronx to process him.

'It's still a piece-a shit,' Martin had said, 'but it's all gotten political.'

Tom knew that. He knew you knew that. But he couldn't stop. More, more satire. Sherman didn't give a crap about Wall Street anymore. Fuck it, he was now a celeb with Judy's shithead friends. Kramer was balling the juror, saw a chance to make a name on the Sherman case, didn't give a fuck that the other black guy who had been with Lamb was a crackhead scumbag. Fallow was given more stories, the case was out of control, JAIL NOT BAIL, Maria's husband died and she came back and dicked over 'Shuhman', but Sherman's lawyer had got him to wire her and . . . STOP, STOP, STOP, please. Tom stopped. He'd done enough. Finish it up any old how.

The *New York Times*. A year later: Sherman McCoy has been arraigned after Lamb died last week. Peter Fallow has won the Pulitzer Prize. The Mayor has been re-elected. And Kramer has been suspended. Who would a thought it?

THE REMAINS
OF THE DAY

Kazuo Ishiguro

I T SEEMS increasingly likely I shall be making the expedition that has been preoccupying my imagination. And in Mr Farraday's Ford, at that. I had been dusting the mantelpiece in the banqueting hall when Mr Farraday approached me.

'You do realise, Stevens,' he said, 'that I don't expect you to stay here while I'm away. Why don't you take the car and have a break?'

'Very good, sir,' I replied noncommittally before returning to my duties. Mr Farraday is an American and likes to indulge in something called banter, and I feared this might be an example of that genre. But when he mentioned it again several days later, it occurred to me it might be an opportunity to visit Miss Kenton, who had written me a letter in which she had indicated she was not entirely happy in Devon where she had lived for the past 20 years and might be open to returning to Darlington Hall. Her presence would be welcome. Since Mr Farraday had bought the Hall after the death of Lord Darlington, the number of staff had been reduced from 117 to 27 and the limescale had built up on the downstairs lavatories accordingly.

Tonight I find myself in Salisbury. I have retired to my room early since the manners of the lower orders are not at all to my taste and, as I starch my pyjamas, I contemplate the necessary qualities for those who aspire to join the highest ranks of service as a butler. Without question, the most essential is dignity, something I like to think both my father and I displayed in our careers. Yet no one could match Mr Neighbours. He was serving drinks at a glittering party hosted by his employer, the Marquis of Cholmondeley-Bottom, when the King loudly expelled foul-smelling wind.

'That was quite uncalled for, Neighbours,' the Marquis said quickly.

'I'm most terribly sorry, sir,' Neighbours replied. 'I shall take myself outdoors and kill myself to make amends.' Truly a legend among butlers. We shall never see his like again. Not least because he blew his head off with the Marquis's hand-tooled 12-bore shotgun.

It has been an honour for me to be close to the most important events in history throughout my career. Some of you may now remember Lord Darlington as a man who made unfortunate political judgments. Let me say that in the 1930s it was not at all clear the Nazi Party were fascists and that Lord Darlington's motive for inviting them to the Hall derived purely from the humanitarian concern that no German and English aristocrats should ever again find themselves on opposing sides in a conflict.

Darlington Hall was extremely busy during the 1930s and I was grateful that Miss Kenton had proved such an admirable appointment in her capacity as leading maidservant. Without her peerless ability to fold napkins neatly, diplomatic relations between England and Germany would undoubtedly have deteriorated. Yet she was not without her faults. Her attempts to place flowers in my quarters and to engage me in conversation at moments of high stress when I was polishing the silver were most unwelcome. Still more unwelcome were her suggestions that my father, who had come to work at the house in his retirement, was no longer up to the job of emptying out His Lordship's chamberpot due to his tremor.

'I will be the judge of that,' I said testily. 'But may I say I have not yet noticed any urine stains on the carpets.'

Matters came to a head at a top-secret meeting of the utmost national importance, attended by Mr Churchill and Herr von Ribbentropp. As I was collecting the ash from Mr Churchill's cigar, Miss Kenton announced that my father was dying and that I should come quickly.

'Do you not realise that the country will be in peril if I fail to attend to Mr Churchill, Miss Kenton?' I said. 'Please tell my father to hang on before he croaks.'

Once the negotiations between Mr Churchill and Herr von Ribbentropp were complete, I allowed myself to visit my father briefly. 'You've been a good son,' he said. 'Have I been a good father?' A bell rang. 'That is Lord Darlington,' I replied. 'If I do not refill his glass with port, the country will be at war within hours.' My father died some time that night. 'His Lordship's meeting was very successful,' I said to Miss Kenton the following day. 'We should congratulate ourselves.'

As I drive onwards through Dorset, it occurs to me you might be finding it hard to believe any manservant could be quite so repressed and self-deluded, and that I owe more to the imagination of someone familiar only with a national caricature than reality. My sense of duty does not allow me to comment further on this, save to point out my primary role for Mr Ishiguro is to be an unreliable narrator, and therefore if I have allowed myself to look more stupid than I perhaps am, it is out of loyalty to his high-minded literary endeavours.

A butler cannot afford to be distracted from his master's service. This was never clearer to me than when Miss Kenton informed me she was leaving Darlington Hall to get married. 'Very well,' I said. 'But I haven't got time to discuss this now as His Lordship has requested I should misinform his godson about the Birds and the Bees.'

That evening, as I was passing Miss Kenton's room, I heard sobbing. I realised then that, for no reason apparent earlier in the book, she had formed a romantic attachment to me and had merely decided to get married to another man to make me jealous. It struck me also that I too had what people refer to as 'feelings' for her, but I didn't enter her room because His Lordship had summoned me to tie up his laces and, had I failed to attend to his shoes, a faux-pas might have been committed that would have brought the country to the brink of war once more.

In the interests of pathos, I may have inadvertently allowed some Devonians to believe I was a man of distinction in my own right through my allusions to the famous men I have stood nearby, though I was careful not to mention the name of Lord Darlington. It is barely 10 years since the war ended and people are still surprisingly judgmental about His Lordship's friendship with Oswald Mosley and are reluctant to recognise his anti-Semitism as patriotism.

I fear I may once more be overloading my self-delusion for the benefit of Mr Ishiguro's pathos, so as I drive away from Cornwall I would like to conclude by saying that I had an extremely enjoyable 20-minute meeting with Miss Kenton, or Mrs Benn as she has been called for the 20 years since we last met.

'I have had an extremely unhappy life,' she said, 'but I don't think it would help to leave my husband for you after all this time.'

'I totally agree,' I said. 'I was thinking the same thing. Our literary duty is to live a life filled with regret for what might have been.'

'And what will you do, Mr Stevens?'

'I'm going to try to learn to smile. If I can just get away from Mr Ishiguro for a moment.'

POSSESSION

A. S. Byatt

Roland Michell gave his credentials: part-time research assistant to Professor Blackadder, who had been editing the Complete Works of the Victorian poet Randolph Henry Ash since 1951. In return, the librarian handed over one of Ash's books and Roland retreated to one of the dustier recesses of the London Library. On opening the book, he founded two sheets of paper.

Dear Madam, Since our unexpected conversation at Crabb's breakfast table, I have thought of little else but English myth and dull literary allusion of interest to no one but writers who take themselves far too seriously. We must speak again.

Very interesting, thought Roland. It cannot be Miss Byatt to whom Ash addressed this correspondence, for though the sentiments may fit, post-modernism was not a trait associated with Byatt and other Victorians. He placed the letters in his jacket pocket and went home.

'Did you have another boring day?' enquired the nondescript Val of her equally nondescript partner. To have called them lovers would have spoken of a depth of emotion not to be found in this book.

'Indeed I did,' Roland replied. 'And you?'

'Oh, yes. Working for a solicitor is most satisfactorily dreary.'

'It is perhaps unfortunate that all of us present-day characters should have been made into two-dimensional academic stereotypes,' said Professor Blackadder as Roland entered his office.

'That would certainly explain why no one ever mentions you

have the same name as Rowan Atkinson's character in the television comedy series,' Roland answered.

'Good Lord,' A. S. Byatt exclaimed. 'What's a television?'

Roland knew it was incumbent on him to inform the professor of his find, yet he chose to keep it to himself, electing instead to seek out the more superficial help of Fergus Wolf, the blond departmental Love God.

'Um, I was wondering if you could give me a hand,' enquired Roland. 'It seems that Ash may have met a woman at one of Crabb Robinson's salons. It can only have been the little-known poet Christabel La Motte. Do you know anything about her?'

'Not a lot. Except I shagged Maud Bailey, the only academic specialising in her work, at a Lacanian conference on Feminist Semiotics in Victorian Poetry. She was a bit of a goer – ooh er, know what I mean? Everyone thought she was a lezzer, just like Christabel.'

Deep in the temperature-controlled vault of the Randolph Henry Ash Centre at the University of American Caricature, Professor Mortimer P. Cropper let out an evil laugh. 'Mwa-ha-ha. By hook or by crook, I shall own every Ash artefact come what may.'

Roland knocked gently on the door of the Women's Studies department at Lincoln University. 'Come in to my garden,' said Maud, tucking her blonde hair into a headscarf in case she may be thought attractive. 'So what do you think of Christabel's poetry?

'*At the risk of simplifying the scansion / It reads a bit like Emily Dickinson,*' said Roland.

'Bravo,' cried A. S. Byatt from afar, admiring her own genius.

'Excellent,' said Maud. 'Now it so happens I am conveniently distantly related to the La Mottes, so perhaps you might accompany me to Seal Court where Christabel lived out her final years in solitude. Though I doubt we shall gain access, as the present owners, Sir George and Lady Joan Bailey, are extremely unfriendly.'

'Thank you for preventing my wheelchair from o'er turning,' said Lady Joan. 'However can I repay you?'

'You could let us have a rummage around for some correspondence,' replied Roland. 'But where to start looking?'

'Remember the lines from Mesulina,' Maud exclaimed. '*For those who come searching, long after I'm dead / I've hidden the letters under the bed.*' They raced upstairs. There they were – a host of golden epistles!

My dear, The fire of Prometheus blazes deep within me, Your friend Randolph.

My dear, It is quite awkward what with my house-mate, Blanche Glover, and all that, Your friend Christabel.

My dear, Hyperion's blessings fall on Albion / As my poem drones on and on / Pray read my epic 'Swammerdam' / And let me pierce your bearded clam, Your ardent friend, Randolph.

My dear, The wonders of your verse / Would be greater if more terse. But I'll meet you anyway, Love Christabel.

My dear, I don't know why you suddenly want all your letters back and for me to contact you no more, but I shall do as you say, Yours R. H. Ash.

'Gosh,' gasped Maud. 'Scholars will have to rethink the history of Victorian Romantic poetry. It appears Ash was not devotedly luxorious to his wife Ellen and that Christabel might not have been a lesbian feminist icon.

'See the parallels in Ash's and Christabel's poems. In Ash we find, *Like ancient varnish runs deep / In darkest dales of tangled bushes,* and in Christabel, *An ash I take into my mouth / As soon as I am north of Louth.* Ash did not go alone unto Yorkshire as we thought! This is why Blanche committed suicide! Perhaps we will turn up some more documents if we look hard.'

'Count on it.' A. S. Byatt smiled. 'For I cannot resist showing off my ventriloquist talents.'

The Journal of R. H. Ash. *By Apollo's swollen Penisneid! Awoke to find Christabel's blood on my thighs. Perhaps Blanche does not* *have a dildo after all. Now Christabel has fled, wither I know not.*

The Secret Diary of Ellen Ash, aged 43 and three-quarters. *Randolph has come back from Yorkshire. He went with that bint but I'm not going to say another word as he's come back without her.*

The Even More Secret diary of Sabine, aged 17 and two-thirds. *Zut alors, ma cousine Anglaise Christabel 'as cerm to stay wiz us. She is vair obviously pregnant. Mais non! She has disparue and come back wizout ze bébé.*

'It is so exciting to be on this literary trail with you,' said Maud, 'especially as you aren't interested in the grubby sex thing.'

'Good God, no,' exclaimed Roland. 'Literary marginalia are far more stimulating.'

'But if you fancied a bunk-up, you could have one.'

'As long as we can still read poetry to one another.'

'There's no time for that. A. S. Byatt has wasted so much time showing off her erudition, we're going to have to wrap the book up in an eighty-page Harry Potter-style romp.'

Roland returned to his flat to see Val. 'I'm sorry it didn't work out with you,' he said, 'I've been a bit Possessed.'

'Don't worry,' Val replied. 'I've hooked up with a solicitor who coincidentally just happens to be handling the gripping issue of who keeps the letters. Hurry, there's not a moment to lose. Mortimer Cropper is plotting to exhume Ash's body illegally and retrieve the missing items Ellen placed in the coffin.'

'Mwa-ha-ha, soon everything will be mine,' cried Cropper, as a gothic storm broke and a yew tree pinned him to the ground.

'Not so fast,' said Maud, Roland, Blackadder, Val and the Coincidental Solicitor, as they discovered a last letter from Christabel that Ellen had concealed.

I kept the baby and she's being brought up by my sis. Don't worry, she's not being made to read your ghastly poetry, Love and kisses, C.

'So you are a direct descendant of Christabel, Maud,' everyone gasped. 'Then the letters are legally yours.'

'Thrice darn it,' snarled Cropper.

'Gosh,' said Roland, 'I've been offered a new job. Which is quite nice. Perhaps we should do the sex thing a bit more.'

Randolph Ash rolled in his grave. 'For what it's worth, I did know about my daughter, but Christabel never got my message. Hey ho, some events vanish without trace.' But by then, no one was listening so no one would ever know.

AMERICAN PSYCHO

Bret Easton Ellis

ABANDON HOPE ALL ye who enter here is typed in bold but Timothy Price knows that won't stop you literary hipsters from drooling over the excess of yuppy alienation. 'Stanford, Vassar, Blaupunkt, D. F. Sanders, Ermenegildo Zegna, Ralph Lauren,' he says as we take a cab from the downtown trading floor of Pierce & Pierce to my girlfriend Evelyn's apartment on the Upper East Side.

He's talking too much, the coke must have been cut with amphetamines, we pass a poster for *Les Misérables*, I really want to see that show, but I can't let him get away with all those lists. Lists are my thing. They're what I do. All I do. 'AIDS, niggers, Jewboys, Nazis, junkies,' I reply, taking out my cock. All this transgression has given me a hard-on and I need to masturbate.

'I think we've all got the point of the book by now,' she says, flashing her $1,500 Prada wool-crêpe dress and helping herself to tuna sushi served from the heads of midgets.

'Tough shit,' I say ogling some hardbody, who I can tell wants to fuck me. 'There's still another 370 pages to go.' I lie on the floor and knock out 7,000 abdominal crunches. Man, I am so halved. Ripped. 'This fucking Cristal is non-vintage,' I sneer, adjusting my Brooks Brothers shirt. 'I'm outta here.'

We take a cab to my apartment. There's a dwarf in the lobby. It's Tom Cruise. He lives here too.

'I love your movies, Tom,' I smile.

'I hate your books, Bret,' he replies.

I go upstairs and get on my sunbed. It's been seven hours since

I last took some rays and I can feel my tan fading. 'That's better,' I say, putting on my $97,000 polar-bear-skin coat. 'Let's go to all the latest trendy clubs and restaurants so I can overpay with my platinum Amex card.'

At work, my secretary, Jean, is making up to me. She's a decent enough hardbody, but I don't fancy her enough to fuck her.

'You've got lunch at Serrano's booked for one, Mr Bateman,' she says. 'You're such a wonderful man.'

'No, I'm not. I'm a fucking psycho,' I laugh. She pretends not to hear and I'm tempted to fuck her throat and tell her to choke on the irony, but I've got some porno movies to take back to the rental store and I've got dinner with Courtney.

'You know Luis is a queer,' I tell Courtney, as we wolf down giant panda carpaccio. Luis is Courtney's boyfriend and he'd tried to suck my cock after I'd half-strangled him in the corridor.

'You can fuck me in the ass if you want,' she says.

I would, but I can't be bothered. Instead I go into a pointless chapter about the rock band Genesis.

'The French do existential futility so much better, don't you think?' a derelict beggar says. 'You Yanks just scratch the surface with a few brand names.'

That does it. I pull out my $750 hand-tooled Sabatier knife and cut out his eye, slash open his abdomen and stuff his pancreas up his ass. 'Fuck you, you nigger cunt.'

There's blood on my collar and I need to change. I get in a cab with Donald Trump. 'I'm so excited to be part of your postmodern fantasies, Patrick,' he drawls. 'Pleased to have you,' I say. 'Give my best to Ivana. I hope she's wiped my cum off her tits.'

I try to book a table at Dorsia. It's booked solid. My shithead brother calls. He's got a table at Dorsia. How dare the cunt? We eat pan-seared Aborigine scrotum and I pick up the bill. It's only $765,000. Cheap.

Armani, check. The *Patty Winters Show*, check. Lord & Taylor, check. Gloria Jose, check. I call an escort, Christy, and get her to come and fuck me and this hardbody Alison. They both come in squirts as I ram three-foot dildoes up their asses. Alison goes home so I drill Christy to the floor, amputate her arm and bite off her tits. I'm feeling warmed up. I take a limo and decapitate the driver after he drops me at Paul Owen's apartment. I slice off his leg and shove the foot in his arse. The bitch squeals like a pig.

'What have you been doing?' Evelyn asks.

'I've been wandering around New York hacking people to death.'

''Course you have, dear. Now run along and do 23,000 crunches.'

I'm tempted to take a blowtorch to her cunt, but I can't be bothered any more. The only people taking my grossness seriously are 17-year-old disaffected middle-class males wearing too-skinny jeans. Still, I guess someone is still listening so I'd better give them something else to wank about. I pick up Bethany and nail her to the floor, before shoving a rat up her cunt to eat her insides. The blood pools interestingly as I daringly eat her nipples and sphincter.

'When did you last see Paul Owen?' I'm being interrogated by some detective and I'm trying to create some tension with my mental disintegration, but it's pointless as everything's the fucking same and no one gives a toss. I shrug and my $47,000 Hermès suit creases. 'He's been seen in Paris.' Wow! How thrillingly postmodern. Perhaps it was all a fantasy.

I go to the zoo and feed a child to the lions, and then go back to my apartment. I put on a $900 tie. I then put on another $900 tie as the book is so badly edited no one has noticed I already had one on. Jesus. That editor is going to die. She only has to read this shit. Imagine what it's like to write.

Fuck. I remember I need to go round to Paul Owen's apartment to store the chick stiff and to eat some more labia. Weird. The place smells of flowers and there's no blood. 'Have you come to rent the apartment?' a woman asks. I nod. 'Did you see the ad in the *Times*?' I nod. 'There was no ad,' she rasps. 'Now fuck off before I call the Feds.' Wow! How thrillingly postmodern. Perhaps it wasn't all a fantasy.

'I've just seen Paul Owen in Paris,' says Timothy Price, bizarrely reappearing 350 pages later wearing an Agnès B, blah, blah. Wow! How thrillingly postmodern. Perhaps it was all a fantasy.

I feel like I'm losing it. I can't be bothered to fuck. The coke is shit. And I can't get a table at Nando's. 'I know who you are,' says the cabby. 'You're the serial killer. I recognise the Rolex.' 'Fuck you, Abdullah,' I yell. 'Say a word and I'll eat your larynx.' Wow! How thrillingly postmodern. Perhaps it wasn't all a fantasy.

'How've you been?' Craig McDermott asks, knocking back an Absolut in Barcadia.

'You know how it is,' I say, my hand shaking, 'killing people, eating them, that kind of thing.'

'Do shut the fuck up,' Evelyn groans. 'Not even the fucked-up male teens are reading any more.'

GENERATION X

Douglas Coupland

BACK IN THE late 70s I flew up to Manitoba to see a total eclipse of the sun. It was like the lights went out. This book reads like they never came back on.

Fifteen years later, Dag, Claire and I are hanging out in California. Dag has just vandalised a car, Claire has been on a date with the yuppy from hell. We have been cheated out of our inheritance. Where is the effortless superiority we were told was our birthright? What do you see?

'We see apocalyptic images,' say Dag and Claire.

I do too, so we drive east. We're out in the car playing a game of trying to shock the reader. We fail, so we wind up in the constipated town of Palm Springs near the Mojave Desert. We head nowhere for a picnic and start telling each other stories.

I'm sorry, I've been a bit vague here. Let me tell you about Dag. He turned up a year ago and I got him a job in Larry's bar. He used to work in Toronto but he upped sticks when he got Sick Office Syndrome.

Capitalism sucks. So we dropped out, name-dropped South American novelists and smoked. Now we trade on a basement lifestyle, doing the worst jobs available just to look hip. Plus we're too dopey to do anything else.

Claire talks about Nostradamus and how incomplete people are somehow more complete. She is our ideal companion. 'Let me tell you two mystical nowhere guys a story about a mystical nowhere place called Texlahoma,' she says. 'There was this astronaut called Buck who needed help to return to a far-off planet. Arleen and Darleen didn't love him enough to die for him. But Serena did.'

Look, I never said these stories had a meaning. Wake up and smell the Starbucks. This is postmodernism for the blank, brand-name generation; all we're doing is filling space, killing time.

Claire and I never fell in love. It was too much effort. Like writing this. Still, I've nothing else to do, so I might as well continue. I'm Andy, 30, an ectomorph, as stick-thin as my ideas. Here's a story I never told Dag and Claire. 'Edward found life a hassle so he stayed indoors for ten years smoking a pipe. When he went out again he realised he was a bumpkin. The End.'

Dag demands I tell a story. 'I went to Japan once and came back home when I was shown a picture of Marilyn Monroe's jet-black bush,' I say. 'I needed to read Rilke's letter within me.'

'That's deep and meaningless,' Dag says, though he and Claire have never had a relationship. 'This is my end-of-the-world story. It's 31 December 1999 and you're arguing with friends about shopping malls and then you die.'

McNovel: a ramble with no real beginning or end about three ambitionless stoners who think they are too cool to breathe.

Five days ago Dag disappeared. Oh, he's turned up in Nevada. 'I needed to know more about nuclear mushroom clouds,' he says.

Dag is back. He gives Claire some trinitite; she freaks out, thinks it's plutonium. Who cares? Everyone has a grumpy yuppy in their life; Claire's is Tobias, an east coast banker. He comes to visit. He's bland and smug; unlike Dag and me, who are just bland.

'What's he doing with Claire?' Dag asks. 'She's got a brain.' Can't say I'd noticed. I'm more worried about going home for Christmas. My parents are so boring they don't even recycle.

We're by the pool and Claire's friend Elvissa appears. No one really knows what she does, but then no one really cares either. Tobias says we're all fakes. So we tell stories about our favourite real experiences before Elvissa goes off on one about a bloke who gets his balls shot off and his eyes pecked out by hummingbirds. At least I think that's what it was about – I nodded off.

Tobias dumps Claire and Elvissa leaves at the same time. I listen to some more stories and laugh in the wrong places. Hell, we just needed a laugh. Any laugh. Dag says he wants to own a hotel in the California Baja. Elvissa shows up in a nunnery. You can see why I needed a laugh.

I light thousands of candles in my parents' house. It's a Vietnam thing. Apparently. Claire phones from New York. She went to see Tobias; it didn't work out. Surprise. They were both too self-obsessed. She now wants to go out in the desert with a dowsing stick to find water.

Dag and I go to a party and accidentally torch an Aston Martin. I wake up to find that Dag and Claire have left. There's a message. 'We've gone to open a hotel for washed-up losers in Mexico. Come and join us.' I get in my car and start driving. An egret scratches my head, and a group of disabled children love bomb me. What the fuck?

Hubris: Dag, Claire and Andy have just opened their 23rd themed organic hotel in California. They are concerned about the credit crunch and moan a great deal about how useless the younger generation are these days.

TRAINSPOTTING

Irvine Welsh

Sɪᴄᴋ Bᴏʏ ᴡɪs tremblin. Ah wis tryin no tae notis the cunt. He wis bringin me doon.

– Rents. Ah goat tae score.

– Aw, ah sais.

Ah wanted the radge to fuck off soas ah cid watch ma Jean-Claude Van Damme vidjo.

– Youse a cunt, he snaps, bustin me mooth wiz a hammer.

We tae the bus roond to Swanny's. He's holdin n awl so we coak up wiv Raymie.

– Youse goat ta use ma werks, he sais.

– Ah wannae tell the radge to fuck off, that he can shove his AIDS urp his erse, but I need the skag. The shite ODs soas ahm erff the hook. Alison sais ah should visit Kelly whos had an abortion. Ah cannae be ersed.

Ahve goat masen a flat an ahm gonnae come off the skaggie this taime. Ah mean it. But first ah needs some stuff tae take the edge off the turkis. Know what ah mean? Ah scores sum opium an sherves it oop ma erse. Ah canna feel a mighty shite comin on. Ma kecks are soaked with diarrhoea an the toilet is trashed. Thens ah remember tha droogs. Ah scoop through tha shite till ah fins it an stuff it bak up me erse and lick ma fingers.

Junk Dilemmas No 63: *Thrillin the poncy London literati wi scuzzy Edinburgh smackheids doant disguise the fact this is jez sum vaguely connected shert storis.*

– Is sum cunt moanin thers no real structure? sais Begbie. Jaysis, whass the radge expect erf a bunch of junkis? Ahl fuckin beat the shite of the erse. Lets fuck im over, Sick Boy.

Ah sais nuthin. He is a cunt, but hes a mate n aw. Anyways, ahd raither be shagging sum burd.

Ahm sittin in me room trying tae find a vein in ma cock. Iss nae tha big a best o taimes, but noo is drippin blood an covered wi ulcers. Tommy cames in.

– Ah needs sum junk, he sais.

– Yer nae do drugs, I ansas.

– Ah dae noo.

Oh my God, where am I? Who are you, more like. I'm Dave, I've appeared from nowhere, but I rather thought you'd like to know I can also mix things up with standard English. I remember picking up Gail in the pub but I don't remember whether I shagged her when she took me home. I hope not, because I've shat, pissed and thrown up in her bed.

– Ah had a wee accident, I say to her mum, handing her the sheets. The shite dribbles on the floor and she slips over, breaking her leg. Seems like a good moment to leave.

Junk Dilemmas No 69: *Canna yers get awa wi jes thinkin up gross shite an writin it doon? Check the fuckin sales figgers, sais Irvine. The thing aboot nihilism is thas nae fuckin point tae anythin. Sers yer canna dae wha ye laike.*

Wah yer doin, Franco? Ma burd ersks. Ah tell the cunt ter main her ern biznis an heid ter the station wi Rents. So were on the train an Rents sais, I canna remember what we goan tae London. Have na clue masen. Sum crime or otha.

Renton had been clean a while and wasn't at all sure why this chapter was in the third person. But then his tiny cock was as hard as rock so he wasn't that bothered.

– S na verra big an iz covered wiv scabs but ahll shag thas any wa, sais Dianne.

As she wiped the spunk from her cunt, he noticed she was only about 12 years old. Ah best fuck off, he thinks. Can you get us sum blow? she sais. An cum an meet ma parents?

Ah shoots a dog wiv mer air rifle and then it bites its oaner an then ah pulps tha boath and the polis thinks ahm a fuckin hero laike Sean Connery.

An thas a fuckin pointlis chapta n aw, Sick Boy. Is ma turn agin an Irvine wannae tra tae git a bit deep ba givin me sum back stora, how ma disabled brar deid, how all tha shrinks tra tae mak sense a wha ah became a junky. Fact is ahs a junky cos ahs a addict. End a. Choose life? Why?

Junk Dilemmas No. 73: *If thers oan thin moar depressin than reidin aboot junkies shootin up, rippin oan another off an pishin and shittin is knowin losers laike tha radge Guy Ritchie will be tossin thessen off into their Armani fuckin suits wiv the vicarious excitement an glama.*

Ahm well fucked na. Couldnae resist bangin up agin an naw mi habits back an mi parents have kidnapped ma. Sweatin, dreamin a dead babies. Jaysis, Irvine's tryin tae hard wiv tha kaind a symbolism. The cunts goat the idea hes naw writin som important fuckin master werk nay jez scribblin down a load a scuzz. Next the cunt will be havin me goan on aboot sectarian-ism. Spoke tae fuckin soon. Naw mi twat o an elder brar go hisen kilt in Northern Ireland. Ahm ment tae be sad but ah doant giv a fuck. Think ahll jez shag his pregnant burd at the funeral instead.

I'm going to save you trying to guess who this is now. It's me, Dave, again. I've got AIDS now. It should have been Rents. I've never shot or fucked a bloke. Just fucked a girl who was raped by some sick radge. Just watch me get my revenge.

Tha reminds ma. Ah had a bloke suck ma off once and ah thought ah should tra fuckin Antonio in tha erse. Tha cunt came on ma face befor ah got rained ta it. Ah wis gonnae beat him up but he sais doant kill ma, Rents, ma boyfrien ha kilt hisen.

Junk Dilemmas No. 78: *If yer characters are barely conscious, what state dya reckin ya readers a in ba naw?*

Ah havnae clue whether ahm off the droogs a na naw. Came tae think a it, ahve lost all trace time-scale or where ah fuckin is. Jez pass i off as stylish junky chic. Suck on tha Bill Burroughs. An Coupland you can stick Generation X reet up yer erse. Generation X? Choose Generation XXX.

I'm glad I dumped Rents and went to university. He was a bright bloke but going nowhere. Money's tight, though, so I'm working as a waitress. I fucking hate some of the clientele who hit on me though. See this lot. I've dunked my tampon in the soup, filled the wine with infected piss. My cystisis is well bad. And I've shat in the chocolate pudding. Cunts don't even notice. Nice.

Tha wuz ma ex burd Kelly, ba tha wa. Check out Swanny. His leg bin amputated but he still shoots into tha stump. An thas Tommy. Another poor cunt dyin a Aids. An thas psycho Begbie, beatin the shite outta some radge tha lookt a him tha wrong wa.

Junk Dilemmas No. 84: *How comes it taks 350 pages tae sa tha junkis are lyin, cheatin, scumbags? N whas all tha borin stuff tha maks up 99% o a junkis lif?*

Ahm well strung oot an ahve had enuff a this shite. Ahm gonnae end it all na. Me an Begbie fucked off tae London wiv a load a smack an flogged it for 16 grand. An ahve ripped Begbie off n aw. So ahm on the train to Amsterdam. An youse can all fuck off. Choose life. Choose an endin. Choose ana endin.

HIGH FIDELITY

Nick Hornby

MY DESERT ISLAND top five break-ups: Alison Ashworth, Penny Hardwick, zzzzz . . . No room for you in that lot, Laura. Thing is, we're just too old to make each other really miserable.

Alison? One day she snogged me, the next she snogged someone else. Penny? She wouldn't let me grope her so I dump her and she knobs Chris Thompson. Etc, etc. You're getting the picture, right? I meet someone, I make some lists, she gets bored and I get dumped. I was 35, running my own nerdy record shop, and had already made 19,621 lists by the time we met, Laura, so if you'd wanted to fuck me up you should have got to me earlier.

That was then, this is now. Laura leaves first thing on Monday. 'I'm not sure I know what I'm doing, Rob,' she says. I can tell she knows that I'm thinking that I know what she's thinking so I just go inside and rearrange my record collection to make the covers follow the colours of the spectrum.

Barry is already at the shop by the time I arrive. 'How was your weekend?' he asks. I think about telling him about Laura but then I think we don't really have that kind of relationship so I reply: 'I made a list of all the anagrams you could make out of "Solomon Burke is God".'

'Cool,' says Barry. 'Did you include "I'm a sad twat"? Now, how about we see this cool American country and western singer, who once recorded with someone who knew Nanci Griffith, play in the pub later?'

I go home to make a list of the top five lists I have ever made, and as I walk in the door the phone rings. It's Laura's best friend, Liz. 'I'm sorry Laura's left you,' she says. 'I'm sure it won't work out with her and Ian.'

This is the first I've heard of a bloke called Ian but I think that Liz doesn't know that I've never heard of him so I decide to tell her that I'm about to go out to a gig. Marie LaSalle opens with a sublime cover version of Boney M's 'Brown Girl in the Ring' and I start crying and Marie comes up to me after the gig and we talk for a bit and then I go home and write down her set list.

Liz phones again. 'You are a complete bastard,' she yells, before slamming down the phone. There are two explanations. 1. Laura has told her that I had an affair when she was pregnant and had an abortion. 2. I can't think of another one, but it looks better as a list.

I find a letter on the stairs addressed to a Mr I. Raymond. The penny drops. Ian is the neighbour I know as Ray. I throw away all my Stevie Ray Vaughan records and go to see Marie play.

'Even single girls get horny,' she says. 'Why don't you come back to my place for a one-night stand?'

I think about whether she's thinking about whether my dick will be too small or if I will come too quickly but we go back and have some angst and the sex isn't too bad and we both know after we've done it that we won't be doing it again and I tell her that is OK by me even though it isn't really though it sort of is as well.

I go home and make a list of all the things a lad-lit book needs. 1. All the blokes are complete losers with dead-end jobs and an emotional inadequacy marginally offset by a self-deprecating self-awareness. 2. All the women are completely sorted with fantastic jobs and are capable of long-term mature relationships. 3. That's it.

I worry that my inadequacies aren't inadequate enough so I stalk Laura by calling her 351 times and make jokes that aren't jokes really about whether Ray is any good in bed and then visit my exes to find out why they dumped me and am only a little surprised when they all tell me it was because I am an arse. Those that remember me, that is.

I am in the shop not selling any records when Laura calls to tell me that her father has died and she wants me to come to his funeral. I make a list of the five most predictable endings to a book and say yes.

'You know,' says Laura, 'when my dad died, I realised it wasn't Ray that I wanted at the funeral, it was you. We've made so many lists together that I couldn't be bothered to start making new ones. So shag me in the car and we can get back together, have babies and live happily ever after.'

I'm thinking this sort of bogus catharsis is just about the most unconvincing psychological resolution I've ever come across but I think I won't say so because I can't think how else to wrap things up and besides Hollywood loves simplistic endings so I just say: 'I've realised that I couldn't commit to you before because I was worried you might die. Will you marry me?'

Laura smiles. 'Maybe later, once I've patronised you a bit more,' she says. 'After all I am still a successful lawyer earning five times as much as you and you are still a useless arse. So why don't I arrange for Marie to play a gig in your sweet little shop and organise a club night for you to DJ?'

The dancefloor is jumping, the night is going well. Barry takes me to one side. 'I can just about accept that you've made all us blokes look like complete dicks,' he says. 'But what I can't forgive is you paving the way for copycats like that knobber Tony Parsons.'

ENDURING LOVE

Ian McEwan

T HE BEGINNING IS simple to mark. Clarissa, me, a picnic, a
shout. What idiocy to be racing into this story. Knowing what
I know now it's hard to evoke the figure of Jed Parry, running, like
me, towards the child in the balloon.

I'm holding back, delaying the moment in a virtuoso display
of literary knowingness. Clarissa and I had enjoyed a childless
marriage in our art-deco London flat and the picnic was to
celebrate her return from America where she had been
researching Keats. She called me her complicated simpleton; really
I was just a simple complication.

I smelled urine as I reached the basket. Parry, along with two
men whom I later knew to be Lacey and Logan, caught up and for
a while we steadied it. Then the wind caught the balloon and it
began to lift. I do not know who was first to let go; but Logan was
left hanging by the rope before falling 300 feet to the field below.

The beginning is an artifice, but then it always is. I could have
started somewhere else, a leisurely breakfast, perhaps. But how
else do you posit extreme moral choices in the most improbable
way? I ran down the hill – it was all downhill after that dramatic
beginning – and urinated strongly to demonstrate my usual
forensic attention to bodily functions. The skeletal structure had
collapsed and I told Parry there was nothing we could do. 'We
could pray,' he said. 'There's no one up there,' I replied.

Clarissa and I tried to make sense of the day's events. She
whispered Miltonian sweet-nothings as she caressed my balls,
before I reasserted my mammalian selfishness by making love to

her with my Darwinian prowess. 'You're such a rationalist, Joe,' she cried. 'I love you more than ever.' The phone rang and I recognised Parry's voice, whispering, 'I love you.' 'Wrong number,' I told Clarissa.

Why did I lie? Who knows? I made my way to the London Library to study neural activity in the amygdala, of which there would be precious little if I continued with such overwrought divisions between the religious and the rational. I spotted Parry stalking me and returned home to find several love letters on my doorstep.

I eventually told Clarissa about Parry; she dismissed me as a fantasist and our lovemaking became more perfunctory, though never less than brilliant on my part. As I left the house, lamenting that I had failed to win the Nobel Prize for physics and was working as a hack for *UFO Today*, I was followed by Parry. 'God loves you, I love you and you love me,' he said.

The police were as uninterested in his harassment as Clarissa. 'If we take it seriously,' the officer pointed out, 'there's no chance for you to explore the lacunae of psychosis or the dualist split between religion and science.'

Let's look at things from Clarissa's perspective. Not because it's enlightening, but because it's a cute shift. She doesn't believe him. She uses the historic present. She's a total bore. Is that enough?

Dear Joe, I still love you. Thanks for loving me, Yours Jed, Kissy Kissy

'Why are you writing to yourself?' Clarissa asked for no good reason. 'For the same reason I've ransacked your desk looking for evidence of an imaginary lover I know you don't have,' I cried. 'Because we are drifting apart and our love is not enduring.'

I met Logan's widow and, after I lectured her children on moral relativism, she told me of her fears that her husband had been with a mistress on the day of the accident. A thought flashed through my hippocampus. Parry was suffering from de Clérambault's syndrome, a homo-erotic psychosis that no one but me had ever heard of. He was lost in a solipsism equal to my own. God, I was clever!

It was Clarissa's birthday and, despite the unenduring nature of our love, she perked up when I gave her a first edition of Keats' love poetry. As we ate our lime sorbets in a restaurent, a masked gunman burst in and shot the man sitting next to us. I saw Parry stop the gunman and then rush out.

'I was eating an apple sorbet,' I told the police later. 'He meant to kill me; Parry stopped him when he saw he had got the wrong man.' Why did I lie to the police about the sorbet? To demonstrate the unreliability of memory? 'We still don't believe you,' the officer answered. 'The victim was an MP who's been a target before.' I compounded this improbability by arranging to buy a gun from some hippies in Sussex. 'I'd stick to writing about things you know,' they shouted as I left.

Clarissa rang. 'Parry's taken me hostage.' I drove home to find him wielding a penknife. 'Forgive me, darling,' he cried, putting the blade to his throat. I pulled out the gun and skilfully shot him in the arm to prevent him killing himself.

Dear Joe, You were right but you were wrong, too, Clarissa.

'Your husband wasn't having an affair,' I said to Logan's widow, introducing an Oxford don and his student mistress with a *deus ex machina* flourish. 'He had given them a lift instead.' 'So,' she replied, 'my love wasn't very enduring either.' 'No,' I agreed, 'but at least I've wrapped up all the loose ends.'

APPENDIX: Here's a bit of clever clogs trickery about de Clérambault's syndrome that some reviewers might take as a journal reference. What laughs! Oh, and J and C got back together and adopted a child. Which is nice.

THE GOD OF SMALL THINGS

Arundhati Roy

MAY IN AYEMENEM is a hot brooding month, where the days are long and humid, crows gorge on bright mangoes and too many overwrought descriptive passages pile up in a car-crash of a creative writing tutorial.

But forget about that, because it was early June , the time when the monsoon breaks, the yellow bullfrogs etc, etc . . . , when Rahel returned to the house. Baby Kochamma was still alive. She was Rahel's baby grand aunt, but Rahel hadn't come to visit her. She had come to see her dizygotic twin, Estha, from whom she had been separated for 23 years.

Her mind inevitably went back to a deeper, more secret, poetic space. A space when Life was full of Beginnings and no Ends, before Edges, Borders and Capital Letters began to appear. She remembered what the Orangedrink Lemondrink Man did to Estha even though he never actually told her what happened. But these are Small Things.

And that was before they were nearly born on a bus, before Ammu and her father were divorced, before Ammu died at 31, a dieable viable age, before the unthinkable became thinkable and Sophie Mol died at 7, a dieable, non-viable age, before Estha was Returned, before she had gone to Canada to get married, before she had got divorced. But these too are Small Things.

Even before Sophie Mol's funeral, the police found Velutha by the river. A river with a rushing, rolling, fishswimming sense. A river swollen, engorged with meaningless imagery. Yes, it had all begun with Sophie Mol in the days before the Love Laws were rewritten.

It was a skyblue day in 1969 when Rahel found herself in a fictive time-slip. She gasped in amazement as the skyblue Plymouth pulled up and her uncle Chacko got out and talked about how Pappachi started drinking after a moth wasn't named after him and used to beat up Mammachi until he warned him off, how he had been a Rhodes scholar, had married Margaret and had a child, Sophie Mol, how she had left him, how he had returned to Kerala to run Mammachi's Paradise Pickles and Preserves factories, how he was a supporter of the Keralan Communist Party run by Comrade Pilla, how . . .

'Stop, Uncle,' Rahel said. 'There are too many names, too many things going on. I can't keep up.'

'That's the whole point,' Chacko replied. 'This is India, a land of sensory and poetic overload, a land where small boats bob in rippling water of green silk, a land teeming with literary prizes for those who can find the right imagery to win them. But these are small things.'

'Is there a God of Small Things?'

'There must be if I won the Booker.'

Rahel went off to find her dizygotic twin. 'Stel klat sdrawkcab ot eno rehtona,' she said. 'Yhw dluow ew tnaw ot od taht?' 'Esuaceb sti eht tros fo suoitneterp parc sniwt od ni siht dnik fo koob.'

It took Rahel a few moments to realise she was now back in 1992 as she passed the tumble-down factory where no trees now grew and an elephant lazily etc . . . She thought deep thoughts of the Love Laws, Small Things and why Estha hadn't spoken for years since he was Returned.

'We are going to the movies,' said Ammu. 'And when we get back, Margaret and Sophie Mol will have arrived from England, now that Margaret's second husband Joe has died.'

They got into the skyblue Plymouth and drove past sun-burnished banana sellers, sheltering under parched palms etc . . . , towards Cochin. 'I need a drink,' said Estha, as the nuns began singing in *The Sound of Music*.

'Come here,' said the Orangedrink LemonDrink Man. 'If you hold my penis, I will give you a free drink.' Estha did as he was told and after some hot fluid had been deposited in his hands he returned to his seat. He didn't quite know why it had happened, or what relevance it had to the story as he never mentioned it again. It was probably another of those Small Things.

Sophie Mol had arrived by the time they returned and was being fussed over by everyone. 'Ti skool ekil ew era llams sgniht won,' Rahel said to Estha, as Ammu, Chacko and Baby Kochamma ignored them. 'Don't be horrid to us, Ammu,' they begged. 'If you talk like that, I shall love you a little less,' she replied. And so the Love Laws began to get rewritten. In a Small Way.

Rahel remembered that every piece of Indian fiction required a dream sequence, so as she sat down next to the silent Estha, she went into a prolonged unnecessary reverie of Kathakali dancers that reminded her of just how Indian she really was.

A deep longing burnt deep in Ammu's vagina as she lay in the bedroom whose walls would soon learn their harrowing secrets. She needed Velutha's hard, lithe Untouchable body and he needed hers. It was against the Love Laws yet the Love Laws could not contain the primal urges of a dark sexuality unleashed. And hopefully breaking the Love Laws would only be a Small Thing.

In the abandoned house, where vapid vinegary fumes etc . . . , where Ammu conjoined with Velutha in sentences of disaggregated phrases, there Rahel and Estha found a broken boat. 'Please mend it for us, Velutha, so we can cross the Swirling, Forbidden River.'

'Take me with you,' begged Sophie Mol. 'I've had enough of all this relentless Indianness.'

As they reached the middle of the Swirling, Forbidden River, the boat capsized. Rahel and Estha swam to safety; Sophie Mol was swept under. 'Ho raed,' the dizygotic twins said. 'Stel epoh sti tsuj a Llams Gniht.'

It was a Big Small Thing. Chacko was crazed with grief and blamed Velutha. 'Arrest the Untouchable,' he ordered the police. The police came for Velutha with batons. He was of a caste of no consequence. He did not survive the night in the blood-stained cell, where rivulets etc . . .

'It was not Velutha,' Ammu wept. 'I have been having an affair with an Untouchable.'

'That's even worse than Velutha killing Sophie Mol,' yelled Chacko.

'The only way to save our honour is to get the twins to lie,' said Baby Kochamma, fingering her silken scarf with pleasure at her niece's discomfort.

'It was Velutha,' said Estha. The last words before he was Returned to the north by train, the last words Rahel ever heard him utter.

Rahel pulled Estha close. It was the first time they had touched one another in 23 years. They undressed silently and conjoined in the Quietness and Emptiness like stacked spoons. There had been no reason for them to sleep together, but it seemed like the sort of ending the chatterati might like.

'It's only a Small Thing,' Rahel said.

'It might have been for you, but it's been a fucking Big Thing for me,' Arundhati replied. 'It's taken me four years to write and it's still not very good. I'm not doing that again in a hurry.'

HARRY POTTER AND THE PHILOSOPHER'S STONE

J. K. Rowling

Mr and Mrs Dursley, of number 4 Privet Drive, were proud to be the comedy formula fall guys who featured at the start of every Harry Potter book. They were both very stupid; but above all they were embarrassed that Mrs Potter was Mrs Dursley's sister. That Tuesday morning Mr Dursley had left for work, paying no attention to the unlikely phenomena of a cat reading the newspaper or men flying around in cloaks, until he overheard an owl talking about Harry Potter. Surely it couldn't be . . . ?

Albus Dumbledore appeared in Privet Drive. 'So it's true,' said Professor McGonagall, 'that James and Lily Potter have been killed by You Know Who.' 'You mean Voldemort,' Dumbledore said. 'But he couldn't kill baby Harry, inflicting only a wound that has left a scar upon the boy's forehead. And now we must leave the orphan with his only living relatives, the Dursleys.'

Nearly ten years had passed since the Dursleys had displayed a total lack of curiosity on discovering James and Lily had been killed and their son Harry abandoned on the doorstep. Then Harry, too, was not the most inquisitive of children. He never questioned why he was forced to sleep in the cupboard under the stairs, why snakes could talk to him, or how it was possible that the Dursleys' son Dudley was even stupider than his parents.

One day a letter arrived for Harry. Uncle Vernon threw it

straight in the bin. Immediately, thousands more letters landed on the doorstep. Uncle Vernon tried to scoop them up but was swept away by a giant.

'Oi've come ter take yer away from these Muggles and get yer ready fer Hogwarts, the school for wizards,' said Hagrid.

'But he's going to the local comprehensive for oiks,' replied Uncle Vernon, for there could be no worse fate for any child than to go to a state school.

'Yer not, Harry,' said Hagrid, 'for yer parents were great wizards who died tryin' ter save yer life.'

As usual Harry showed little interest in the fact his parents had possessed magical powers – or indeed that they were dead – and happily climbed on the back of the giant's motorbike as it soared through the air to Diagon Alley, to get Harry kitted out for school.

'First we must go ter Gringott's Bank ter get out the gold yer parents left for yer,' said Hagrid.

'Am I rich?' asked Harry.

'In ten years time yer will be a multi-millionaire Hollywood film star, Harry.'

Harry collected his gold galleons, bought his wand and headed to platform nine and three-quarters at King's Cross station for the Hogwarts Express.

'Cor, look, there's Harry Potter,' said Ron Weasley, who was also starting school.

'It's Harold Potter,' said Hermione Granger, another first year, keen to establish her credentials as a prissy know-all.

Once more, Harry expressed no bewilderment that he appeared to be something of a celebrity among his new friends and settled back to enjoy a toad sandwich. A blond boy with a cruel sneer opened the carriage door. 'You look like a member of the Hitler Youth,' said Harry. 'I guess we're going to be lifelong enemies.' '*Jahwohl!*' cried Draco Malfoy, clicking his heels.

They were greeted on their arrival by the headmaster, Professor Dumbledore, who took them through to the Great Hall where the

Sorting Hat was waiting to allocate the new pupils into Houses. 'Hooray,' yelled Harry, Ron and Hermione, 'we're in goody-goody Gryffindor.' 'Hooray,' yelled Malfoy, 'I'm an evil Slytherin.'

Harry raced off to find his dormitory and soon settled easily into the routine of boarding school life. But because he was a bit dim it took him longer to understand he was a naturally brilliant young wizard of whom everyone but himself had heard.

'This magic is easier than I thought,' he said, after a Dark Arts lesson with Professor Quirrell.

'I know what you mean,' said J. K. Rowling. 'Who would have thought an Enid Blyton boarding-school book could still prove so popular in the 1990s?'

Harry, Ron and Hermione immersed themselves in the daily school routines – the lessons, the amusing run-ins with the Fat Lady, a naughty rule-breaking outing into the Forbidden Forest, and, of course, Quidditch, a game at which Harry naturally excelled.

'It's all quite fun,' said Harry, 'but I can't help noticing we are well over half the way through the book and nothing has actually happened.'

'You've not seen nothing yet,' Ron replied gloomily. 'In the later books when everyone is far too scared to edit J. K. she drones on for hundreds of pages.'

Hermione sensibly decided something needed to be done. 'Why don't you put on that Invisibility Cloak that someone conveniently sent you and go and explore Hogwarts,' she said.

'Gosh,' said Harry on his return. 'I'm sure that Professor Snape is trying to steal the Philosopher's Stone that is being hidden inside the Mirror of Erised which is being protected by a three-headed dog.'

'Thank goodness no one can get past the three-headed dog,' cried Hermione.

'Arh, now yer come ter mention it,' said Hagrid, 'since oi talks like a bumpkin, oi is incredibly dim and oi told a stranger how ter get past Fluffy the dog in exchange for a dragon.'

'Never mind,' said Harry, 'it's always useful to have an idiot to move the plot along when we hit an impasse. But now we must rush back to Hogwarts to prevent Professor Snape from giving the Philosopher's Stone to Voldemort to bring him back to life.'

'How can you say You Know Who's name?' shrieked Ron.

Harry put on the Invisibility Cloak and headed several hundred miles beneath Hogwarts. He reached the Mirror of Erised and gasped. 'It's you.'

'Of course,' Professor Quirrell cackled. 'Have you really read so few books as to imagine the baddy would turn out to be the obvious villain, Snape?' A bolt of lightning rent the air and Harry fell unconscious.

'Congratulations, Potter,' said Dumbledore three days later, suspecting that a few explanations were in order. 'You have saved the world from Voldemort again, though luckily I turned up to finish off Quirrell. Voldemort must find another way to return to life.

'And while I'm about it, I'm going to arbitrarily award Gryffindor hundreds of extra House points so they win the House Cup.'

'Hooray,' yelled Harry, Ron and Hermione.

'Boo,' booed Malfoy.

'Isn't boarding school a hoot?' said Hedwig the owl.

ATOMISED

Michel Houellebecq

THIS BOOK IS primarily the story of a man who wanted to take the French philosophical tradition of Sartre, Camus, Foucault and Deleuze to its nihilistic conclusion. At the time of his disappearance, <u>Michel Houellebecq</u> – sorry, Djerzinski – was considered a serious candidate for the Nobel Prize, though his true significance as one of the principal architects of the metaphysical mutation that opened a new era in world history would not be understood for many years.

Michel wondered whether he should touch his colleague's breasts but he'd long since realised his cock was only fit to piss, so he said his goodbyes and went home. He ate a Monoprix meal, threw his dead canary in the garbage and phoned his half-brother Bruno. So began his first night of freedom away from the university.

Post-war France was a difficult and troubled society and Janine had stopped reading Heisenberg's autobiography and had relentlessly pursued the nomadic modern by having two sons by different fathers. Michel was born in 1956, Bruno in 1958, and after their fathers had inevitably disappeared, presumed dead, the boys were brought up by their grandmothers.

It's not as difficult as you might think to segue from scientific and philosophical debate on the nature of ontology and the molecular structure of meaning and happiness to the personal narratives of Michel and Bruno, providing you stick to a threadbare, dissociated style. You just have to keep your fingers crossed that the readers don't realise either that the intellectual arguments are not as rigorous as you imagine them to be or that your main intention is to be childishly shocking.

It is the late 1960s. Bruno is at a boarding school in Meaux. He is an Omega male, always bullied by the older boys who piss in his mouth and rub shit on his clothes. The highlight of his day is to position himself opposite girls and try to make himself spontaneously ejaculate by looking up their skirts. Michel is at school elsewhere, beloved by Annabelle who dreams of becoming his wife. Michel does not know how to touch her, so when they go to an ashram she gets fucked by the guru. She has an abortion and writes to Michel, but he is too consumed with the quantum potential of Griffiths history in Hilbert spaces to be arsed to reply. He shows no emotion when his grandmother dies. And neither do you, other than the ennui that comes with the numbing sense of predictability.

Sexual desire is the preserve of youth. It makes no allowances for sagging labia or flaccid penises and with his sole unpaid-for sexual encounter limited to forcing some sperm on to the pubic hair of a surprised teenager who would later commit suicide, in the mid-1980s Bruno decided to take a vacation to the Lieu de Changement, an atavistic commune based on Frédéric de Cantec's observations of primitive societies where people came together to fuck each other stupid.

For a long time no one wanted to fuck him, though this allowed Michel plenty of scope to indulge his own penchant for writing about masturbation, unattractive genitalia and the sexual predilections of sodomites, Arabs and Wogs. Mysteriously, a 40-year old woman with gnarled breasts, called Christiane, one day took a shine to him, and after he had prematurely ejaculated into his pants they became lovers, attending many orgies together where their sexual organs were rendered leathery and chlamydial by over-exertion. For the first time in his life, Bruno experienced happiness.

The excruciating inevitability of bourgeois capitalist alienation continued into the 1990s as Michel's search for manufactured controversy led him to conclude that perfect reproduction was impossible while DNA was stored in a double helix. Yet he too was not immune from a desire to be provocative, so when Annabelle contacted him again after more than 30 years he decided to meet her.

After a few disappointing failures in which his penis refused to become erect, he limply managed to ejaculate into her arid vagina as a reward for her desire to have a baby. Unfortunately Annabelle was required to have yet another abortion as tests revealed she had ovarian cancer. This did not respond to chemotherapy and she died shortly afterwards. Michel went home and had a Monoprix meal and resumed his circular deliberations on whether human consciousness could be reduced to a field of probabilities in a Fock space.

Bruno was in a Fock space of his own. During the weekdays when he was not with Christiane, he continued to visit prostitutes, indulge in casual racism and masturbate while fantasising about the time he had observed his mother's inelastic vagina being serviced by toyboys in her crushingly symbolic attempts to reclaim her own youth. He was still, in his way, happy until Christiane became paralysed after fucking 30 men at a party while giving him a blow job. She hadn't meant to be fucked quite so rigid, but her entire skeleton collapsed with osteoporosis. It surprised no one when she committed suicide 30 pages later.

By 1999, Michel had still got no further with his research into the ideal method of reproduction when he got the call to say that his mother was dying. He collected Bruno from the mental hospital where he had been detained after making inappropriate sexual demands on teenagers at the school where he was teaching and travelled to the south-west of France. Bruno had called her a miserable old whore and promised to piss on her ashes, but Michel made sure he didn't get round to it. Instead they just chucked them out of the train window and went home.

Michel moved to a university in Galway where his work on the

Copenhagen Project and the demystification of God and reality continued apace until his disappearance in 2009. It was presumed he had killed himself, having discovered the only potential for happiness was in cloning, but a more educated guess might be his disappointment at realising his attempt to write the *fin de siècle* work of European gravitas had lapsed into pure comedy.

It is 2070. Yawn. The world is full of women clones. Yawn. Everyone is happy. Yawn. History exists. Yawn. It is elemental. Yawn. It is inexorable. Yawn. The species that envisaged its passing has brought it about. Yawn. This book is dedicated to Me. I mean Mankind.

DISGRACE

J. M. Coetzee

FOR A DIVORCED man of fifty-two, David Laurie has solved, to his mind, the sex problem rather well. Every Thursday he spends ninety minutes with Soraya. They fuck – he rather more intensely than she, he suspects – and he buys her the occasional gift; but of his job as Professor of Modern Languages at Cape Technical University he says little.

This ideal arrangement comes to an end after he catches her eye while she is out shopping with her sons. Soraya doesn't return his calls and the agency say she no longer works for them. He has been dumped by a prostitute. He is no more than a client to be discarded. Yet he is one of those late-middle-aged men in fiction with an uncanny knack for luring women into bed, so his period of sexual abstinence is not prolonged.

There is a knock on his office door. 'Good afternoon, Professor Lurie,' says a young woman. He looks up to see Melanie Isaacs, an attractive student taking his course on the Romantics. He observes and objectifies her breasts.

'Let me take you out for a drink,' he says.

'I don't think my boyfriend would like that,' she replies.

But she goes anyway and, after he has plied her with whisky, allows herself to go home with him. He removes her panties and thrusts his penis inside her vigorously, while she lies passively on her back. For no obvious reason, he believes himself at the beginning of *un grand passion*.

Melanie never does anything more than allow herself to be fucked, while David never for a moment considers there might be something abusive – or even lacking – in their relationship. It is a beautifully romantic status quo, only interrupted when Melanie's boyfriend lets down the tyres of David's car and the relationship comes to the attention of the university authorities.

'Would you not consider apologising for what you have done?' says the Professor of Religious Studies, who is chairing the enquiry. 'That way you can stay in your job.'

'I will admit my guilt but not apologise,' David says. 'For Melanie is the love of my life.'

'I think the readers will find that psychologically unconvincing.'

'They can think what they want. All that matters is that I present myself as a stripped down man in stripped down prose – a pathetic, masochistic, redundant white man in the new South Africa.'

'Well, you've done that OK. And you've lost your job.'

'Good. I am now on the way to annihilation and disgrace.'

He enjoys the fact that everyone is ignoring him and leaves Cape Town to visit Lucy, his daughter from his first marriage, at her scrubby smallholding in the Eastern Cape. He notices she has become rather plump, not at all the sort of woman with whom he would choose to go to bed. But then she is his daughter, and a lesbian at that, so he supposes it does not matter unduly.

They talk at cross purposes for a while because that is the language of alienation among the newly dispossessed of South Africa, before Lucy introduces him to the dogs and takes him to meet Petrus, the farmer whose land adjoins hers. Petrus is confident, one of the new South Africans who have inherited the Earth, but David thinks he might quite like him anyway.

For a week, he does little. Lucy takes him to meet her friend, Bev Shaw. She is incredibly ugly, but he chooses to overlook that. 'You can come and help me put down unwanted animals,' she says. He smiles. For the first time in a long while he is content. 'I could get used to that kind of metaphor for the old South Africa.'

They see them coming, the two men and a boy. They take the car, shoot the dogs. He tries to resist; they set him alight. Lucy, they take indoors.

'I know what they did to you,' he says to Lucy later.

'I don't want to talk about it,' she replies. 'You were not there.'

They report the theft, the death of the dogs. But not the rape. They go to a party at Petrus's house. They are the only white people. They see the boy. 'He is a thief,' David says. Petrus shrugs. They leave.

David is consumed with anger. He visits Bev. She strips off. She isn't his usual type, but he performs, in the spirit of personal disgrace.

'You have to leave,' he says to Lucy. 'It is not safe for you here.'

'It is my duty to accept the rape,' she says. 'To them I was a symbol of apartheid repression and I must suffer for my post-colonial guilt. It is you who must leave.'

He nods. No one else can follow such twisted logic, but it makes perfect sense to him. He goes back to his vandalised house in Cape Town and fails to write an opera about Lord Byron. His spirits rise; his disintegration is continuing apace.

Everyone continues to ignore him. He will probably never have sex again unless he humiliates himself once more with a prostitute. The prostitute falls asleep mid-coitus. He does not care. The intensity of his self-hatred lifts him to a pitiful orgasm.

He is on a roll. He drives to Port Elizabeth to visit Melanie's father. 'Why have you come?' her father asks. He is not sure that admitting his desire for disgrace and humiliation is a sufficient answer. So he apologises and abases himself on the floor before them all.

Bev calls him. 'I think you should visit Lucy,' she says. Lucy is looking heavier than ever. 'I'm pregnant from the rape,' she says dully. 'I'm keeping the baby and I'm becoming Petrus's third wife.' 'But Petrus is implicated in the rape,' he says. She shrugs.

They visit Petrus. The boy is there. He is Petrus's son-in-law.

His name is Pollux. 'Sounds like bollox,' says David. 'You said it,' laughs Petrus, 'and I'm the master in the new South Africa.'

Lucy resigns herself to the new patriarchy as the necessary price for having been born with exploitative white genes. David is now a mere husk and rejoins Bev killing animals. He becomes attached to a dog but puts him down anyway. The simple present tense and third-rate characterisation has got to him.

'I was doing the mutt a favour,' he says.

The mutt isn't the only one pleased to be put out of its misery.

ACKNOWLEDGEMENTS

Denial is a much underrated psychological trait. If I had realised just how much work this book was going to involve, I would almost certainly never have agreed to it. That it has ever been completed owes as much to the support and encouragement of others as it does to my own efforts.

So thanks are due. In some cases long overdue, most notably to Nigel Wilcockson at Random House for not giving me too hard a time for finally delivering the manuscript two years later than planned.

Step forward also Lisa Allardice, Paul Laity, Pru Hone, David Newnham, Sarah Crown, Richard Lea and Lindesay Irvine at the *Guardian*, for giving me the freedom to develop the book and the editing skills to save me from making myself look a complete idiot on more occasions than I care to remember.

Many thanks also to Professor John Sutherland and Dr David Dwan for their friendship and expertise.

Lastly a big thank you to my family – Jill, Anna and Robbie – for putting up with many years of me having my head buried in a book when I should have been paying attention to them.